Falling in Love with Jesus

Falling in Love with Jesus

STUDIES IN THE BOOK OF LUKE

RUBEL SHELLY

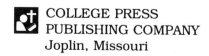
COLLEGE PRESS
PUBLISHING COMPANY
Joplin, Missouri

Copyright © 1998
Second printing 1999
College Press Publishing Company

Printed and Bound in the United States of America
All Rights Reserved

Cover Design: Mark A. Cole

Library of Congress Cataloging-in-Publication Data

Shelly, Rubel.
    Falling in love with Jesus: studies in the Book of Luke/ Rubel Shelly.
      p.   cm.
    Includes bibliographical references.
    ISBN 0-89900-802-X (pbk.)
    1. Bible. N.T. Luke—Study and teaching. I. Title.
BS2596.S47 1998
226.4'06—dc21   98-13868
                                                      CIP

Preface

Paul once gave this charge to a church's leaders: "Keep watch over yourselves and all the flock of which God has made you overseers. Be shepherds of the church of God, which he bought with his own blood" (Acts 20:28). The shepherds of the congregation of which I am a part take this responsibility seriously and believe that it begins with a plan to nourish the church with a healthy diet from the Word of God.

The gospel is taught in our public assemblies and in Bible classes for all ages. We have missionary outreach around the world. Tapes and written materials from this congregation literally go around the world for the sake of making known the truth of the Word of God. One of the most effective things that has recently happened in our church life is the widespread commitment by hundreds of our members to small-group Bible study and interaction.

Our overseers have charged a member of our staff with coordinating the small groups. No one "controls" them or dictates what will happen in them. Each group is free to select its own material for study. No one attempts to monitor the groups to see that people think and say only what someone here wants said. The confidence of our elders is that the Holy Spirit will be active in these groups to nurture people and bring them where Christ wants each participant to be.

In order to encourage the groups to maintain their focus on Christ, the shepherds commissioned the church's ministry staff to prepare materials that could be used widely in the church. The outcome of this charge is in your hands in the form of a study guide for the Gospel of Luke. This has been followed by a similar guide for The Acts of the Apostles. *Falling in Love with Jesus* has been prepared with every member of the church in mind. Young and old, single and married, new convert and mature believer — all can benefit from its use.

Introduction

The Gospel of Luke has been an encouragement to Christians since it first became available in the early 60s of the Christian Era. It tells the life of Jesus through the eyes of a physician and dedicated historian. Luke traveled the biblical lands and interviewed those who were with Jesus in order to tell the story of Jesus as accurately as possible.

The approach of this study of *Luke* is designed to help you get acquainted with Jesus of Nazareth on a personal level. It focuses on each Christian being able to develop a one-on-one relationship with the One who loves them best. It will reveal Jesus to you as the Son of God, Son of Man, and Savior of All. We will draw close to him by celebrating his birth, traveling with him as he preaches, learning his heart through his parables, and sharing once again in the agony of his death and joy of his resurrection.

Two thousand years after Jesus walked the roads of Galilee, we sometimes find it difficult to feel personally involved with who he is. Our desire is that this study of Luke will help you overcome this barrier of time and space and discover the blessing of a warm camaraderie with the love of your life.

Specific Objectives of This Study

Some of the churchwide objectives of *Falling in Love with Jesus* have already been stated above. But here are the specific objectives for choosing to encourage people to study the Gospel of Luke in detail.

♦ This Gospel tells the single most important story in the world for believers. No church that gets sidetracked with secondary issues will thrive within the will of God.

♦ We want members of the church to know the story of Christ thoroughly so they can share it with others. Jesus Christ is the only one who can save, so it is critical that we be able to tell his story correctly and meaningfully.

♦ Systematic study methods like the ones used in this study guide will help you study other parts of the Bible. So we offer this as an example of how to do meaningful study of the Word of God.

How to Use *Falling in Love with Jesus*

These notes must not be given priority over the text of the Bible itself. They are designed to encourage you to read Scripture and think deeply about its content. The notes are based on the New International Version, and all verses quoted directly from the text are from the NIV unless otherwise indicated. Whatever translation you are reading, feel free to underline key words and phrases, jot helpful notes in the margins, and otherwise personalize your study Bible.

The notes here will give you background to Luke, an outline of the book, historical data, and other helpful materials to make your reading of Luke's Gospel meaningful. Because he wrote in a language and culture so different from our own, the goal in these notes is to fill in the gaps on places, events, and terms so your reading will be more profitable.

The notes in this study guide avoid trying to draw conclusions for you about the meaning of what the Holy Spirit led Luke to record. That is your job.

You may choose to use these notes for personal study and quiet time with the Word of God. Here is a plan you might find helpful:

1. Before beginning to read, pray for God to cleanse your heart of anything that would keep you from receiving his instruction. Ask him to guide your reading to show you if there is (a) some sin you need to confess to him, (b) a promise for you to claim, (c) a command for you to obey, or (d) an example for you to imitate.

2. As you start to read, read the section of Luke for study that day aloud. Forming the words with your mouth and actually saying them impresses each one more deeply on your heart. Then read the suggested daily text (i.e., Day One, etc.) aloud.

3. Reflect on the five questions supplied for each day. These are issues for your personal reflection and will lead you to ask God how the material from Luke applies to your personal life. Here you will need to be introspective and honest about your spiritual life.

4. End your quiet time with a prayer that asks God to shape your life by the things you have just studied. Something may impress you powerfully later in the day or week and call this study time back to your consciousness, although you did not realize its significance in your few minutes of study. This is the work of the Holy Spirit in you.

5. [Optional] You may want to keep a personal journal of your thoughts, insights, or prayers that relate to this study. You could get either a loose-leaf notebook or spiral-bound notebook for your notes. These notes will trace your spiritual journey over several months.

Many of you will use *Falling in Love with Jesus* as a member of a small group that meets regularly. Ideally, these groups should have four to ten members. Keeping each group small allows everyone to participate and keeps it from becoming a lecture class. Small-group studies should be interactive and include everyone.

Each member of the group will find the suggestions outlined for personal study and quiet time ideal for daily preparation. Then, when the group meets, you may decide collectively how to use the study guide. You may review the block of text for that week or concentrate on one or two of the sets of questions for daily reflection. Here is a plan you may wish to try and then adapt to your group:

1. As members of your group assemble, greet each other warmly and move to your study location. It will be best to meet at the same time and place. Each person needs to commit to promptness so the group can use its time well.

2. Ask someone to read aloud the entire text that is being studied this time. This will focus everyone's thoughts on the same events and issues.

3. Have someone lead a prayer for the group to be open to God's voice. God speaks to his seeking children from Scripture, but our hearts must be prepared to hear him.

4. Conduct your group study by whatever method you choose. Either work through the verses that have been read or focus on one or more of the sets of reflection questions in the margins. Do not let one or two people dominate the study. The leader's task is to make sure everyone has the opportunity to join the discussion.

5. Relate your personal experiences and questions to the issues on the floor. Each group is to be a safe place where people can talk without fear of being set upon by others or having their confidence betrayed to people outside the group.

6. Close with prayer. Feel free to share special prayer needs with others in your group as they are called for. Pray about people and issues that have surfaced in the discussion time.

In whatever setting you choose to study *Falling in Love with Jesus,* link generous amounts of prayer to the project. As God speaks to you through this written word, answer him in your praise and requests in prayer.

The ultimate goal of a study this intense is to produce spiritual reflection, growth, and change in each person who chooses to participate. The Bible is not intended to be studied abstractly. It is God's powerful instrument to challenge and change hearts.

Additional Study Resources

If you wish to build your personal Bible study library and get useful tools that will help you in future study, here are a few recommendations that might be helpful.

The basic study tool everyone needs is a Bible dictionary. It provides an alphabetical index to the persons and places of the Bible. The best one-volume Bible dictionary on the market is *The New Bible Dictionary*, 2nd ed., edited by J.D. Douglas, et al. and published by Tyndale House Publishers.

A Bible atlas is particularly helpful in the study of the Gospels and Acts. It provides maps, photographs, and other details that help you understand how the geography of the life of Christ and the early church affected what happened then. *The Rand McNally Bible Atlas*, edited by Emil G. Kraeling, is probably the best of its class. Less expensive but still very helpful is *The New Bible Atlas* by J.J. Bimson and J.P. Kane from Tyndale.

If you enjoy the study of history and want a good historical background to the study of the New Testament, you will find Merrill Tenney's *New Testament Times* (Eerdmans) or F.F. Bruce's *New Testament History* (Doubleday) rewarding.

Finally, you may want to purchase a commentary or two on the Gospel of Luke. Remember that commentaries are written by fallible humans such as yourself. It is important — if you read a commentary at all — to realize that you have the right to wrestle with, challenge, or refuse the writer's conclusion about an interpretation. You must make up your own mind when you study the Word of God, for you are the one God will hold responsible for your life under its authority. With these cautions in mind, three quality popular-level commentaries on Luke are Leon Morris, *The Gospel According to St. Luke*, Tyndale NT Commentaries (Grand Rapids: Eerdmans, 1988); Darrell L. Bock, *Luke*, InterVarsity NT Commentary Series (Downers Grove, IL: InterVarsity, 1996); and Mark C. Black, *Luke*, NIV Commentary Series (Joplin, MO: College Press, 1996).

A Final Word

May God bless your study of the Gospel of Luke. As you witness the life of Jesus, may you find yourself falling more deeply in love with him than ever before, and may that experience lead you to a closer walk with your brothers and sisters in Christ.

Outline

Use this space for notes

I. **The Prologue.** 1:1-4.
II. **His Entry into the World.** 1:5–2:52.
  A. Two surprising announcements. 1:5-38.
    1. To Zechariah and Elizabeth. 1:5-25.
    2. To Mary. 1:26-38.
  B. Mary's visit with Elizabeth. 1:39-56.
  C. The birth of the Savior's forerunner. 1:57-80.
  D. The arrival of the Savior. 2:1-20.
    1. His birth at Bethlehem. 2:1-7.
    2. The announcement to shepherds. 2:8-20.
  E. The earliest events of his life. 2:21-40.
    1. The child's circumcision. 2:21.
    2. His presentation at the temple. 2:22-39.
      a. Meeting the requirements of the Law. 2:22-24.
      b. Simeon's recognition of the child. 2:25-35.
      c. Anna's recognition of the child. 2:36-39.
    3. A summary of his infancy and childhood. 2:40.
  F. The years of growth to manhood. 2:41-52.
    1. An incident from his twelfth year. 2:41-50.
    2. A summary of his growth to manhood. 2:51-52.
III. **Preparing for His Ministry.** 3:1–4:13.
  A. John's work of preparation. 3:1-20.
    1. The initiation of his ministry. 3:1-6.
    2. His preaching. 3:7-14.
    3. His heraldic message. 3:15-17.
    4. A summary of his ministry. 3:18-20.
  B. The baptism of Jesus by John. 3:21-22.

C. Jesus' genealogy on Mary's side. 3:23-38.
D. His personal encounter with Satan. 4:1-13.
IV. The Ministry of the Son of Man. 4:14–19:28.
A. An early ministry in Galilee. 4:14–7:50.
    1. His rejection at Nazareth. 4:14-30.
    2. His ministry at Capernaum. 4:31-41.
    3. Working beyond Capernaum. 4:42-44.
    4. The course of his ministry. 5:1–7:50.
        a. Calling his first disciples. 5:1-11.
        b. Healing a leper. 5:12-16.
        c. Forgiving sins. 5:17-26.
        d. Calling another disciple. 5:27-32.
        e. The issue of fasting. 5:33-39.
        f. The Sabbath question. 6:1-11.
        g. Choosing the Twelve. 6:12-19.
        h. The great kingdom sermon. 6:20-49.
        i. Healing the centurion's servant. 7:1-10.
        j. Raising the widow's son. 7:11-17.
        k. His estimation of John the Baptist. 7:18-35.
        l. A sinful woman forgiven. 7:36-50.
B. A later ministry in Galilee. 8:1-56.
    1. Women in ministry to Jesus. 8:1-3.
    2. The activity of his ministry. 8:4-56.
        a. Two kingdom parables. 8:4-18.
            1) The Parable of the Soils. 8:4-15.
            2) The Parable of the Lamp. 8:16-18.
        b. Kinship with Jesus. 8:19-21.
        c. Miracles establishing his kingdom authority. 8:22-56.
            1) Calming a storm. 8:22-25.
            2) Healing a demon-possessed man. 8:26-39.
            3) A miracle within a miracle. 8:40-56.
C. An expanded ministry with the Twelve. 9:1-50.
    1. The mission of the Twelve. 9:1-9.
    2. Feeding a great multitude. 9:10-17.

3. The prediction of his death. 9:18-27.
4. The Transfiguration. 9:28-36.
5. Healing a demon-possessed boy. 9:37-45.
6. A rebuke of pride and intolerance. 9:46-50.
D. Ministry on the way to Jerusalem. 9:51–19:28.
  1. The first phase of the journey. 9:51–13:21.
    a. Rejection by a Samaritan village. 9:51-56.
    b. A rebuke of halfhearted discipleship. 9:57-62.
    c. The mission of the seventy. 10:1-24.
    d. The Parable of the Good Samaritan. 10:25-37.
    e. A visit with Martha and Mary. 10:38-42.
    f. Teaching about prayer. 11:1-13.
    g. Rebuking blasphemy and unbelief. 11:14-36.
    h. Rebuking hypocrisy. 11:37-54.
    i. Encouraging the disciples to boldness. 12:1-12.
    j. Warning against covetousness. 12:13-21.
    k. Warning against anxiety. 12:22-34.
    l. A call to watchfulness. 12:35-48.
    m.The divisive influence of the Savior. 12:49-59.
    n. A call to repentance. 13:1-9.
    o. Conflict on the Sabbath. 13:10-21.
  2. The second phase. 13:22–17:10.
    a. The "narrow door" of the kingdom. 13:22-30.
    b. The message to Herod and a lament over Jerusalem. 13:31-35.
    c. Jesus as a Pharisee's guest. 14:1-24.
    d. The cost of discipleship. 14:25-35.
    e. Parables about lost things. 15:1-32.
      1) The Lost Sheep. 15:1-7.

2) The Lost Coin. 15:8-10.

3) The Lost Child. 15:11-32.

　　f. The Parable of the Shrewd Manager. 16:1-13.

　　g. Replying to the Pharisees' reaction. 16:14-18.

　　h. The rich man and Lazarus. 16:19-31.

　　i. Warnings to the disciples. 17:1-10.

　3. The third phase. 17:11–19:28.

　　a. The Samaritan leper. 17:11-19.

　　b. The coming of the kingdom. 17:20-37.

　　c. The unrighteous judge. 18:1-8.

　　d. A Pharisee and a publican. 18:9-14.

　　e. Jesus and the little children. 18:15-17.

　　f. Encountering a rich young ruler. 18:18-30.

　　g. Another prediction of his death. 18:31-34.

　　h. Events at Jericho. 18:35–19:28.

　　　1) Healing a blind man. 18:35-43.

　　　2) The conversion of Zacchaeus. 19:1-10.

　　　3) The Parable of the Pounds. 19:11-28.

V. A Final Ministry in Jerusalem. 19:29–21:38.

　A. His triumphal entry. 19:29-44.

　B. Cleansing the temple. 19:45-46.

　C. Questions and challenges *from* his opponents. 19:47–20:40.

　　1. The setting for the events. 19:47-48.

　　2. A question about his authority. 20:1-19.

　　3. A question about tribute money. 20:20-26.

　　4. A question about the resurrection. 20:27-40.

　D. Questions and challenges *for* his opponents. 20:41–21:4.

　　1. His question about the Messiah's sonship. 20:41-44.

　　2. His warning about the hypocrisy of the

scribes. 20:45-47.

    3. His admiration of a widow's giving. 21:1-4.

E. Revelations to his disciples about the future. 21:5-36.

    1. The destruction of the Jewish temple. 21:5-7.

    2. The fall of Jerusalem. 21:8-28.

    3. An appeal for vigilance. 21:29-36.

F. Summary statement about his work in Jerusalem. 21:37-38.

VI. The Death and Resurrection of the Son of Man. 22:1–24:53.

A. The conspiracy against Jesus. 22:1-6.

B. The Last Supper. 22:7-38.

    1. Preparing for the event. 22:7-13.

    2. Instructions about a kingdom meal. 22:14-20.

    3. Interactions with his disciples. 22:21-38.

        a. The announcement of impending betrayal. 22:21-23.

        b. A dispute over kingdom importance. 22:24-30.

        c. Peter's denials foretold. 22:31-34.

        d. Announcing a change in their circumstances. 22:35-38.

C. The Mount of Olives. 22:39-53.

    1. His agony in Gethsemane. 22:39-46.

    2. His betrayal and arrest. 22:47-53.

D. Peter's three denials. 22:54-62.

E. The "trials" of Jesus. 22:63–23:25.

    1. Before the Jewish rulers. 22:63-71.

    2. Before the civil rulers. 23:1-25.

        a. The initial hearing before Pilate. 23:1-7.

        b. An examination before Herod Antipas. 23:8-12.

        c. Resumption of the trial before Pilate. 23:13-25.

F. The crucifixion. 23:26-49.

    1. Events on the way to Golgotha. 23:26-32.
    2. Events at Golgotha. 23:33-49.
       a. Crucifixion and mockery. 23:33-38.
       b. The penitent thief. 23:39-43.
       c. The death scene. 23:44-49.
G. The burial. 23:50-56.
H. The resurrection and appearances. 24:1-49.
    1. The empty tomb. 24:1-12.
    2. The walk to Emmaus. 24:13-35.
    3. Appearing to the apostles. 24:36-49.
       a. Proof of his resurrection. 24:36-43.
       b. The last words to the apostles. 24:44-49.
I. The ascension. 24:50-53.

Week One

Introduction to the Gospel;
Luke 1:1-4 (Point I of outline)

The *central figure* of the Gospel of Luke is Jesus of Nazareth, and the *unifying theme* of the third Gospel is that Jesus offers salvation to all humankind. Because this is so, we may justifiably give it the subtitle "Falling in Love With Jesus."

The author of the Gospel of Luke clearly loved Jesus and had no hesitation about offering him to others for their love. He had seen something compelling about Jesus that touched his heart. Yes, he had fallen in love with him. His life had been radically changed because of that love, and the mission of his life was to let others in on the wonderful truth of Jesus' power to save sinners.

As we begin our study of what one writer has called the "most beautiful book in the world," there are some basic questions that need answers. Just what is a *Gospel*? Who is the author of this one? What circumstances moved him to write it? What is its central and unifying theme?

Literary Genre: What Is a Gospel?

If the word "gospel" is spelled with a lower-case *g*, it refers to the core truth of the Christian faith. It is the message of salvation for all on the basis of God's grace that has been enfleshed in Jesus Christ. Of all the truths that collectively make up the total body of information that pertains to the Christian faith, it is the gospel that is, to use Paul's language, "of first importance."

"For what I received I passed on to you as of first importance: that Christ died for our sins according to the Scriptures, that he was buried, that he was raised on the

Day 1
Beginning Our Study

Read 1 John 1:1–3:10 to learn about John's experience of "falling in love with Jesus."

1. State your reason for being involved in this study of Luke.
2. What does the phrase "falling in love" mean to you? What experiences do you associate with it?
3. How did Luke come to love Jesus? How was John's experience different?
4. When and how did *you* fall in love with Jesus?

Day 2
Luke's "Gospel"

Read 1 Peter 1:1–2:12 about the significance of what has been "passed down" to each of us.

1. What impressions of Jesus were passed to you as a child? How have they matured over time?
2. How was the gospel originally taught to you? What is "Good News" to your life?

3. At what point in your life did you begin to seek God? What moved you to do so?
4. If you could select someone to write about your life, what kind of person would you choose?
5. What do you want your children and best friends to remember about you?

Use this space for your own notes

third day according to the Scriptures, and that he appeared to [a multitude of witnesses]" (1 Cor. 15:3-5a).

When we speak of the gospel in this sense, there is one and only one gospel. It is the good news that salvation is offered to undeserving people on the merits of Christ's finished work at Calvary.

When we spell the word with an upper-case *G*, however, it has a different meaning; it identifies a particular literary form. As distinct from the thirteen epistles of Paul, for example, there are four Gospels. In each of the *four Gospels*, the author's purpose is to tell the *one gospel story* for a particular audience and from his own sources of information about Jesus.

When we use the term Gospel to designate a special type of literature, what is the distinguishing feature that sets a writing of this type apart from an epistle or an apocalypse? Although some older books would offer the descriptive term "biography" as a rough equivalent, few writers today would do so. While a person's biography would attempt to survey his complete life story, F.C. Burkitt has calculated that all the information about Jesus in the four Gospels of our New Testament covers a total of only about forty days from Jesus' life. Neither is it correct to call the Gospels mere "history." To be sure, they are historical, but the Gospels clearly have a higher purpose than simply to set down facts about Jesus.

In terms of the types of literature we know, perhaps it is most helpful to think of the Gospels as *tracts* designed for wide distribution in the first-century world. They are relatively short documents that set forth Jesus as the Son of God who alone can save us. Circulated among non-Christians, the Gospels presented the basic "salvation truths" about Jesus that could bring someone to faith in him; circulated among people who were already Christians, they preserved the memory of Jesus' saving work, offered his life as a model for imitation, and contained his teachings for study and reflection.

No one of our four Gospels — not even all four of them combined — provide a complete biography of Jesus Christ or a full history of his life and work. But any one of them — for they originally circulated separately — was (and is!) adequate to bring a seeking heart to a saving encounter with the Son of God.

The nature and purpose of a Gospel is most clearly summarized near the end of the Fourth Gospel, written by the apostle John: *"Jesus did many other miraculous signs in the presence of his disciples, which are not recorded in this book. But these are written that you may believe that Jesus is the Christ, the Son of God, and that by believing you may have life in his name"* (John 20:30-31).

The Author of the Gospel of Luke

The relevant facts about Jesus that could bring people to salvation were first shared and circulated orally. The gospel was preached by apostles and evangelists. People whose hearts had been captured by his love told their friends about Jesus. Parents taught what they knew of him to their children. Eventually, bits and pieces of this information were committed to writing.

The final stage of a Gospel's production was reached when the Holy Spirit guided someone to write — from personal observation, oral reports, and written sources — a tract such as the Gospel of Luke. The ultimate factor at work in this process, which guaranteed both a correct presentation of the facts and their power to convince seeking hearts of Jesus' power to save them, was the Holy Spirit. *"For prophecy* [i.e., statements of God's will for humanity] *never had its origin in the will of man, but men spoke from God as they were carried along by the Holy Spirit"* (2 Pet. 1:21).

Day 3
The Man Luke

Read Philemon for insight into personal relationships among first-century Christians.

1. What were the personal interactions between Luke and Paul? How did they become dear friends?
2. Does their relationship remind you of anyone in your own life?
3. What does the term "friend" mean to you?
4. How does your relationship with Jesus open the door to friendships with others who love him?
5. How does the church create the opportunity for meaningful relationships in your life?

19

Of the four Gospels preserved for us and circulated in the New Testament, the third Gospel is distinctive as to its authorship. Of the four men chosen by God to write history's most important information, only *Luke* was a Greek and only he produced a sequel to the Gospel that bears his name.

Luke has the distinction of being the only non-Jewish person to write any part of the New Testament. At Colossians 4:10-17, Paul lists several coworkers in his ministry. In verses 10 and 11, he names the "only Jews among my fellow workers." Luke is therefore included among the Gentiles whose names are given. Both his occupation and special relationship to Paul are contained in these words: *"Our dear friend Luke, the doctor, and Demas [Dē´-məs] send greetings"* (v. 14).

From Philemon 24, we learn that Luke was with Paul during the latter's two-year imprisonment at Rome. And from 2 Timothy 4:11, we discover that he was still standing by the great missionary apostle near the end of Paul's life.

The sequel to this Gospel by Luke is the Acts of the Apostles. Together, these two books cover the account of Christianity's earliest days from the birth of Jesus to the time of Paul's first imprisonment at Rome in A.D. 62. Paul's personal physician almost surely wrote both volumes during the period A.D. 60-62. [Note: More will be said about the circumstances that moved Luke to write this material in the study of 1:1-4.]

In terms of the total number of words, Luke in his two volumes contributed more of the content of the New Testament than any other writer.

Day 4
The Theme of Luke's Gospel
Read Jonah 3-4 to glimpse God's passion for saving all people.

The Theme of the Gospel of Luke

Luke's theme is one you might suspect him to emphasize because of his own background and experience. As a Greek, he writes to explain that *Jesus*

Christ is the Savior of All Humankind. Although Jesus was a Jew, Luke was led by the Holy Spirit to present him as the Savior of both Jews and Gentiles. From his "dear friend" Paul, he had learned this: *"I am not ashamed of the gospel, because it is the power of God for the salvation of everyone who believes: first for the Jew, then for the Gentile"* (Rom. 1:16).

Luke's method of telling the story of Jesus focused on the stories of individuals who met the Savior. As presented by Luke, the love of Jesus knew no bounds. He reached out to prostitutes (7:36-50), Samaritans (17:11-19), tax-collectors (18:9-14), and a dying thief (23:39-43).

Who would *not* fall in love with such a character as Jesus? Who would be afraid to come to him? Who would have to fear rejection by him?

There is a legend that Luke was not only a physician but a painter. Whether or not there is any truth to that legend, a close reading of his Gospel makes it clear that he saw Jesus through the eyes of an artist. The picture he painted of him with words has drawn many a person to fall in love with the Savior.

I. The Prologue. 1:1-4.

The opening verses of the Gospel of Luke affirm the confident historical base on which Christian faith rests. We do not embrace myths and fables, hoping against hope that there is some value to these tales. We embrace only those documented facts of history that students such as Luke have "carefully investigated" and preserved in writing for us. We have "certainty" for the things offered to us about Jesus.

With the methodology of a trained scientist, Dr. Luke scrutinized the written materials that had begun to circulate among believers. He also had contact with "eyewitnesses" to events from Jesus' life.

1. The Jews had a hard time sharing God with other people. Why? Is this a common human experience?
Cf. Isa. 51:4.

2. When have prejudice and stereotyping hindered you from loving others? Have they ever kept churches you know from evangelism?

3. God extends love and forgiveness to people we may have rejected. What problems can this create? Where have you been touched by this dilemma?

4. Pray for God to open your heart to all those he loves and accepts.

Day 5
God-Lovers

Read Luke 14:1-15 and 19:1-10 to learn of two persons who fell in love with Jesus.

1. What does the name "Theophilus" mean? What do you understand the significance of this name to be in 1:1-4?

2. Why is it so important for Luke to share the Jesus story with others? What was his goal?

3. Name some people you have known who had

Luke's passion for sharing Jesus.

4. Identify some key people you know who are God-lovers. What specific features of their lives mark them as men or women in love with God?

5. Pray for God to open your heart to appreciate Luke's portrait of Jesus.

Guided as he was by the Holy Spirit in this process of reading and interviewing, he had determined to "write an orderly account" of the central events of faith for a man named "Theophilus" [Thē-ă-fĭ-ləs]. (cf. Acts 1:1). Since this proper name means God-lover, we cannot be certain whether he was a personal addressee for this tract or whether the extremely literate Luke was reaching out by the use of this name for all whose hearts were open to making a response to God's love for them as witnessed in Jesus.

By means of our careful study of the Gospel of Luke today, any one of us may become a Theophilus (i.e., Lover of God). If you are new to the story of Jesus, our prayer is that you will fall in love with Jesus through this study. If you are a believer already, our prayer for you is that your love will become deeper and richer through the experience that lies ahead.

Week 2

Luke 1:5-80 (II A to II C in Outline)

II. His Entry into the World. 1:5–2:52

A. Two Surprising Announcements. 1:5-38.

Throughout the Gospel of Luke, there are scenes of unexpected events that bring great delight to the participants. The first two are particularly surprising and joyous. One has to do with the possibility of an aged but childless couple having a baby in their "sunset years"; the other announces the impending birth of a child to a woman who is a virgin. One is amazing; the other is unprecedented. Both are by divine intervention and focus on the coming of the long-awaited Redeemer of Humanity.

1. To Zechariah [Zĕk-ə-rī´-ə] and Elizabeth. 1:5-25.

During the reign of Herod the Great, who ruled Judea as a vassal king under Rome from 37-4 B.C., a most unusual announcement was made to a godly couple. The man was a Jewish priest named Zechariah, and his wife of many years was named Elizabeth. Their personal character and religious devotion were above reproach. But there was a major sadness that had been with them during their adult years. They had been unable to have children.

While we sometimes associate life's disappointments (e.g., handicap, bankruptcy, childlessness) with God's displeasure or punishment, the history of this couple proves conclusively that this is too glib an assumption. While *some* human suffering is certainly traceable to sin in the sufferer's past, not all can be accounted for that way.

As Zechariah was carrying out his duties at the

Day 1
The Ministry of Angels

Read Hebrews 1:1-14 in order to be aware of the ministry of angels on behalf of Christians.

1. What have you been taught about angels? What questions do you still have? What do you personally believe?
2. What insights came to you from a close reading of Hebrews 1?
3. What sorts of activities are associated with angels in these texts: Josh. 5:13ff; Dan. 9:17-23a; Matt. 18:10; and Heb. 13:2?
4. Reflect on the role angels may have played in your life to this point.
5. What comfort do you get from the promise that angels "serve those who will inherit salvation"?

Day 2
The Story of Zechariah and Elizabeth

Read Psalm 86 to see a prayer this godly couple might have prayed repeatedly.

1. Describe this couple as you see them from the text. Did their holiness exempt them from disappointment? When have you felt that life has cheated you?

2. Do you see any evidence that they were bitter over their disappointment? How do you tend to respond to disappointment?

3. How did God surprise this couple? Share a situation when God brought surprise out of your tragedy.

4. Characterize Zechariah's response to Gabriel. Unbelief? Shock? Natural surprise? Are you ever like him when you get an answer to prayer?

5. Elizabeth saw her pregnancy as God's act of removing her "disgrace." Reflect on times of God's grace in removing "shame" or "disgrace" from your life.

temple one day, a heavenly visitor startled him at the incense altar which stood just before the curtain separating the Holy Place from the Holy of Holies. The unnamed angel spoke immediately to alleviate his fear and to explain the purpose behind his visit. Zechariah was told that the many prayers he and his wife had prayed for a child were about to be answered. Yet he was not simply told, "You're going to have a baby." The announcement was much more specific and detailed than that.

The startled priest was told that his wife would have a son and that his name was to be John. Furthermore, he was told to raise his son John under the requirements of a Nazirite vow (cf. Num. 6:1-12). The most important thing he was told, however, was that John would function by the power of the Holy Spirit to fulfill the prediction of Malachi 4:5-6. This could only mean one thing to a pious man such as Zechariah: his son was to be the forerunner of Israel's Messiah.

Such news was both personally and theologically "too good to be true" for Zechariah to accept at face value. How could he know this was not merely a dream? What sort of sign could the angel give him that all this was from God? In a tone of rebuke against his unbelief, the angel told the aged priest that he would be unable to speak until the promised child was born. As with every act of judgment God has ever brought against unbelief, the penalty against Zechariah for his doubt was intended not to destroy but to discipline. At the end of this episode, it will be obvious that his nine months of silence were significant in strengthening his faith in God.

When Zechariah came from within the Holy Place to the worshiping crowd outside the temple, it was apparent to everyone that something had happened to him. Unable to speak and to explain what he had witnessed, he could only gesture to the crowd. They perceived that he had had a "vision" (i.e., revelation from the Lord) but had no idea of its content. When his week of temple service was complete, Zechariah returned home to his wife. Soon thereafter Elizabeth conceived a child and praised God for removing the "disgrace" of her childlessness (cf. Gen. 17:16-17).

2. To Mary. 1:26-38.

Before carrying through with the story of the birth of John, Luke interrupts that narrative to tell of a second angelic visitation to a young woman of Nazareth named Mary. When Elizabeth was six months along in her pregnancy, Gabriel was sent to tell Mary that she would also have a son.

Unlike elderly Elizabeth, Mary was little more than a child. It was customary at the time for a girl to be "betrothed" in her early teens, usually to a man considerably older who had proved his ability to work at a trade and support a family. Betrothal was a formal ceremony that legally pledged a man and woman to marriage, but it did not confer the rights of marriage. Specifically, the couple did not have the right of sexual intercourse and were expected not to begin living together until one year from the time of their betrothal.

Remembering that Luke was a physician, we can understand his stress on the virginity of Mary at the time of this announcement. He was not an ignorant man from a superstitious time. He knew where babies came from and went to great lengths in his narrative to stress the *miraculous conception* of Mary's child.

Mary reacted to an angel's presence much as Zechariah had months earlier at Jerusalem. She was frightened by it. So Gabriel said, "Do not be afraid, Mary, you have found favor with God." The specific nature and degree of "favor" given her was tied to the birth of a son who would be "Son of the Most

Day 3
The Announcement to Mary

Read Esther 4:1-17 for an incident when God unexpectedly called a young woman to noble service for him.

1. What surprise came to Mary? How was this very different from the one that came to Zechariah and Elizabeth?
2. Empathize with Mary and her situation. How would a pregnant teenager be viewed in her time and place? How kind would you likely have been to her as a citizen of Nazareth?
3. Try to articulate the degree of faith required for Mary to respond as she did in v. 38.
4. Describe someone's experience who has exemplified great faith and devotion in your experience. How has that example deepened your own faith?

High" (cf. 1:35) and who would rule from the "throne of his father David" (cf. 2 Sam. 7:12-14).

Mary was startled at the prospect of having a child and asked how it could be in view of her virginity. Gabriel acknowledged her chastity and explained that the Holy Spirit would bring about the conception miraculously. Her child would, in fact, be the Son of God rather than the offspring of any human father. With her head surely reeling from such a prospect and all it could entail, Mary humbly offered herself as a servant to the Lord to fill whatever role heaven chose for her. What marvelous faith in one so young! In witnessing such trust in God, surely we are given insight into why this girl rather than some other was chosen to provide Jesus his human form.

At the close of his announcement, Gabriel mentioned what was happening with Zechariah and Elizabeth, Mary's own cousin. The older woman's pregnancy was thus offered as a confirmatory sign to Mary of God's presence in what had just been announced to her.

B. Mary's Visit with Elizabeth. 1:39-56.

It appears that Mary made immediate preparation for and started on a trip to see her cousin Elizabeth. The trip would have been a difficult one of over sixty miles, yet she did not hesitate. Whether moved of God to make the trip or anxious to confirm her own situation with a visit to assure herself about the impending birth of a child to her aged cousin, we cannot be sure.

When the two women greeted each other, Elizabeth was filled with the Holy Spirit and prophesied. She both repeated the angel's message about Mary's favored status before God and blessed her for the faith she had exhibited in God's power to fulfill his promise.

Here Luke recites a song of Mary. Whether com-

Day 4
Mary and Elizabeth Together

Read Ruth 1:1-18 to see another example of a safe relationship between two women who supported each other.

1. Why do you suppose Mary sought the company of Elizabeth at this critical time? Why would they be natural confidantes for each other?

2. How do you choose a confidant in times of stress? What elements of your personality

posed on the spot or over days of reflection, it is one of the most beautiful sections of biblical literature. In its first stanza (1:46-48), she celebrates God's goodness to her. In the second (1:49-50), she praises his mercy to all who fear him. The third stanza (1:51-53) contrasts his judgment of the proud with his goodness to the humble. The final one (1:54-55) stresses her confidence in Yahweh's work to keep the promises made to Abraham and all his descendants through the child to be born of her.

Mary apparently returned to Nazareth just prior to the birth of Elizabeth's son. The visit with her cousin had confirmed the faith of both these mothers-to-be. We can only speculate as to what they must have talked about in anticipating the careers and interactions of their sons.

C. The Birth of the Savior's Forerunner. 1:57-80.

When Elizabeth's pregnancy had come to full term, she gave birth to a healthy son. When neighbors and friends gathered on the eighth day following his birth for the infant's circumcision, someone gave voice to the assumption that he was to be named after his father, Zechariah. Readers of Luke's text almost sense a tone of horror in Elizabeth's voice as she protests and says that he is to be named John.

At this point, Zechariah comes back into the drama. The crowd asked him about the naming of his son, so he asked for writing materials. He wrote: "His name is John." With the writing of those words, his experience had come full circle. What had begun with doubt at the angel's announcement had grown into full faith and acceptance of the divine will.

Then his speech returned, and he began to give praise to God. Just as Mary had composed a hymn earlier, so now Zechariah sang to the glory of God.

might draw people to you?

3. Notice that the focus of their time together was not each other and their babies — but God. What brought them to this unifying theme? Cf. vv. 35,41.

4. Share how God's Holy Spirit has united you with another person at a particularly important time in life.

5. How does the sense of being a "kindred spirit" with another believer show itself?

Day 5
The Birth of John the Baptist

Read Psalm 119:49-56 to see the value of God's promises in upholding us.

1. What is the best example of a promise that has been kept to you?

2. How does John's birth represent a promise kept? What did this mean for the faith of his parents?

3. Describe Zechariah's "testimony" at the end of this episode. To whom does his song give praise? Why? For what purpose?

4. What does v. 66 imply about the expectations people attached to John? What would be his relationship to Jesus?

5. What promise from God are you most eager to see come to pass?

It is interesting that his song focused on the Messiah rather than on his own son. Only one of its five stanzas is about John, with all the others in praise of Jesus.

Stanza one (1:68-69) speaks of the redemption of Israel as something already done. This is a common device of Old Testament prophecy in that something promised by Yahweh is spoken of in advance of its fulfillment as already done. The second stanza (1:70-72) acknowledges the Lord's salvation as the fulfillment of his long-standing promises made to the patriarchs of Israel. In the third stanza (1:73-75), the nature of God's salvation is heralded as a complete redemption that will "enable us to serve him without fear" in the presence of former enemies and oppressors. In the fourth stanza only (1:76-77) is John recognized; he is to be God's prophet who heralds the arrival of Messiah and gives all who hear him the knowledge of salvation. The fifth stanza (1:78-79) completes the song by praising the Lord for bringing divine light into the world's darkness through the appearance of Messiah.

As with the song of Mary earlier, this hymn from Zechariah is pure celebration of the nature and actions of God. It is neither Mary's submission nor Zechariah's doubt-become-faith that is to be praised. It is God himself and God alone, for salvation through Jesus Christ is altogether an activity of his grace to us.

Through the events of the Gospel of Luke to this point, the stage has been set for the appearance of the Son of Man. Having crafted the preliminaries of his Gospel so as to have his readers eager for his arrival, Luke has us ready to witness the event of fulfillment that brought God among us.

Week Three

Luke 2:1-40 (II D to II E in Outline)

D. The Arrival of the Savior. 2:1-20.

No birth has ever been so anticipated as that of Jesus of Nazareth. Since the first announcement to Adam and Eve that a redeemer would come to their descendants in human form (cf. Gen. 3:15), divine revelation through a variety of prophets has pointed to his coming and work. All of God's holy purposes from eternity past would be realized in him. *"In the past God spoke to our forefathers through the prophets at many times and in various ways, but in these last days he has spoken to us by his Son, whom he appointed heir of all things, and through whom he made the universe"* (Heb. 1:1-2).

Luke's account of the birth of Jesus is perhaps most notable for its restraint. Against the tendency of most to overestimate the importance of human achievements, this Gentile physician recounts the events of heavenly fulfillment with the language of understatement.

1. His birth at Bethlehem. 2:1-7.

Since Mary lived in Nazareth (1:26), how did it come about that she was in Bethlehem at the time of her firstborn son's birth? The background to answering this question comes to us from events not recorded by Luke. Perhaps because he was familiar with the Gospel of Matthew — one of the written accounts of Jesus' life that may be included in the statement of 1:1 — Paul's physician-friend did not repeat that story.

From Matthew 1:18-25, we know the following about Mary's relationship with Joseph. When he

Day 1
All Things Center in Jesus

Read Isaiah 53 as an example of a prediction centering on Jesus from 700 years before his birth.

1. What do you understand Gal. 4:4-5 to mean? How does history focus on Jesus?
2. What event or person in your life made you see the need to center everything on Jesus? What are your personal obstacles to keeping life focused on him?
3. Which of these are most helpful in keeping Christ at the center of your life: Church involvement? Family prayer/devotions? Private spiritual disciplines? Other?
4. What difference do you sense when you are centered on Jesus? What happens when you lose focus?
5. Write a brief prayer asking God to center everything in your life on Jesus.

Day 2
The Birth at Bethlehem

Read Matthew 1:18-25 to learn about Joseph and his feelings about God and Mary.

1. What is "providence"? How did a girl from Nazareth wind up in Bethlehem for her baby's birth? Does God still act in world and national affairs to bring about his purposes? Cf. Hab. 1:1-11.

2. Have you ever heard your parents talk about waiting for your birth? Have you ever antici- pated another birth eagerly? Describe the eagerness Joseph and Mary would have felt.

3. The baby was born in an animal shelter. Since Joseph and Mary knew his identity, how must they have felt? Have you ever had to deal with shame over a situation you could not control?

4. What can the church do to help people deal with their guilt and shame? Describe the creation of a safe environment for people attempting to heal from spiritual trauma.

learned that his betrothed Mary was pregnant, he incorrectly assumed that she had broken her vow of faithfulness to him and was considering the best way to initiate a divorce proceeding. Unlike our modern pre-marital practice of engagement, a Jewish "be- trothal" was much more formal and binding. One could not terminate it simply by changing his mind or asking for his ring back. While he was pondering his options, an angel of God appeared to him, explained the miraculous conception of Mary's baby, and gave him the chance to be involved in these ful- fillment events by telling him to "take Mary home as your wife." What scandalous talk that would precipi- tate in Nazareth! Without hesitation, Joseph obeyed Yahweh's command and joined Mary to await the birth of God's son.

Toward the end of the pregnancy, word reached Nazareth of a Roman decree requiring Israelite fami- lies to participate in a census. Thus Joseph had to make a trip to his ancestral home of Bethlehem. Unwilling to be separated at so critical a time, the couple made the sixty-mile trip together. With the restraint already mentioned, Luke indulges neither his own nor our curiosity about how difficult a trip it must have been for them.

Overcrowded as Bethlehem would have been from an influx of people answering the census order, the weary couple was unable to find lodging in an inn. Thus it came about that history's most important birth took place in a shelter meant for animals and Jesus was laid in a manger (i.e., feeding trough). Tradition says the shelter was a cave, yet the language of the text would allow either that or one in the open air. From the very beginning of his life on earth, Jesus was identified with the humble and poor.

Without any evidence that they were conscious of it, Joseph and Mary had participated in the fulfill- ment of an Old Testament prophecy from Micah 5:2

that the Messiah's birth would take place in Bethlehem. At the very least, Caesar Augustus certainly issued the census order without any intent of bringing about the fulfillment of a biblical prediction. History and each individual life belong to God. We need not be aware of his sovereign workings to be part of a plan he is bringing to completion.

2. The announcement to shepherds. 2:8-20.

The first announcement of the infant's birth was made that same night to some shepherds living with their flocks in the area nearby. From extrabiblical literature, we know that many of the sheep raised at Bethlehem were destined to become temple sacrifices. One can hardly miss the irony of this birth announcement to men whose job was to prepare appropriate sacrifices for the altar at Jerusalem.

Although King David had been a shepherd and in spite of the fact that their animals would be offered at the temple, shepherds of Jesus' day were social outcasts. It was not simply their contact with animals and thus with uncleanness but their general reputation as men who would accidentally (!) end a day with more sheep than they had when they led their flocks into shared pasture. It was to the outcasts and dispossessed that Jesus would one day offer the kingdom of God. These fortunate shepherds were allowed to represent their kind as the first to offer worship to the child born to be king — not only King of the Jews but King of all.

The angel who appeared to them told them that the child they would visit that night was "Christ the Lord." The Greek word *Christ* translates the Hebrew *Messiah*, and *Lord* is the term used in the Greek version of the Old Testament (the Septuagint) for *Yahweh*. The shepherds were not left to judge the baby's identity but were given that information by revelation.

At the end of the single angel's announcement, a

Day 3
The Announcement to Shepherds

Read Psalm 23 to find a shepherd writing about his work – and seeing God in it.

1. Imagine that you are president of a PR firm in charge of bringing Christ to earth. How would you have done it? To what people would you have sent the notices?

2. Shepherds were the first people to hear of the birth of Jesus. What was their status in the social order? Why would the first word of Jesus' arrival come to them?

3. Who are the "best prospects" for hearing about Jesus in any generation? Cf. Matt. 9:9-13; 1 Cor. 1:26-31. Do churches ever have trouble linking up with such people? Why? How can this be corrected?

4. Characterize the shepherds' response to the announcement. Why do you think they were so eager to respond? What

excuses might they have offered for staying at their job that night?

5. How quickly do you respond to God's call? How prone are you to make excuses? What adjustments have you made recently to God's claim on your life?

**Day 4
The Early Events**

Read Leviticus 12:1-8 for background on the ceremony that called the new family to the temple.

1. Jesus' parents had a heart for God. What procedures did the Law require at a child's birth? How did Joseph and Mary deal with those duties?

2. The formative influence of a family on a child is apparent. Why do you think God chose these two to be Jesus' parents?

3. What impressions do parents make on children by their concern to live out their spiritual duties? By neglecting them?

4. Recall some decisions made in your family of origin that affected you deeply. What choices are before you in your home today that will affect others significantly?

host of others joined him to praise God in a heavenly chorus celebrating the significance of Jesus' birth. Then the shepherds "hurried off" to find the baby and his parents. By telling others in Bethlehem about the events they had witnessed that night, they "amazed" those who heard them. For the larger story he was telling, Luke found it more important to relate that "Mary treasured up all these things and pondered them in her heart."

E. The Earliest Events of His Life. 2:21-40.

Although Luke was a Gentile writing for fellow-Gentiles, he nevertheless told the story of Jesus' early life correctly in terms of its Jewish setting. Without giving details of the circumcision and purification rituals following the birth of a son, he did find it important to present this family as pious and obedient under the Law of Moses. He also told of two inspired responses to the infant's presence at Jerusalem for his mother's purification ceremony. With a marvelous economy of words, twenty verses tell all we know of Jesus from Luke for the period between his birth and twelfth year.

1. The child's circumcision. 2:21.

Under Jewish law, males were to be circumcised when eight days old (Gen. 17:12). This physical mark served to identify one with the covenant God made with Abraham. To reject it was to reject Yahweh.

2. His presentation at the temple. 2:22-39.

a. Meeting the requirements of the Law. 2:22-24.

Since contact with blood created ritual uncleanness, the Hebrew Torah required a ceremony of purification for women after childbirth (cf. Lev. 12:1-5). After the birth of a son, a woman was to wait thirty-three days after his circumcision for the purification ritual. Still another ritual associated with the birth of a firstborn son was his presentation and redemption (i.e., buying back) with an offering (cf. Num. 18:15-16). These two ceremonies are treated together in the Gospel of Luke.

Two otherwise obscure points in the narrative are of great interest. First, the purification was "their" (rather than "her") purification. This likely includes not Jesus but Joseph, who surely was forced to deliver Mary's son in the animal shelter and who thus contracted blood defilement. Second, the sacrifice offered for the infant son's redemption (i.e., birds rather than a lamb, cf. Lev. 12:6-13) was appropriate only for the poor. Again, the coming of the Son of Man identified him in every particular as one associated with the disenfranchised.

b. Simeon's recognition of the child. 2:25-35.

When Jesus was being presented at the temple some five weeks after his circumcision, he was recognized by Simeon. A devout Jew, the Lord had revealed to him that "he would not die before he had seen the Lord's Christ." On the day Mary and Joseph were present with Jesus, the Spirit moved him to go into the temple courts. There he encountered Jesus and recognized him as the promised one. In a song reminiscent of those from Luke 1, he praised Yahweh for the coming of the one who would bring salvation to "all people." That this term included all nations and races is clear from the next line that praises Jesus as "a light for revelation to the Gentiles." We cannot be surprised that our Gentile writer, Luke, would cite this revelation.

In a more personal statement to Mary, Simeon predicted her son's work within Israel. His ministry would be the background for the rise and fall of many. It would also serve to reveal the character of those with whom he interacted. Finally, he also foresaw the grief of heart that would come to Mary from his treatment at the hands of those he had come to save.

Day 5
Who Can Recognize Jesus?

Read 2 Corinthians 3:7-18 to find Paul's comments about some whose hearts could not see Jesus.

1. Tell the story of two people recognizing Jesus at the temple. What effect would this have had on Joseph and Mary to reinforce their faith and commitment?

2. Simeon and Anna recognized Jesus' true identity. How?

3. Are some people more spiritually sensitive than others? Why?

4. Why wasn't everyone in Jerusalem given the information Simeon and Anna received?

5. How can we make our hearts more open and responsive to Jesus' presence?

c. Anna's recognition of the child. 2:26-39.

Consistent with the observed fact that Luke gives more prominence in his Gospel to women than the other Gospels do, we read next of the appearance of an elderly prophetess named Anna. As Mary and Joseph were pondering what had been revealed to them through Simeon, Anna appeared and began to speak about the child among all those who were still clinging to the promise of the Messiah's appearing (i.e., the one who would redeem Jerusalem).

3. A summary of his infancy and childhood. 2:40

With all the legal requirements at Jerusalem satisfied, Joseph and Mary left the city and returned to their home city of Nazareth. There Jesus would grow to manhood. The first twelve years of his life are summarized by Luke's statement that "the child grew and became strong; he was filled with wisdom, and the grace of God was upon him."

[Note on the Chronology of the Life of Jesus: Luke is the only writer of a Gospel who offers dating clues for the birth of Christ. In a form typical for his time, he dated the event in the reign of Caesar Augustus and during a time when Quirinius [Qwĭ-rĭ̄-nē-əs] governed Syria (2:1-2). Augustus was emperor from 27 B.C. to 14 A.D., and Quirinius was the military legate of Syria 10-7 B.C.

[As to the census itself, we have records from the one in Egypt from A.D. 20 and a mention in Josephus of one in A.D. 6. Since Luke says the one associated with Jesus' birth was the "first census," and in view of the Roman practice of taking a count of the population every fourteen years, the initial one must have been called for around 9/8 B.C.

[Finally, Herod the Great — who murdered several babies at Bethlehem in an effort to destroy the newborn King of the Jews (cf. Matt. 2:1ff) — died in 4 B.C. This collection of hints allows us to date Jesus' birth within a relatively narrow window.

[The birth could not have taken place after Herod's death in 4 B.C. and could not have happened before Caesar's call for a census in 9/8 B.C. Thus the most specific we can be is to say that Jesus was born between 8 and 4 B.C.]

Week Four

Luke 2:41-52 (II F in Outline)

Day 1
Influencing a Child's Faith

Read Deuteronomy 6 to find what Israelite parents were to do in forming the faith of their children.

1. Did you ever get separated from your parents? What was happening in your life at age 12?
2. What is your most vivid childhood memory of religious life?
3. What family experiences might have prepared Jesus for his conversations at the temple?
4. How could Deuteronomy 6 still guide a family's spiritual life? Compare your childhood experiences with this model.
5. Do we depend too much on church and Bible School to train children? Where does the primary responsibility belong? How can church and family partner in the process?

F. The Years of Growth to Manhood. 2:41-52.

The only thing Scripture records for us from the boyhood of Jesus is found in this section of Luke. It is not a videocassette, only a snapshot. But what it reveals of the boy Jesus is significant for what it tells about the direction he chose for his life while still so young.

The town of his youth was Nazareth. It was an insignificant city that is never mentioned in the Old Testament, Josephus, or Talmud. Nathanael would later be inclined to dismiss Jesus because he was from a town that was so small and undistinguished (cf. John 1:46). The city depended on agriculture for its livelihood and was so small that it likely needed only a few craftsmen. Jesus' family was one of that limited number, and he would have learned Joseph's carpentry skills as he grew to manhood (Matt. 13:55). Later, he would draw some of his object lessons from the experiences he had in a carpenter's shop by talking of plows, yokes, etc.

Jesus likely received little formal education. All Jewish children, however, were taught at the synagogue. They were taught the Torah (i.e., the five books of Moses) by heart. As they grew older, the children would have begun participating in discussions of its meaning. Jesus' interest in such studies is reflected in a visit he made with his parents to Jerusalem when he was twelve years old.

1. An incident from his twelfth year. 2:41-50.

At age thirteen, a Jewish male became a "son of the Law" and was from that time on counted a full member of the synagogue and held accountable as an adult for conforming his behavior to the instructions found in Scripture. To prepare him for what would later in Jewish history be known as his *bar mitzvah*, a boy was allowed to participate in holy festivals for a year or two before his thirteenth birthday.

A major requirement of all males in Israel was participation in the three "pilgrim feasts" of Judaism. From wherever they were in the world, Jewish men were supposed to travel to the temple in Jerusalem to celebrate the festivals of Passover, Pentecost, and Tabernacles (Exod. 23:14-17). For those who were scattered in the far reaches of the Roman Empire, one feast per year would have been a major investment of time and effort. For devout Hebrews who lived closer, the obligation to all three festivals was considered mandatory.

After observing that Joseph and Mary went "every year" to observe Passover, Luke goes on to tell the events of a particular pilgrimage when Jesus was twelve. The setting for this episode seems strange to us but fits the time and place very well.

How could Joseph and Mary not miss Jesus for a whole day of their trip back to Nazareth? For modern families who travel together by car or on planes, it sounds incredible that people could go so long without missing their child. But people in Jesus' time traveled on foot and preferred to be in large groups for the sake of protection. As pilgrims moved from Galilee toward Judea, they linked with caravans arriving from even greater distances and then continued to pick up others as they got closer to the holy city. Thus thousands of people moved together across the landscape. Unlike our preferred way of traveling by families or small groups, they moved in huge groups that sorted out into subgroups of nursing mothers, chattering older men, single women, playing children, etc.

Day 2
The Value of Ritual

Read Exodus 12 for background to the Feast of Unleavened Bread.

1. What is "ritual"? Share a family ritual from your experience that shaped your faith and life.
2. What was the nature of the Passover Festival? How was the whole family involved in it?
3. Are there things you want to pass on to your children and grandchildren? What are you doing to achieve that goal?
4. Is it possible for people to "inherit faith"? Contrast inherited and personal faith.
5. Describe a ritual you would like to implement in your family.

37

Day 3
The Word of God

Read Psalm 119:105-136 about loving and desiring the Word of God.

1. Did your childhood give you the opportunity to learn Scripture? Describe your earliest memories of Bible study.

2. His knowledge of Scripture led Jesus to make an early life commitment to the Father. Compare that to your experience.

3. Do you understand the importance of daily time with the Bible? Why is the Bible so critical to Christian living? Tell how you find time for personal Bible study.

4. Are your daily experiences different when you forget or neglect Bible study?

5. Children are passionate about church and the Bible. How do we maintain that spirit among adults?

Visualizing such a scene, it is not so hard to understand how Joseph and Mary could have moved with a mob of people on the assumption that their son was with his younger friends in the group. Although their departure without him was unintentional, his act of remaining behind seems to have been altogether deliberate. Our text informs us that "the boy Jesus stayed behind in Jerusalem." It was a choice rather than an accident on his part to remain in the temple precincts.

It was on the third day following their initial departure that Joseph and Mary found Jesus. The words of Mary to her son reflect both her personal stress and a rebuke of what he has done. "Son, why have you treated us like this?" she asked. "Your father and I have been anxiously searching for you." The response from Jesus gives us not only the first recorded words of the Son of Man but a significant insight into his entire life. "Why were you searching for me?" he asked. "Didn't you know I had to be in my Father's house?"

Jesus' reply to Mary should not be read as reflecting disrespect toward his mother but as surprise. His surprise would have been that they had not come directly to the temple when they missed him. In other words, he was not rebuking them for looking for him (which was only natural!) but expressing a degree of shock that they would not have known to go to the temple to find him. After all, they had taught him to love the law and house of God.

[Note: The KJV has Jesus speaking of "my Father's *business*" here. The translation "house" is surely correct. One can be busy with the Father's work anywhere and at any time. It was the house (i.e., temple) of God that held special attraction to Jesus when he and his family went to Jerusalem.]

It is also important to note that Jesus was already speaking of "my Father." Although he was only twelve years old and had no supernatural powers of insight, he was beginning to sense a special and perhaps unshared relationship with God. Although it was not without precedent for Jews to speak of God as "*our* Father," we know no parallel to this strong reference to "*my* Father."

Why had Jesus stayed behind at the temple? We are not left to wonder. Luke tells us that he was absorbed in studying the Word of God with the teachers gathered in the temple compound. He was "sitting among the teachers, listening to them and asking them questions." A common educational method of the time was to gather around competent teachers for extended periods of question-and-answer exchange. Jesus was not only able to engage in such discussions with adults but to do so impressively. "Everyone who heard him was amazed at his understanding and his answers."

Most students of this text see it as a great compliment to the family experience Jesus had with Mary and Joseph. "These words are thus a revelation of the life in the home at Nazareth. It was not by a miracle or due to some divine attribute, but because of the training he had received from his pious parents, that Jesus at the age of twelve was a master of the Scriptures, and had learned to reverence and adore all that was related to them and to the worship of God. Is it not possible for parents today to awaken in the hearts of their children a love for the house and the Word and the will of God?" [Charles R. Erdman, *The Gospel of Luke* (Philadelphia: Westminster Press, 1966), p. 44.]

As an insight into the total human experience of Jesus, few texts are more revealing than this one. By his twelfth year, his heart was possessed by a firm resolve to be active in pursuit of the Father and in obedience to the divine will.

Both Jesus and his parents were struggling at this

Day 4
Godly Family Life

Read Ephesians 5:21–6:4 for Paul's vision of a Christian family.

1. Luke says Jesus obeyed his parents. Why is submission to authority an important lesson for all of us to learn?

2. Do you ever have problems with authority? Describe a situation where obedience to God came only with great difficulty.

3. Authority is sometimes abused. Describe how this can happen between parents and children, husbands and wives, elders and churches.

4. How does falling in love with Jesus purify the other relationships of your life?

point to understand how they fit within the divine plan that was unfolding around them. While Luke lets us know that Joseph and Mary "did not understand what he was saying to them," we are only left to wonder how much Jesus himself saw clearly at this point. Did he have an idea of being the Messiah yet? Did he see his sonship to God as unique and unshared?

Day 5
A Balanced Life

Read Proverbs 3 to see the value of living one's whole life under the rule of God.

1. Explain the "balance" in Jesus' life as reflected at Luke 2:52. Do you have difficulty with balance in your life?
2. *Wisdom* refers to intellectual growth. How do you nurture your intellectual life?
3. *Stature* refers to physical development. How do you honor your body as a temple of the Holy Spirit?
4. *Favor with God* refers to a relationship with God. How do you nurture your relationship with Father, Son, and Spirit?
5. *Favor with men* refers to social development. How do you nurture your relationships with the people around you?

2. A summary of his growth to manhood. 2:51-52.

At the conclusion of this interesting event, we learn that Jesus returned to Nazareth with his parents and was submissive to their authority. Over the next eighteen years, Jesus lived in Nazareth, continued his education at the synagogue, and worked as a carpenter.

The fact that only Mary is mentioned in this summary of the remainder of Jesus' boyhood lends credibility to the theory that Joseph died early in his life. Luke does not mention him again. This raises an interesting question in light of the fact that Jesus had four brothers and some sisters (Matt. 13:55-56). If Joseph did leave Mary a young widow, Jesus would have had a special degree of responsibility to care for the family because of his position as the oldest male child.

Until he was about thirty years old, Jesus matured in a balanced way. Luke records that he "grew in wisdom and stature" (i.e., intellectually and physically). To this he adds that he "grew . . . in favor with God and men" (i.e., spiritually and socially). In his comments on this verse, Leon Morris writes: "In the similar summary in the case of John the Baptist (1:80) there is nothing equivalent to *in favour with . . . man*. Probably there was an early difference in personality. John's sternness precluded him from anything like attractiveness."

Regardless of the differences in their personalities, Jesus and John were linked closely in the divine will. Luke examines John's preparatory work before pursuing more data from the life of Jesus.

Week Five

Luke 3:1-38 (III A to III C in Outline)

III. Preparing for His Ministry. 3:1–4:13.

A. John's Work of Preparation. 3:1-20.

All four Gospels point to the importance of John the Baptist's career as background to the work of Jesus. He was the first prophet to appear in Israel for 400 years. Breaking the centuries of silence, he announced the nearness of the Messiah and called people to repentance and baptism in anticipation of his appearance. Luke preserves several details of his teaching that are found only in this Gospel.

1. The initiation of his ministry. 3:1-6.

Preaching in the region of the Jordan valley, John offered "a baptism of repentance for the forgiveness of sins." Repentance is an inner determination to turn away from sin, and baptism was the sign of repentance that John required of people. It was also a rite of cleansing known to the Jews through both their many ceremonial washings and the baptism of proselytes to Judaism. As would later be the case with Christian baptism, repentance and baptism constituted a person's appeal to God for spiritual cleansing (cf. 1 Pet. 3:21).

John's ministry in advance of the public appearance of Jesus was a fulfillment of Isaiah's prediction of "one calling in the desert" to prepare the Lord's way. Using the Eastern imagery of a king making a journey, Isaiah had prophesied of one who would prepare the highway before him by straightening roads, filling valleys, and smoothing rough spots

Day 1
John the Baptizer

Read Matthew's overview of John's ministry from Matthew 3:1-12.

1. Contrast the personalities and behaviors of Jesus and John.
2. Is it difficult for you to accept "unusual" people? Can parents expect children to be alike?
3. Comment on John's self-description at John 3:27-30.
4. Describe someone who "prepared the way" for your life of faith.

(Isa. 40:3-5). The obstacles John sought to remove from Christ's path were not physical ones but those spiritual hindrances that could be dealt with only through repentance and cleansing from God. Once he appeared, not only would the Jews benefit from the Messiah's presence but "all mankind" would be called to salvation.

**Day 2
Repentance**

Read Psalm 51 and Joel 2:12-17 for some insights on repentance.

1. Define "repentance." What is "fruit in keeping with repentance"?
2. How did John personalize his preaching to different groups?
3. Why would people flock to hear a preacher calling for repentance?
4. Was there a time in your life when repentance was God's primary message to you? What fruit has come from your repentance?

2. His preaching. 3:7-14.

As John's preaching began to draw large crowds, it appears that many were offering to receive baptism at his hands as a superstitious rite that might spare them God's judgment. Since baptism is meaningless except as it bears witness to a transformation of one's heart, John denounced them and refused their request for baptism. He called such persons a "brood of vipers" who were looking only to appease their guilty consciences.

Unless his hearers were willing to actually forsake their sins and change their lifestyles, his baptism would be useless to them. Thus he challenged them to produce evidence (i.e., fruit) of their repentance. Furthermore, he warned them against thinking that their descent from Abraham would be enough to save them.

John called people who were accustomed to substituting ceremonies and rituals for practical righteousness to stop playing their silly religious games. He demanded that they turn away from sin and embrace a life of compassion for the poor. Tax collectors — notorious in that day for their greed and dishonesty — were told to prove their repentance by collecting no more money than the law actually required. The Jewish soldiers who accompanied and helped the tax collectors were likewise told not to extort money by force or false charges and to be content with their own wages.

No wonder John was causing such a stir. His preaching was bold and direct. It treated real-life issues. It translated the meaning of religion into practical terms for everyone who heard him.

3. His heraldic message. 3:15-17.

John's impact was so powerful that many began to wonder aloud about the possibility that he was the long-awaited Christ. Rather than having his head turned by such flattering speculation, he immediately disclaimed it. At the same time, however, he made it clear that he was in service to the Christ for whose appearance he was also waiting.

John's personal humility is attested by the two things he said about himself in relation to the coming Messiah. For one thing, he said he was not worthy to untie the sandal thongs of the one to whom the people were comparing him. For another, there was the difference he made between the baptism he taught and administered and the one Christ would initiate. John baptized people in water as a sign of their repentance and eagerness to receive the Messiah. The Messiah himself, though, would "baptize you with the Holy Spirit and with fire." Baptism with the Holy Spirit would be a possibility for those who accepted him in true faith; baptism with fire would be the fate of all those who remained impenitent before him.

John was merely preparing the way for Christ. Jesus himself would be the one to separate the wheat from the chaff, taking the former into his barn but burning the latter with unquenchable fire.

4. A summary of his ministry. 3:18-20.

John was a faithful prophet who fulfilled his ministry of preparation. As with faithful prophets in general, John was not revered by his generation but rejected, imprisoned, and eventually killed. Although the actual termination of John's ministry did not come until after Jesus had started his own, Luke proceeds to tell us of the event that closed it in

Day 3
The Kingdom of God

Read Micah 4:1–5:5 for some of the literature that caused Israel to desire the Kingdom of God.

1. John announced the coming of the Kingdom of God. What is the kingdom? What do you think John's hearers understood it to be?

2. Why would word of the kingdom excite so many people?

3. What issues excite and draw large crowds today?

4. What expectations and dreams drive your life? How many of them have a distinctly spiritual focus?

order to focus his narrative on Jesus. Unwilling to spare anyone from God's call to repentance, he rebuked Herod the tetrarch for seducing his (half-) brother's wife and for "all the other evil things he had done" (cf. Matt. 14:1-12). Although a humble man, John was also courageous. He would not spare even the Herods from God's call to repentance.

**Day 4
Baptism**

Read Romans 6 to learn about Christian baptism.

1. What was the purpose of John's baptism? How is it like Christian baptism? How different?
2. Reflect on your baptism. Have you been baptized? What caused you to see the need for baptism? What changed at your baptism?
3. From Romans 6, explain the symbolism of baptism.
4. What affirmations came to Jesus at his baptism? How does baptism bring affirmation to someone today?

B. The Baptism of Jesus by John. 3:21-22.

When one first reads of this baptismal scene, it is nothing short of astonishing. Not only is the Son of God submitting to baptism at the hands of his messenger, but he is receiving a baptism associated with repentance and cleansing from sin. Why should the greater submit to baptism at the hands of the lesser? What sin did Jesus offer for cleansing?

First, Jesus allowed John to baptize him in order to affirm his genuine identification with those he had come to save. He shared our humanity in fact, not merely in appearance. Since this was the case, he was obligated to acknowledge every commandment from God and to indicate his attitude toward divine authority. Jesus insisted that John's ministry was indeed given by the Father (7:24ff). Thus he was obligated to "fulfill all righteousness" by submitting to it (Matt. 3:15; cf. Heb. 2:14).

Second, Jesus was not baptized to be cleansed of personal sin. He was without sin himself (Heb. 4:15), but his identification with the issue of taking away sin was affirmed in the act.

The baptism at the hands of John was thus a sign of Jesus' own humility and obedience to the Heavenly Father. It was used by heaven to endorse him as the Messiah and marks the beginning of his ministry in the flesh. "The closest modern parallel to Jesus' baptism — though of course it is not at all the same — is the selection of a presidential candidate at a political convention. At this ancient 'convention,'

44

however, there is only one elector who speaks, only one vote that counts." [Bock, p. 77.]

Luke alone records the detail that Jesus "was praying" at his baptism. As a matter of fact, Jesus was constantly in communion with his Father while on earth. It therefore comes as no surprise for us to learn this fact.

As Jesus was praying, the Holy Spirit made his presence and approval known when he "descended on him in bodily form like a dove." Some believe that Jesus' endowment with supernatural powers was initiated here and that the pre-public ministry time of his wrestling with human weakness and temptation were therefore identical with our own. His temptations were absolutely authentic, and he had no miraculous power to offset human weakness prior to the Spirit's descent. All depends on exactly what we understand Jesus to have "emptied" himself of when he was born into a limited, human, infant body (Phil. 2:7, NASB).

In addition to the visible presence of the Holy Spirit, the Father's presence and approval were made known audibly. He leaves no doubt of either the identity of the one who has just been baptized by John (i.e., "You are my son") or of his attitude toward him (i.e., "whom I love; with you I am well pleased"). And if Jesus is the Son of God who is loved by the Father, how could we not fall in love with him ourselves? Luke's Gospel makes a powerful case for doing so.

The public presentation of himself to undertake the dual role of Messiah and Suffering Servant was a breathtaking event. Yet it may be a bit misleading to call this a "public" event, since there is no evidence that any human witnesses were present beyond Jesus and John. If others were present and witnessed it, it seems highly unlikely that no reference would be made to their reaction. (Compare John 12:27-30.)

Day 5
Your Family Tree

Read 2 Kings 15 and mark the phrase "just as his father had done."

1. Reflect on some good things that came to you through family heritage. What is the value of reflecting on one's family tree?
2. What things from your heritage do you want to change for future generations?
3. What surprising or unusual characters do you see in Jesus' family tree? What do you learn from this?
4. The church is a "new family tree" for each believer. How does this fact help us break unhealthy cycles and form healthy patterns for the future?

C. Jesus' Genealogy on Mary's side. 3:23-38.

If Jesus was born around 6 B.C., he would have been 32 years old at the start of his public ministry. Luke simply records that he was "about thirty years old when he began his ministry."

On the heels of Jesus' endorsement as the Son of God, Luke offers his genealogy as further proof of the claim. Although the common assumption of his contemporaries was that Jesus was the son of Mary's husband (i.e., "He was the son, so it was thought, of Joseph"), Luke wants it clearly understood by his readers that the virgin-conceived Christ was in fact God's son rather than Joseph's. Thus the lineage offered does not stop, as does the one in Matthew, by tracing the ancestry that proves him to be "the son of David, the son of Abraham" (Matt. 1:1). Luke traces his roots past Abraham, Noah, and Adam to God.

There are significant differences in the genealogies found in Matthew and Luke. Many scholars believe the best explanation of this phenomenon lies in the different purposes of the first and third Gospels. Matthew was a Jew who wrote for Jews, so he traced the *legal* ancestry of Jesus that would prove his right to David's throne and to the title Messiah. Luke was a Gentile writing for Gentiles, however, so he traced the *actual* ancestry through Mary that would prove that Jesus was the Savior not only of the Jews but of all humankind.

Week Six

Luke 4:1-13 (III D in Outline)

D. His Personal Encounter with Satan. 4:1-13.

No one you know has ever been exempted from temptation. You fight your own battles every day and would think it unfair for anyone else to live on this planet and not have to deal with its challenges. Since the redemptive purpose of the Incarnation demanded that Jesus share our humanity in order to free us from the power of Satan (Heb. 2:14), it was necessary for him to have to deal with temptation as well. Scripture affirms this in these words: "We have [a high priest] who has been tempted in every way, just as we are — yet was without sin" (Heb. 4:15b).

Before Jesus could take it upon himself to defeat Satan for us at the cross, he first had to face and defeat him personally in the experiences described in this section of Luke's Gospel. This text is therefore not only dramatic and fascinating but is also integral to the telling of his story.

What a confrontation it must have been. What is summarized here in brief narrative must have been extended episodes of lies, challenges, and provocations that were occasionally punctuated with charm and subterfuge. For Jesus or us, temptation would be easy to resist if it came with a uniformly ugly face and menacing growl. Satan is not only capable of coming at human beings in his more straightforward nature as a "roaring lion" (1 Pet. 5:8), but he also "masquerades as an angel of light" (2 Cor. 11:14).

Both Matthew (4:1-11) and Luke tell of the wilderness temptation in some detail, while Mark (1:12-13) merely tells that it took place. They tell of the

Day 1
Satan

Read Revelation 12 for a summary of Satan's career as God's arch-enemy.

1. Satan is the "ruler of this world" (John 12:31; Eph. 2:2). How did he achieve such a status in God's world?
2. Why was it necessary for Jesus to have this dramatic encounter with Satan?
3. Recall a time when God rescued you from Satan's assault. Pray and thank God for his mercy in that situation.
4. Name some ways that you believe Satan is working to destroy the things that are precious to God in our time.
5. What will be Satan's final fate?

Day 2
Temptation

Read Genesis 3 to learn of Satan's first encounter as the tempter.

1. Define "temptation." Distinguish life's tests and discipline from the things that Satan uses to draw people into evil (cf. Jas.1:12-15).
2. What was the essence of the Eden temptations? Jesus' wilderness temptations?
3. What is Satan's most common route of attack in *your* life? His most effective attack?
4. Do you fear Satan? Guard against his attacks? Describe your strategy for resisting him.
5. Jesus told his disciples to pray: "Deliver us from the evil one." Take some time now to offer this prayer for yourself and others.

same three temptations but in a different order. The point of temptation — whether Jesus' or ours — is always the same. It is an invitation to please oneself rather than God. The point of such a test at the inauguration of Jesus' public ministry is therefore apparent. Luke shows that the Lord fixed his heart from the beginning on honoring the will of the Father and not on self-seeking goals. No wonder he could love Jesus and present him to others so they could fall in love with him too.

One should not think that this was Jesus' first encounter with Satan and temptation. As he grew up in Nazareth and gradually became convinced of his role as the Messiah, he must have been tempted to be arrogant and to resist submitting to parental authority. And there must have been the everyday stresses that come to everyone in the process of growing up, learning a trade, and dealing with people. The point of this one-on-one confrontation at the very beginning of his public role was that Satan hoped to derail his purpose at what might have been considered his most vulnerable and insecure moment. With neither followers nor track record, this would be the ideal time to isolate and overwhelm him.

The setting for the temptation is ironic. He had just been baptized by John, filled with the power of the Spirit, and affirmed in his identity as the "beloved Son." Surely part of his reason for withdrawing to a deserted place and fasting for forty days was to heighten his sensitivity to the will of God for his work. That time of triumph and seeking after God became the platform for Satan's attack on him. Does that sound familiar? Just at the moment when things seem to be going well and when we are consciously seeking God, Satan sets a trap to destroy us.

The *first* temptation was for Jesus to use his just-received miraculous powers for personal benefit. Had not a voice from heaven just called him "Son"?

Then how could it be improper for him to prove the genuineness of that relationship by turning stones to bread as his forty-day fast ended? If only Satan had known the heart of a godly man better, this might have become a more powerful temptation. A compassionate Jesus in the midst of a crowd of hungry people might be pressured to use his powers for them. But he would not profane his position or powers for personal satisfaction. He responded to the tempter by quoting from the Old Testament. It was far more important for him to honor his Father in holiness than to have a meal that day. Human beings are more than creatures with physical needs. We are in the image of God and are called to honor our likeness to him by putting spiritual things before material concerns.

The *second* temptation in Luke's account was an offer by Satan to deliver "all the kingdoms of the world" to Jesus in exchange for his worship. Although the world was created by God, the Bible admits that its allegiance has been yielded to Satan and evil. Thus, as the "prince of this world" (John 12:31), Satan was offering something that was genuinely under his power. Furthermore, it was something that Jesus wanted for himself. If men and women would give their allegiance to him, he would lead them to the Father. Merely to have the allegiance of others — without regard to the price paid for it — is an evil ambition grounded in selfish ambition. Thus Jesus could not be seduced by the devilish scheme put before him. He turned Satan down a second time by quoting Scripture. This time the text he cited affirmed that God alone is worthy of worship. Jesus would seek a transfer of loyalty by men and women who were under Satan's authority, but he would seek them via the divine route of obedience, submission, and a cross rather than through disloyalty to God. It seems much harder for some of

Day 3
Confidence in Living

Read 1 John 1:6–2:17 to learn of Christian security in relation to sin.

1. Who is the person mentioned in Romans 4:8? Relate this verse to 1 John 1:6ff.
2. What difference would it make in your life to believe that you are the person of Romans 4:8? Are you that person?
3. How confident are you about your security in Christ? About facing each day's share of difficulty or temptation? Explain your answer.
4. Imagine that you are talking to a child. Tell her how to live in confidence and hope before the Lord.

5. When did your heart become settled in God's promise to save and protect you to the end?

Day 4
Forgiveness

Read Psalm 51 where David deals with his awful sin with Bathsheba.

1. From Psalm 51, what do you hear as David's greatest heartache about his sin?

2. Describe the way you feel when confronted by your own spiritual failures. Compare that to David's self-description.

3. What does the word "forgiveness" mean in your life?

4. Do you think David had to struggle with accepting God's forgiveness? Have you ever had such a struggle? How did you resolve it?

us to keep our vision clear. We tend to think that a noble end may be sought by any available means. Holy ends must be sought by equally holy means.

The *third* temptation was nothing more nor less than an appeal to Jesus' vanity. Perhaps he was challenging Jesus to seek an immediate following by doing something spectacular in the crowded temple precincts. Even worse, he may have been chiding him to do a pointless miracle by putting himself in harm's way and presuming on God's grace to deliver him from the reasonable consequences one could expect from such an action. In either case, Satan was prompting the Son of God to put heaven to the test by acting foolishly. It is not faith that causes one to take foolish risks but presumption, and Jesus would not act presumptuously. He turned down this temptation by citing a biblical text that prohibits putting God to the test. God's people in every generation are to be willing to face danger in order to do their duty, and he will send his angels to minister to them — as he sent them to Jesus in the Garden of Gethsemane before his betrayal and death. "Courting danger" is an invitation to destruction. It is what many of us do in making career choices, spending money foolishly, or walking into relationships where we know the spiritual atmosphere is unhealthy. Presumptuous and foolish behavior is sinful in itself and leads to an even greater likelihood of more sin to come.

When this period of temptation ended, Satan is said to have "left" Jesus. But he did not leave for good, only "until an opportune time" to resume his attack. Temptation will never end for any of us until our lives here are finished. Therefore we can never drop our guard against Satan.

These verses remind practically everyone who reads them of the first encounter of the human race with Satan. In the Garden of Eden, Satan sought to plant doubt about the goodness of God and the reality of his relationship with Adam and Eve. "When the woman saw that the fruit of the tree was good for food and pleasing to the eye, and also desirable for gaining wisdom, she took some and ate it. She also gave some to her husband, who was with her, and he ate it" (Gen. 3:6). Here the offers from Satan appear to have appealed to physical satisfaction (i.e., something good to eat), visual appeal (i.e., pleasing to look at), and personal vanity (i.e., able to confer an advantage). The threefold similarity here with the emphasis of the temptations put before Jesus is striking.

Also, John wrote of the world's appeal and warned: "For everything in the world — the cravings of sinful man, the lust of his eyes and the boasting of what he has and does — comes not from the Father but from the world. The world and its desires pass away, but the man who does the will of God lives forever" (1 John 2:16-17). The pattern is discernible again: cravings (i.e., personal satisfaction), lust of the eyes (i.e., visual appeal), and boasting (i.e., vanity). The Bible seems to teach with considerable consistency that there are three primary avenues through which evil enters a human heart. With so much specific warning, one would expect us humans to do better than we do. Our continual failure before Satan's efforts to entice us into evil attests both our weakness and his persistence.

No one who is vulnerable before any temptation needs to fear that Christ cannot understand his or her situation. He has been where we stand. And he has given us confident hope that God's power to overcome evil is greater than Satan's power to ensnare. Jesus' victory over sin proves that Satan cannot have the final word. Now that sin has had its power broken and the devil's stranglehold on the race has been challenged, there is no reason for us to cringe in fear before evil.

Day 5
Strength for the Battle

Read Psalm 119:89-115 for affirmations of the value of the Word of God in battling temptation.

1. How did Jesus respond to each of Satan's temptations? What insights come to you from that?
2. List the key terms from Psalm 119 that describe David's attitude toward the Word of God.
3. Make a list of terms from your own experience that summarize your attitude toward the Word of God.
4. How has obedience to God brought peace to your life?
5. Is there any adjustment you need to make in your attitude toward or personal experience with the Bible? What will you do today to bring about that adjustment?

Week Seven

Luke 4:14-44 (IV A 1 to IV A 3 in Outline)

Day 1
The Focus of His Ministry

Read Isaiah 61 for the full setting of the text Jesus read in the Nazareth synagogue.

1. Of all the texts about the Messiah, why do you think Jesus chose this one to read? What blinded his hearers to his application of the verses to himself?
2. Define the focus of Jesus' work from these verses.
3. Which of these activities best fits your life need today? Why?
4. How well do these verses describe churches today? What relevance do they have to church ministry? Explain your answer.
5. Might you have sided against Jesus that day? Have you ever resisted his good news of freedom and release for yourself?

Day 2
Rejection

Read Isaiah 53 for a prediction of Jesus' rejection.

1. How hard is it for you to go back home? To meet people who knew

IV. The Ministry of the Son of Man. 4:14–19:28.

A. An Early Ministry in Galilee. 4:14–7:50.

After telling about Jesus' baptism and temptation, Luke devotes an extended amount of space to an early ministry of the Son of Man in Galilee. We are not to understand that Jesus did nothing in Judea and waited until he returned to Nazareth to start teaching. To the contrary, Luke lets us know that reports of his earliest works reached Nazareth before he did. Thus he arrived in his hometown to be greeted by curiosity and skepticism by the people who had known him as a child, adolescent, and young man.

Luke probably tells about the ministry sequence because of its defining nature for Jesus. It sets his agenda as a work of compassion and grace that was heralding the Kingdom of God. It illustrates his unique and authoritative style of teaching. It shows the power of the Holy Spirit at work in him to perform miracles. And it reveals how his work generated not only eager response from his hearers but also fierce opposition.

1. His rejection at Nazareth. 4:14-30.

By the time he reached Nazareth, Jesus had already established a reputation in several synagogues as a masterful teacher. From his own words at verse 23b, it appears that he had experienced a particularly impressive reception at Capernaum [Kə-pər'-nā-əm]. News about his message — and perhaps about his miracles — had come to the attention of his family and friends there. They were eager to get an explanation of what they had heard or to witness for themselves something of what had been reported.

Following his weekly custom of synagogue worship, Jesus was in place at the Nazareth synagogue on a Sabbath. Perhaps as an honor to him, he was asked to read from the prophets. This reading was typically the second one in a synagogue assembly, following a reading from the Torah. Whether Jesus asked for the Isaiah scroll or had it handed to him by the guidance of divine providence, we cannot say. But when he received the scroll, he very deliberately unrolled it to the section that corresponds to Isaiah 61 in our chapter-and-verse editions of the Bible.

Adopting a respectful posture of standing to read the Holy Scripture, Jesus stood and read the Hebrew text. The section speaks of a ministry to people in distress by God's anointed, the Messiah. After respectfully rolling up the scroll, he assumed the customary Jewish teaching posture by sitting down before speaking. With eager eyes fixed on him, the people waited to hear what he might claim. There was no hesitation or ambiguity. "Today this scripture is fulfilled in your hearing," he said.

Although the first impressions of the fickle group were positive (i.e., "All spoke well of him and were amazed at the gracious words that came from his lips"), they were mixed with a heavy dose of skepticism. "Isn't this Joseph's son?" they kept asking. In other words, "Can we really believe that someone so well-known to us has been chosen by Yahweh as his 'anointed one'?"

Jesus chose to confront their skepticism directly. He first quoted two proverbs they would have known and applied them to the situation. The former (i.e., "Physician, heal yourself!") seems to say

you "back when"?

2. Describe what Jesus had been doing before his return to Nazareth. What sort of curiosity can you imagine about him?

3. Why did the people at Nazareth reject Jesus?

4. Try to imagine the impact of rejection on Jesus. On his family.

5. Think of a time of rejection in your own life. How did God enable you to deal with it?

that they were expecting him to rescue his reputation by performing miracles of the sort that had been attributed to him during his work there. The latter (i.e., "No prophet is accepted in his hometown") is an ancient version of our familiarity-breeds-contempt theme. He then moved to cite the examples of two Old Testament prophets (i.e., Elijah and Elisha) who were not appreciated by the people who knew them best and who should have benefitted most from their ministries. As a matter of historical fact, the widow who took care of Elijah (1 Kgs. 17:8ff) and the Syrian leper healed by Elisha (2 Kgs. 15:1ff) were both Gentiles.

So direct a confrontation that included an appeal to Gentiles was more than the synagogue crowd would tolerate. Their skepticism turned to anger, and they ran Jesus out of town. They were ready to throw him off a cliff, which would have been a prelude to stoning him. At that point, Jesus appears to have performed his one and only miracle for the people of his hometown. He escaped their intentions without having to fight or flee. He simply "walked right through the crowd and went on his way." Insofar as the biblical record goes, this was the beginning and end of Jesus' work at Nazareth. The Gospels say nothing about Jesus ever visiting Nazareth again after this disappointing Sabbath event.

2. His ministry at Capernaum. 4:31-41.

In sharp contrast to what happened at the synagogue service at Nazareth, Luke moves quickly to tell of another Sabbath event in Capernaum. It has a happy ending. It results in a man's release from demon possession and a city's rejoicing in Jesus. This is one of five episodes in the Gospel of Luke where someone is healed on the Sabbath.

As Jesus began his teaching at Capernaum, people were "amazed at his teaching." Specifically,

---

Day 3
Savior of All

Read Acts 15:1-32 for an early discussion of racism in the church.

1. What did Jesus indicate about God's acceptance of Gentiles? How so? With what effect on the people listening?
2. How did racism hinder the first-century church? Cite specific instances.
3. React to this statement: "Racism is no longer a problem for Christians."
4. What prejudices have you been forced to deal with in your life? Do you understand their origins?
5. Suggest some ways Christians can be forces for reconciliation in our world.

their amazement traced to the "authority" his message had. Most scholars see this as a reference to Jesus' style of teaching, as well as its wonderful content. Typical rabbinic style consisted of quoting first one and then another revered authority on the meaning of the scriptural text. By contrast, Jesus was both bold and original in his treatment of the Word of God. His teaching rang with the sort of authority that genuine prophets of the Old Testament possessed. Just as they cried out "Thus says the Lord!", so did Jesus speak in the authority of one filled with the Spirit of God.

As he taught that day, "a man possessed by a demon, an evil spirit" interrupted him. Although we know very little about demon possession, it will not do to explain it away as an ancient description of mental illness. During the personal ministry of Jesus, he was establishing the phenomenal claim that "all authority in heaven and on earth" belonged to him (Matt. 28:18). It was therefore necessary to demonstrate not only his power over nature (e.g., stilling storms), mankind (e.g., healing disease, discerning hearts), and death (e.g., raising Lazarus) but also over spiritual powers. Thus did he confront and cast out demons who had taken control of the bodies and/or minds of helpless persons. Without the contortions and incantations of so-called exorcisms, the Spirit-empowered word of Jesus was enough to rebuke and cast out demons.

In this confrontation, one of the strangest things related in all the Bible happens: Jesus' mission and true identity are confessed by a demon! "Have you come to destroy us?" asked the demon. "I know who you are — the Holy One of God!" Jesus rebuked the shrieking demon and cast it out of the man. In a scene that must have frightened those who witnessed it, the demon "threw the man down before them all and came out without injuring him."

Day 4
Sabbath Traditions

Read Matthew 15:1-14 for a fuller view of Jesus' problem with human traditions.

1. Define "tradition." Are all traditions harmful? When do they become problematic?
2. Explain how Sabbath traditions had come to be oppressive in Jesus' time.
3. Name a religious tradition that has been helpful to you. One that has been harmful.
4. How does one challenge religious tradition without creating tension and problems?
5. Can you identify a tradition in your personal or church history that is hurting people? What do you suggest doing about it?

Day 5
Jesus' Compassion

Read Mark 7:24-37 for an account of Jesus' compassion at work.

1. What is "compassion"? Where does this trait belong in Christian character?

2. Try to imagine what it would have been like to deal with a demon-possessed person. Would you seek out or avoid such a person? Why?

3. What enabled Jesus to deal with such difficult persons? Why would he not feel compelled to avoid them?

4. Describe the sort of person with whom you have the greatest personal difficulty. How has godly compassion enabled you to deal with such people?

5. What resulted from the encounter between Jesus and the demon-possessed man? Recall an experience when your compassionate outreach produced an unexpected outcome.

Leaving the synagogue that day, Jesus went to the home of Simon Peter. There he healed Peter's mother-in-law. Dr. Luke reports that she had been suffering from a "high fever" that Jesus "rebuked" and cured instantly. The completeness of the cure is stressed in the fact that the woman "got up at once and began to wait on them."

Word of this miracle and of the casting out of a demon earlier in the day had traveled rapidly that day. Thus, as the sun was setting (i.e., the Sabbath ended at sundown Saturday), "the people brought to Jesus all who had various kinds of sickness." If we take the word "brought" literally, we understand why they had to wait until sundown. Carrying burdens was forbidden on the Sabbath, so they had to wait for that holy day to end before loading makeshift stretchers with the diseased bodies of the people they loved. Jesus did not merely make some sign of blessing in the crowd's direction and pronounce the people whole. Luke notes that he laid his hands on each person who was healed. Little details of this sort seem to have fascinated Luke. He had fallen in love with a compassionate Jesus who would not turn away from diseased and (under the Law of Moses) "unclean" persons.

In the course of the miraculous healings that afternoon and evening, more demon-possessed persons were set free. But Jesus put a stop to the testimonies to his deity by the demons. He "rebuked them and would not allow them to speak, because they knew he was the Christ." While this appears strange to us, it probably relates to two things: (1) Jesus wanted his words and works to speak for themselves (cf. 7:18-23) and (2) he had no desire to have the primary early testimony to his identity given by such evil witnesses as evil spirits.

3. Working beyond Capernaum. 4:42-44.

With the success of that Sabbath behind him,

Jesus could have made Capernaum his permanent base of operation and drawn great numbers of pilgrims there. This was not his Father's agenda, however, and he would have no part of such a plan.

Early the next morning, he escaped to a "solitary place" to pray and to get away from the mob he knew would come (cf. Mark 1:35). Talking with the crowds later, he resisted their pressure to stay in Capernaum. He told them that the Father had sent him to "preach the good news of the kingdom of God to the other towns also" and left. Luke tells us that he began a preaching tour that eventually took him not only to other synagogues in Galilee but into Judea.

Week Eight

Luke 5:1-39 (IV A 4 a to IV A 4 e in Outline)

Day 1
Discipleship

Read John 13:1-20 for a perspective on the imitation of Jesus.

1. Define these terms: *disciple, master, apostle.* How did Jesus teach his followers?
2. What made Peter drop his nets after a night of fruitless work? What background did he have with Jesus?
3. What frightened Peter about this miracle? Why did he react as he did?
4. Does *fear* or a *sense of sinfulness* ever intimidate your discipleship? Describe how you have worked through one of these situations.
5. What motive for discipleship is highlighted in John 13? How does it relate to Peter's experience here? To your own?

4. The course of his ministry. 5:1–7:50.

Luke devotes the next three chapters to tracing some of the significant events of Jesus' early Galilean ministry.

a. Calling his first disciples. 5:1-11.

One of the first things Luke tells about the public ministry of Jesus is his selection of certain disciples to be his associates and trainees in kingdom matters. He then launches into events involving the teacher and his pupils. The setting for instruction Jesus used with these men was not unlike that of Socrates and Aristotle with their pupils. A "school" at that time was more often a teacher traveling with men who would observe, listen, and ask questions. So the early disciples (i.e., students) were trained and groomed. Then, from their number, Jesus ultimately chose apostles (i.e., ambassadors) to represent him to others.

Because of his later importance to the apostleship, the first disciple whose calling Luke tells about is Simon Peter. Since they were his fishing partners, the same story also accounts for the calling of Peter's brother, Andrew, and another pair of brothers named James and John.

Only a short distance from Capernaum, Jesus was beside the Lake of Gennesaret [Jĕn-nĕs´-ə-rĕt] — better known to most of us as the Sea of Galilee. There he was besieged by people who had heard about his deeds in Capernaum. As he taught, the crowd grew until it was ultimately difficult to address the people. So he asked the owner of a nearby boat to permit him to sit in his vessel and to use the water as a natural platform and loudspeaker system. That boat owner happened to be Peter.

After Jesus had taught the people from the boat-pulpit, he focused his attention more specifically on Peter. The fisherman had presumably stayed in the boat he loaned to Jesus and had heard all that had been said. He was not asked to give his opinion of the lesson, but he was urged to put the boat still further out and to drop his nets. Peter told how fruitless fishing had been the night before. Instead of using this as an excuse for not doing what Jesus had asked, however, he indicated something of his response to the teaching he had heard. "Master, we've worked hard all night and haven't caught anything," he said. "But because you say so, I will let down the nets." It was faith in Jesus rather than anything he had reason to expect out of his own experience that moved him that day. Peter's faith prompted obedience.

No sooner had the nets been dropped than they began to fill. Wrestling with them by himself, Peter could not pull them in without tearing the nets. So he called for his partners who were still on the shore, and they worked together to bring in a huge catch. So many fish were put into the two boats, in fact, that they were overloaded and began to sink.

This was no extraordinary stroke of good luck. Peter knew immediately that he was witnessing a miracle. The great gathering of fish had happened because Jesus had somehow acted in this setting. Peter's sense of awe before this holy man caused him to exclaim, "Go away from me, Lord; I am a sinful man!"

Jesus' response to the humble and confessional statement Peter made must have surprised the fisherman. Jesus neither disclaimed the fact of the miracle nor left Peter to wonder what its meaning might have been. It was an acted parable. It was the basis for making a second request of Peter and his

Day 2
Fishers of Men

Read 1 Peter 4:12–5:11 about living for Christ in a hostile environment.

1. What was the life of a Galilean fisherman like? What adjustments would have to be made in leaving that life for Jesus' new calling?
2. Peter saw and accepted Jesus' power and authority. Did he understand how Jesus did the miracle? Is understanding a prerequisite to following Christ?
3. Do you struggle with *understanding* God versus *accepting his will*? Explain.
4. From 1 Peter, compare the mature apostle's counsel to his early experiences. What process brought him to maturity in his faith?
5. We admire Peter and other "giants" of faith. Can we reach maturity in Christ without the same *process of refining* they endured? Where are you in that process?

friends. "Don't be afraid," he told him. "From now on you will catch men." Peter, Andrew, James, and John immediately retired from the fishing business to become full-time students of the Galilean who had astonished them that day.

[Note: Although the Lukan text could be read as indicating that this was the first time Jesus and these men had met, other Gospel information lets us know that Andrew and Peter — likely James and John also — had had the benefits of John the Baptist's identification of him and a private interview with the new rabbi before this episode (John 1:35ff). These four did not follow Jesus on a whim or because of some mesmerizing power he exercised over them. They had come to believe in him through what they had seen and heard. The Lord never asks people to follow him blindly and without evidence of his identity and authority.]

b. Healing a leper. 5:12-16.

In an unnamed Galilean town, Jesus met a man "covered with leprosy." No disease of antiquity was more feared than leprosy. Among the Jews, a diagnosis of this disfiguring and debilitating disease meant that one had to live away from his family and in quarantine from the rest of the community (Lev. 13:42-46). He could not, of course, participate in events of the synagogue or temple. He was reduced to a miserable existence that became increasingly difficult as the disease progressed. Perhaps only such things as AIDS and the Ebola virus are modern parallels.

The text suggests that the suffering man had learned of Jesus' ability to work healing miracles and had sought for him. When he found him, he had no reservations about his power to cure leprosy. It was only his compassionate willingness that remained an unknown for him. In a pathetic scene, the leper threw himself face down on the ground and begged, "Lord, if you are willing, you can make me clean."

**Day 3
Compassion**

Read Micah 6:6-8 for insight on the true worship of God.

1. What was the status of lepers in ancient times? Have you ever felt you were the spiritual equivalent of a leper? Describe that time.

2. The leper was concerned about Jesus' willingness to heal him. Have you ever struggled with God's willingness to accept, forgive, and heal you? How did you resolve that struggle?

3. Who are some of the significant people who have reached out to you at crucial times? What difference did it make in your life?

Then, in a scene as tenderly powerful as the previous one was pitiful, Jesus did an unexpected thing that must have shocked the sick man and caused the disciples watching him to gasp. Although he certainly did not have to do so to effect a miracle, Jesus not only spoke the words of healing (i.e., "Be clean!") but also entered the poor man's world of uncleanness (i.e., "He reached out his hand and touched the man"). Anyone who touched a leper was immediately ceremonially unclean himself. So Jesus deliberately cut himself off from certain privileges of his own health in order to accept the liabilities of someone else's malady. It was a microcosm of the purpose behind the Incarnation. "Since the children have flesh and blood, he too shared in their humanity so that by his death he might destroy him who holds the power of death — that is, the devil — and free those who all their lives were held in slavery by their fear of death" (Heb. 2:14-15).

Made well immediately, the just-leprous man was told by Jesus to follow the instructions of the Law of Moses about purification (cf. Lev. 14:1ff). Strange as it sounds, though, he was also told not to tell anyone how he came to be healed. Jesus apparently did not want miracle cures to become the focus of his ministry lest it distract from his primary work of preaching the message of the kingdom. This interpretation of his intention is supported by Luke's comment that the crowds around Jesus were soon so large and demanding that he often "withdrew" himself in order to focus himself on the Father's work through prayer.

c. Forgiving sins. 5:17-26.

The next miracle account in Luke's Gospel adds the element of confrontation between Jesus and the religious establishment of his time. "Pharisees" were so conservative and orthodox that they were inclined to go beyond the actual requirements of the Law of Moses to impose demands that seem silly to modern

4. What life experiences have taught you to reach out to distressed people?
5. What situations are most difficult for you to address with compassion? Is there a person or situation you can reach out to this week that needs your compassion?

**Day 4
Forgiveness**

Read Psalm 103 and reflect on God's wonderful forgiveness.

1. Why did his friends bring this man to Jesus?

61

Why do you think Jesus raised the issue of forgiveness?

2. Do we sometimes confuse our wants and needs when we pray? Can you recall an instance when you went to the Lord with a request he graciously satisfied in an unexpected way?

3. Which is most difficult for you: giving forgiveness, seeking forgiveness, or accepting forgiveness? Cite an example that confirms your answer.

4. How does forgiveness allow or create healing? What amazing things have you seen happen in an atmosphere of genuine forgiveness?

readers — who may not have reflected seriously on our own peculiarities of interpretation. "Teachers of the law" were professional teachers (i.e., the "scribes" of older versions) who might be either Pharisees or Sadducees. The close association of these teachers with the Pharisees (cf. v. 30) likely signifies a group of "concerned brothers" who were bringing a few of their top-gun teachers and debaters to pass judgment on the orthodoxy of the young rabbi from Nazareth.

On this particular day, Jesus was teaching a tightly packed crowd from inside a Palestinian house. Such houses were typically built with flat roofs and exterior staircases by which a family could go up at night to catch any evening breezes. Space for latecomers to get close to Jesus inside one of these residences would have been difficult to find. One group of latecomers was on a mission, however, and would not be stopped by the press of a crowd. They had brought a paralyzed friend on a stretcher. Thwarted in their attempt to get into the house, they climbed the outside stairs, tore away part of the roof, and lowered the man into the room.

For the sake of such determined faith on the part of the paralyzed man's friends, Jesus said, "Friend, your sins are forgiven." This opens the interesting possibility that the man's physical problem traced to some evil deed and its consequences. Without dwelling on that point, Luke proceeds to tell us of the antagonism of the Pharisees and teachers of the law who had witnessed and heard what was happening. They regarded Jesus' statement as blasphemy and were thinking (correctly!) that God alone has the authority to forgive sins. Jesus' response was to verbalize what they were thinking and to challenge his challengers.

Jesus pointed out that it was an easier thing to *say* (i.e., merely to verbalize) "Your sins are forgiven" than to say "Get up and walk" to such a man. How so? It is one man's word against another's to say the former, for there is no necessarily observable difference between a saint and a sinner. On the other hand, to tell a paralyzed person that he can get up and walk will immediately validate or falsify the speaker's claim to divine power. Thus, in order to prove that he was speaking and acting by divine authority in all things, Jesus put himself on the spot. He told the man to rise and walk — and he did! He was strong enough to pick up the stretcher on which he had been brought to Jesus. He left for home, praising God. Aside from the Pharisees and teachers who were embarrassed and angered by what had happened, everyone else left that event "filled with awe" of God's power.

d. Calling another disciple. 5:27-32.

As Jesus was leaving the house — and perhaps the city — he passed by a man named Levi or Matthew (Matt. 9:9-13). He was a tax collector, which likely made him both wealthy and despised. Perhaps with a background of prior contact with Jesus similar to that of Peter and his fishing partners before their call, Matthew was called to join the forming band of disciples. His faith and commitment were evident in the immediate and total response he made to Jesus.

Because he was a wealthy man, Matthew was able to have a "great banquet" in Jesus' honor at his house. Other tax collectors and acquaintances of his were invited to meet and hear Jesus. The Pharisees and teachers of the Law of Moses who saw what was happening criticized Jesus severely — though not to his face. "Why do you eat and drink with tax collectors and 'sinners'?" they asked his disciples. Although they had meant for their question to be a doubt-maker among his fledgling disciples rather than a statement he would hear, Jesus again (cf. v. 22) responded without being invited to do so.

Day 5
Friend of Sinners

Read Luke 15 for Jesus' defense of spending so much time with "sinners."

1. What is meant by the title "friend of sinners"? What attracts sinful people to Jesus? Why is this title meaningful to you?

2. When Matthew accepted Jesus' call, what was the first thing he did? How did it open a faith door to outcasts?

3. Do you agree that each believer is capable of being a faith door for someone else? Explain how you attempt to link others with Jesus.

4. When are your friends most likely to be open to the friendship of

Jesus through you? Are you aware of someone you need to approach soon?

5. What role do fasting, prayer, and other religious expressions have in our witness to Christ?

"It is not the healthy who need a doctor, but the sick," he said. "I have not come to call the righteous, but sinners to repentance." The irony of his remark to the critics who were sniping at him should not be missed — although they most likely missed it altogether.

e. The issue of fasting. 5:33-39.

Another thing that bothered the Pharisees who had come to spy on Jesus at Matthew's party was not only the fact that he had chosen to be with the wrong crowd that day but the general mood of joy that seemed to attend his total life and ministry.

Although the Law of Moses enjoined only one fast per year on the Day of Atonement, the pious Pharisees had come to require twice-weekly fasts (cf. 18:12); John's disciples had apparently adopted a similar tradition. The Pharisees had also worked out a series of set prayers to be said at fixed times. Why were Jesus and his disciples not observing these forms?

Jesus replied by saying that rites and ceremonies were not the essence of true religion. He announced that he was calling people to a new way of viewing and relating to God — one that could not be comprehended or contained by their old ways and legalistic norms. Christianity is not a patched version of what had gone before; neither could it be contained in the old wineskins of Pharisaic forms and cultural expression.

Fasting may be appropriate as a voluntary expression of repentance, grief, or seeking after the Lord; it must always be voluntary for Christ's followers. And while prayer is central to genuine faith, it is the prayer of authentic praise or petition rather than ritual repetition that has power before the Lord.

Week Nine

Luke 6:1-11 (IV A 4 f in Outline)

f. The Sabbath question. 6:1-11.

The episode of healing in which Jesus claimed to have the authority to forgive sins (cf. 5:17ff) made the Pharisees skeptical of him. They accused him of blasphemy when he said it. The fact that Jesus challenged them and proceeded to heal the paralyzed man as proof of his divine authority could not have set well with them. From this point forward in the Gospel of Luke, the Pharisees are bent on exposing Jesus. They become intransigent enemies who will not hear anything he says with an open mind.

Sabbath observance had become both a distinctive and oppressive part of the Jewish religion. The Law of Moses commanded that the seventh day of the week be honored as a day of rest and worship. People were to suspend their normal work routines and celebrate the Lord with their families and friends. But the rabbis had developed an extensive body of oral law (i.e., tradition) that sought to specify exactly what was forbidden and what was allowed on that day. Their many layers of tradition had turned what had been intended as a peaceful and worshipful day into a tense and difficult one. Two tractates in the Mishna (*Shabbath* and *Erubin*) are devoted to working out the details of what could or could not be done during the 24 hours following sundown Friday evening.

His critics must have followed Jesus around, waiting to see or hear something they could use against him. On a day when he and his disciples were walking through a grainfield, they saw something that set them off. Jesus' disciples began to pluck some of the

Day 1
The Sabbath

Read Isaiah 1:10-17 to find an Old Testament prophet talking about the abuse of the Sabbath and other religious rituals.

1. What was the original purpose of the Sabbath commandment?
2. Why do you think so many extra provisions grew up around this commandment?
3. Ritual seems to be easier than true spirituality and following Jesus. Why? Can you think of situations where we value ritual above the original motive behind a biblical command?
4. How do you protect yourself from elevating the letter of the law above its true spirit? From creating artificial choices between "letter" and "spirit" of divine commands?

grain, rub it in their hands, and pop it into their mouths to eat. Since the Law of Moses permitted travelers to "pick kernels with your hands" while passing through someone's field (Deut. 23:25), they did not level a charge of stealing against the disciples. Neither, it would seem, did they challenge their right to "pick" grain on the Sabbath. It appears to have been the fact that they rubbed the heads of grain in their hands. It was a form of threshing, and that was more than they could tolerate.

Since a rabbi was always held responsible for the behavior of his pupils, the Pharisee critics did not challenge the disciples themselves. They went straight to Jesus. "Why are you doing what is unlawful on the Sabbath?" they wanted to know. Jesus' response was not merely to defend what his disciples had done but to challenge the manner in which the Pharisees were accustomed to using biblical rules. He cited an Old Testament example from 1 Samuel 21:1-6 in which David and his army did something that was a violation of the letter of law but for which he received no censure from God or men.

The incident in question is one in which David and his troops arrived at Nob in need of provisions. He asked the priest at Israel's tabernacle to help him secure the things he needed. "Now then, what do you have on hand?" he asked Ahimelech. "Give me five loaves of bread, or whatever you can find." The priest said that he had no supplies on hand. Specifically, he told David that he had no "ordinary bread." He did acknowledge, however, that some just-replaced loaves from the Table of the Presence were still on hand. Called "shewbread" in some translations, twelve loaves of this bread were prepared each week, set on the Table of the Presence in the Holy Place, and replaced the next week. Only priests on duty were to eat this bread. In the absence of what he had called "ordinary bread," the priest

Day 2
A Critical Spirit

Read James 4:1-12 about pride and slander.

1. People sometimes criticize others to elevate themselves. Might this have been at work in this case? Explain your answer.

2. James appears to see a link between *pride* and a *critical spirit*. Do you agree? Explain any relationship you see.

3. Are you generally critical? Critical of certain people or situations? If so, how are you dealing with the problem? If not, how did God teach you to avoid the problem?

4. How does another's criticism affect you? How do you deal with such persons?

5. How do you deal with people who try to "pick someone apart" in your presence?

proceeded to give David and his men the "consecrated bread" to eat.

Jesus had put his critics in a dilemma by citing this precedent. If they were ready to condemn Jesus and his men for breaking the Sabbath law by expending a minimal amount of energy to secure and eat a few kernels of grain, they would also have to condemn David and his army for their technical violation of the law in meeting their need for food. On the other hand, if they could tolerate and defend David's offense as a compassionate act of meeting an obvious need, they would be hard pressed to denounce what Jesus had allowed his disciples to do.

The Pharisees apparently had no answer. They were astute enough to know that the argument by analogy had put them in a very tight spot, so they said nothing. But Jesus pressed his point and announced, "The Son of Man is Lord of the Sabbath." He was neither subtle nor hesitant about announcing his identity to his sternest critics. He had already claimed deity by forgiving sins, and now he used the messianic title Son of Man of himself.

To say that he was "Lord of the Sabbath" was tantamount to saying that Jesus had authority over the laws, rituals, and institutions that Scripture authorizes. He was shutting his critics (and others) up to a very narrow set of options concerning his identity: *Either Jesus is divine, the Messiah, and Lord of humankind* or *he is to be rejected outright.* He left no middle-ground option of neutrality for us. We either believe or disbelieve, acknowledge him to be God or call him a liar.

Although the next event in this Gospel takes place on "another Sabbath," Luke chooses to relate it here because it is an extension of the controversy just recorded. It brings another charge of rule-breaking against Jesus. It also gives him the opportunity to explain another aspect of how the letter and spirit of

Day 3
"Lord of the Sabbath"

Read John 5:1-18 for another case of healing on the Sabbath.

1. Jesus knew that doing certain things on Saturday would bring criticism. Why did he proceed to do them anyway?

2. Did Jesus ever violate the Sabbath law? Jewish traditions about the Sabbath? Explain your answer.

3. How careful should we be about upsetting

67

people by doing things outside the "comfort zone" of their tradition?

4. When should we live within others' expectations of us? Should we ever ignore or violate another's expectations?

5. Can you recall an instance when your behavior violated someone's non-biblical tradition? How did you find out? How did you respond? Are you satisfied with that response now that you reflect on it?

law must be considered simultaneously in interpreting a biblical rule.

On the day in question, Jesus was teaching in a synagogue. There was a man present that day who had a "shriveled" right hand. Perhaps it had been seriously injured in an accident and had healed as a misshapen, useless appendage. Maybe it was the result of a birth defect. Luke the physician gives only the condition, not a history of its origin. Whether Jesus or his critics noticed the man first is not clear. There is no evidence that the man asked Jesus to heal him.

The escalating tension between Jesus and the Pharisees is clear from Luke's comment about the setting for what followed: "The Pharisees and the teachers of the law were looking for a reason to accuse Jesus, so they watched him closely to see if he would heal on the Sabbath."

Knowing the intentions of these onlookers, Jesus chose to force the issue. There was no good reason for not waiting until the next day to heal the man whose hand was atrophied. It was not a life-or-death case; even Jewish tradition made exceptions for things done under such emergency circumstances on the Sabbath. But Jesus chose *not* to wait for the next day in order to avoid controversy. He did something that he knew would bring down the wrath of his skeptics on his head.

Jesus asked the man whose hand was impaired to stand up in the synagogue where he would be in full view of all. The man stood up — whether as an act of faith in Jesus or simply by virtue of a startling request that took him off guard, we are left to wonder. Having spoken to the man to ask him to stand, Jesus spoke next to the people who were watching him to find some fault. "I ask you, which is lawful on the Sabbath: to do good or to do evil, to save life or to destroy it?" The form of the question

68

seems to imply that Jesus believed the withholding of good was morally equivalent to doing evil to another person (cf. James 4:17).

This reading of the situation at hand means that Jesus was actually putting this question to his critics: *Are you afraid that I will violate the Sabbath by healing this man? Should you not fear instead that I might violate this holy day by forcing him to continue suffering limitation and handicap?* One writer sees the issue a bit differently and says: "In attempting to defend the truth of sabbath tradition, [the Pharisees] plot harm on the sabbath, while Jesus seeks to meet needs. Who *is* violating the sabbath? There is a sting in the question" [Bock, *Luke*, p. 116].

On either reading, these interpreters of Scripture had clearly missed the point of the fourth commandment in the Decalogue. Sabbath keeping was a means to the end of honoring God with rest, worship, and celebration. They had made it an end in itself that had become oppressive with its detailed prohibitions. In this particular instance, they had been willing to allow the purpose of the Sabbath for one unfortunate man to go unmet (i.e., giving his cause for worship and celebration) in order to satisfy their zeal for legalistic righteousness.

With the issue squarely on the table, Jesus put his claims to deity and authority on the line. "Stretch out your hand," he said to the man whose hand had been crippled. When he did so, both he and the critical onlookers saw that it was "completely restored." We are not told the man's reaction to being healed and can only assume that he rejoiced. We are told, however, the reaction of the Pharisees who had already set themselves against Jesus. They were "furious" and began plotting against Jesus.

It is a dangerous thing to be caught in a trap of vested interest that will not permit one's eyes to see what is going on right before one's face. Yet that is

Day 4
Personal Worth

Read Mark 5:1-20 to see Jesus responding to people in need.

1. The man whose hand was crippled was viewed differently by Jesus and the Pharisees. What was Jesus' concern for him? What was the Pharisees' concern?

2. Can you recall an instance when Jesus saw someone in need and turned away? What do you make of that?

3. Can you help *everyone* whose need you know? Can you help *someone* whose need you know? Explain the difference in these questions.

4. The world calculates a person's worth on the basis of looks, ability, and money. What is the biblical view of human worth? Which do you live by?

5. What can the church do to help people have a healthy sense of their worth and dignity as human beings?

**Day 5
Interpreting the Bible**

Read 1 Samuel 6:1-11 for the case Jesus cited here.

1. What was the point of David's example to this situation?
2. Jesus' guiding principle about the Sabbath was that it was made for man, not vice versa (cf. Mark 2:27). Show how he applied that principle here.
3. Have you ever put rules over the value of people to God? Ever based your own relationship with God on your ability to keep rules? What relevance do you see for that tendency from this narrative?
4. What effect would it have on our use of Scripture to realize that rules were made for men, not vice versa? Can you think of an issue in biblical interpretation where this point has been missed?
5. Explain how you maintain a healthy respect for biblical authority without becoming a "legalist." How you value people above rules without being a "liberal."

exactly what happened with these people. They had been offended by Jesus' claims and had closed their eyes, ears, and hearts to him. The problem was not with the lack of evidence but with their attitude toward it. Jesus made himself known, but they would not be open to his self-revelation.

As valuable principles of biblical interpretation, two matters stand out from Jesus' Sabbath controversies. First, as Lord of the Sabbath and possessor of all authority (Matt. 28:28), Jesus interpreted the laws and commandments of God with absolute authority and correctness. His flesh-and-blood example of righteousness sets straight some of our pointless controversies over word meanings and fine points of theology. What the professional teachers of the Law of Moses were expecting in view of their interpretations were nothing like the enfleshed righteousness of God that appeared in the person of Jesus of Nazareth. Second, our interpretations of Scripture must respect the principle that the will of God is to liberate, heal, and enrich human life. We have the right to be very skeptical of any doctrine that makes seeking persons' lives more difficult by virtue of dogmatic and burdensome demands.

Week Ten

Luke 6:12-49 (IV A 4 g to IV A 4 h in Outline)

g. *Choosing the Twelve. 6:12-19.*

Having just described the background to a hostility toward Jesus from the nation's religious leaders that would ultimately result in his death at their hands, Luke proceeds to explain the procedure by which Jesus provided for his ministry to extend beyond his own lifetime. From the larger group of disciples attached to him, Jesus selected twelve men who would become his constant companions, assistants in ministry, and agents for the establishment of the church. The term *apostle* means "someone sent as a messenger." As Paul would later explain, the apostles served the church as Jesus' "ambassadors," men speaking for him in foreign territories (2 Cor. 5:20a). The significance of this event to Jesus is evident in the fact that he "spent the [entire] night praying to God" about his selections.

As if to signify both the establishment of a new order and its fulfillment of the old one, Jesus chose the same number of apostles as Israel had tribes. His later ministry would make it clear that everything he and the Twelve did was done to bring the expectations raised through Israel's prophets to completion.

The apostles could hardly have been more diverse or ordinary. The diversity is evident in that one collected taxes for the Romans (i.e., Matthew), while another was apparently aligned with a party of nationalists that was bent on resisting Rome at every turn (i.e., Simon the Zealot); their ordinariness reflects what Paul would later say about the composition of the first-century church in 1 Corinthians 1:26ff. Luke's list corresponds to the ones given in

Day 1
The Apostles

Read Acts 1:15-26 about the qualifications for being an apostle.

1. Jesus prayed all night before choosing the Twelve. What criteria do you think he used in choosing them?
2. Since Jesus prayed about his choice, explain the selection of Judas. Does prayer make your decisions infallible? Can people and circumstances change?
3. How were the Twelve alike? Different? Explain how such a diverse group could stay together.
4. How are you like the people in your church? How different? Explain how God is making you "one body" with them.

71

the other Synoptics (Matt. 10:2-4; Mark 3:16-19), with variations only in the order of the names. A constant in these lists is that Peter's name always comes first and Judas's last. Luke's "Judas son of James" is called Thaddaeus [Thăd´-dē-əs] in Matthew and Mark, reflecting the fact that many people of that time had two names.

Although Luke reminds us that Judas "became a traitor," it is likely that he was faithful at first and perhaps even noteworthy among the disciples. After all, he was the only non-Galilean chosen to the group. The name "Iscariot" is generally understood to identify Judas as a man from Kerioth [Kĕr´-ē-ŏth], a region in Judea.

Following a night in prayer and the appointment of the apostles, Jesus returned to the larger group of disciples following him. Perhaps for the benefit of solidifying the commitment of his new inner circle, he performed a dramatic series of miraculous healings and exorcisms.

Day 2
Blessings and Woes

Read Deuteronomy 28 for an Old Testament set of blessings and woes.

1. How does the start of this sermon "mock" worldly values? Explain the unique perspective of the kingdom of God.
2. What does the term *kingdom of God* mean? Are all church members kingdom citizens? Explain your answer.
3. What is the fundamental insight of God's kingdom people? What life orientation does it create?

h. The great kingdom sermon. 6:20-49.

The sermon that follows the selection of the Twelve bears many resemblances to the Sermon on the Mount (Matt. 5–7). It may be an alternate account of the same sermon, for "level place" of v. 19 need not be anything more than an inviting area on the mountainside that would accommodate a large crowd. It seems more likely, however, that this is another setting for what must have been something of a "keynote speech" that Jesus made again and again to different groups of people. He would not be the first preacher to use a favorite sermon outline more than once.

The sermon as preached here may be outlined as follows: blessings and woes (6:20-26), a life of love (6:27-36), judging others (6:37-42), a tree and its fruit (6:43-45), and the two builders (6:46-49). Whether in this form or in the longer version found in Matthew's

Gospel, this basic sermon on kingdom living should be seen as a *discipleship manual* for all who have committed themselves to follow Jesus as Lord.

The first movement of the sermon draws a sharp contrast between two life orientations. On the one hand, there is an abbreviated list of beatitudes (i.e., kingdom joys for those under God's sovereign rule); on the other, there is a deliberate contrast of woes (i.e., spiritual misfortune of those who are blind to the things of God). Taken together, the two lists "make a mockery of the world's values. They exalt what the world despises and reject what the world admires." [Morris, *Luke*, p. 126.]

The world certainly does not consider people fortunate who are poor, hungry, weeping, and rejected. Yet it is precisely those persons who are most likely to see themselves as totally dependent upon God. Denied the chance to boast of their self-sufficiency, they can boast only in the blessedness of their *spiritual status* before the Lord. Those who are deemed fortunate by the world's standards (i.e., rich, well fed, laughing, and popular) are far less likely to sense their need for God or to seek him. They feel so secure in their creature comforts that they tend to neglect the things of God.

The second movement of this great kingdom sermon focuses on living a life of love. More particularly, it calls the disciples of Jesus to an unnatural (i.e., supernatural) sort of love that embraces even one's enemies and imitates divine love in performing kindnesses where retaliation might be expected.

Granted that there is a significant amount of hyperbole in these statements, they are nevertheless designed to establish a principle for living that will revolutionize personal behavior. There are obvious limits to turning the other cheek and allowing others to keep what they have taken from you! We know there are limits because Jesus himself protested

4. Recall the event that has done most to drive home this insight to your heart.
5. Do you ever find yourself chasing after the things named in vv. 24-26? If so, how do you explain that? How do you keep your vision clear?

Day 3
A Life of Love

Read 1 Corinthians 13 as a reminder of the character of Christian love.

1. What is unique about the biblical concept of love?
2. Jesus states several demands of living by love. Which of the items given here challenges you most? Why?
3. Why do you think Jesus used such extreme language in this section?

Are there limits to turning one's cheek or allowing others to borrow from you? Explain your answer.

4. Jesus links love to spiritual parentage in vv. 35-36. What do you understand him to be saying here? What insight does this give you into your character?

5. Who has been your best example of this sort of distinctive life? Describe his or her impact on your Christian life.

injustices directed at him (John 18:23), and Paul called on the authorities to protect him from an out-of-control mob (Acts 22:25).

The point of these startling commands is not to create a woodenheaded literalism that turns society chaotic or leaves believers to be perpetual victims. It is to establish *perspective*. Against the human tendency to defensiveness, disciples are asked to be vulnerable. Contrary to the desire to retaliate, we are told to pray for those who hurt us. And against the selfish nature so many of us have, Jesus challenges us to generosity. When Jesus said that these calls were for "you who hear me" (v. 27), he was making it clear that they would always be beyond mere casual listeners; these are things that only the committed can embrace. While Jesus himself set limits and boundaries, at the end of his life he was praying for the forgiveness of those who had crucified him. Challenging as this standard is, it is the one that Jesus not only talked about but modeled for us.

This call to a life of love sets the stage for the Golden Rule: "Do to others as you would have them do to you" (v. 31). This is a call for spiritual sensitivity and discernment. Why are some people abusive? Why are they filled with rage? Why do they violate others' persons and property? Many of them are striking out against a world that has hurt and exploited them. So shall we see their behaviors and strike back at them? Jesus asks us to look at such persons with compassion and to give them the chance to be treated another way. Only if we rise above caring for those who are within our natural circles of concern can we display divine parentage. "Be merciful, just as your Father is merciful" (v. 36; cf. Eph. 4:32).

The sermon's third movement grows naturally from the second. People who love others and show mercy have no business criticizing and condemning them; either love rules out a critical spirit, or a critical

Day 4
Judging Others

Read James 2:1-13 about impartiality and fairness.

spirit exhibits the lack of love. The metaphor about measuring grain stresses that generosity of spirit and action is always expected of a kingdom person. The one about following a blind man not only warns us about the choice we make of the leaders we trust and follow, but it also challenges us to set an example that others may safely imitate. Above all else, worthy Christian leaders — whether first-century apostles or present-day church leaders — must prove that they see Christ's path clearly by exhibiting a loving, noncensorious spirit.

Jesus' final word to drive home the point about the absurdity of a critical spirit was a humorous one. He caricatured the person who tends to find fault by comparing him to someone with a huge wooden beam in his eye trying to get a dust speck out of another's. Such a person is nothing less than a "hypocrite" and would better learn to be gentle rather than supercritical (cf. Gal. 6:1). Each of us has enough faults of his own that his time would be better spent in self-examination than in passing judgment on others.

The two closing sections of the sermon are closely related to each other. Both stress the importance of taking Jesus' teaching seriously if one is going to share in the kingdom experience.

The ultimate test toward which professions of faith point is godly character. Thus Jesus likened a tree and its fruit to a person's character and deeds. Just as trees are recognized by the fruit they bear, a kingdom citizen is known by the "good things" that arise from the "good stored up in his heart." In other words, a profession of faith that is genuine will show itself in good deeds. Salvation is always and only by grace, not on the basis of performance and good deeds; yet the fact remains that no one who has been saved can fail to evidence her status with God by her goodness.

1. What life experiences have inclined you toward prejudice or a critical spirit? Tell how you have addressed these biases with God's help.

2. Recall a situation where you were the victim of someone's unfair judgment. How did God help you deal with it?

3. Do you see the humor of Jesus' words here? Have you ever thought of him telling jokes? Laughing? How does his sense of humor make him more human and real for you?

4. Why is it especially important for church leaders to avoid the pitfall of judging others?

Day 5
Choices

Read the famous challenge to choose God found at Joshua 24:14-28.

1. What is a disciple's first duty? How does the parable about a tree and its fruit illustrate it? The parable of the two builders?

2. How does one "choose" the fruit his life will bear?

3. What distinguishes the two builders in Jesus' story?

4. Identify the most important choice before

you today. What are its chief spiritual dimensions? How are you seeking God's guidance in making the decision?

5. Life in Christ still has to face storms of trial. Do trials prove you have made a wrong choice? Is some faith commitment in your life being tested today?

Verse 46 ties the section about trees and their fruit to the final appeal to build on a solid foundation. "Why do you call me, 'Lord, Lord,' and do not do what I say?" asked Jesus. Faithfulness is the primary obligation of Christ's disciples. Obedience is not an optional part of a kingdom life. By means of a rhetorical question, Jesus made it plain that one was indeed a hypocrite who claimed that Jesus was his Lord but then excused himself from daily obedience to his teaching.

Thus the closing admonition of the sermon is in the form of a short parable. Two builders set themselves to the task of erecting houses. One of them "dug down deep and laid the foundation on a rock" for his building. This is a long and demanding process, but it has long-term benefits. On the day when a flash flood comes, that house will survive because of its strong foundation. The other builder may have produced as pretty a house as the first, but it was badly flawed. In his haste to have something to show, he "built a house on the ground without a foundation." When it was tested by a flash flood, it could not withstand the force and collapsed. The life of someone who "hears [Jesus'] words *and puts them into practice*" is resting on a rock-solid foundation and will survive the storms of life, but the person who "hears [Jesus'] words and does not put them into practice" will lose everything.

It is not profession and external show that demonstrate discipleship. It is serious attention to the teachings of Christ, sincere obedience to his commandments,and faithful endurance in times of trouble for his sake.

Week Eleven

Luke 7:1-17 (IV A 4 i and IV A 4 j in Outline)

i. Healing the centurion's servant. 7:1-10.

Jesus' great sermon on the kingdom of God and discipleship had ended with an appeal for people to hear his words and put them into practice. Now that "Jesus had finished saying all this," Luke relates a series of events that illustrate the nature of faithfulness. Stories of a centurion, the widow of Nain, John the Baptist, and a sinful woman all point readers to an examination of the nature of authentic faith. They also contain more incentive for Luke's readers to fall in love with Jesus, just as the physician-friend of Paul had done by learning this material originally.

The first account in the series involves a *Gentile*. Luke's personal background — coupled with his concern to educate the early church about God's desire to save people from all races — would predispose him to want to tell this centurion's story. Moved by the Holy Spirit to do so, it remains in Scripture still to shock readers and to remind us that faith is often found in unlikely places and among unexpected people. Thus we are warned again concerning passing judgment on others (cf. 6:37-42) and called instead to discern the nature of another's heart by the actions he performs (cf. 6:43-45).

A "centurion" was an army officer in command of approximately a hundred soldiers. This man was likely a Roman officer assigned to Herod Antipas and therefore stationed at Capernaum. He was a pious man and probably is to be seen as one of the many "God-fearers" (i.e., non-Jews attracted to Yahweh and the Law of Moses but unwilling to proselyte) of that time. That he was also wealthy and generous is

Day 1
Humility

Read of Jesus as our example of humility in Philippians 2:1-11.

1. Centurions gave orders. How do you see humility in this man's actions?
2. What is *humility*? Do you think about this virtue often? What evidence of humility can you point to in your life?
3. Can you name someone who holds a position of authority and yet models the virtue of Christian humility? Does he or she know of your respect?
4. Explain how the life of Jesus demonstrates humility in its ultimate form.
5. If you could ask Jesus to heal one person who is important to you today, who would it be? Why?

evident from the fact that he had built a synagogue for the Jews of Capernaum (v. 5). Both his character and his significance to the narrative of the Gospel of Luke lead one to think of Cornelius and the importance he has to the Acts narrative (Acts 10:1ff).

The noble character of this centurion is also attested in the fact of his attitude toward a certain slave of his who was critically ill. That he cared enough about him to approach Jesus on his behalf indicates that he did not share the common view of his time that slaves were mere "living tools" who were expendable. Furthermore, in making his request, he exhibited considerable humility by approaching Jesus through "some elders of the Jews" rather than directly. [Note: Matthew's account of this same event does not mention intermediaries and appears to have the centurion approach Jesus personally (cf. Matt. 8:5-13). While the Bible's critics have tried to cast the two accounts as contradictory, they are irresponsible in doing so. What one does through an appointed agent is correctly attributed to the person himself.]

Because the centurion had been a friend to the Jewish community in Capernaum, the elders of that community were willing to bring his request to Jesus. In fact, they "pleaded earnestly" with Jesus on his behalf and insisted that the centurion "deserves" a response from Jesus because of his kindnesses to the Jews. Jesus responded to their plea by going with them in the direction of the centurion's home.

As they approached his house, the centurion sent a second delegation of representatives to Jesus. This time the message he sent was, if anything, more remarkable than the first. Perhaps as further evidence of his humility or perhaps out of concern for Jesus' being criticized about entering a Gentile house, he expressed the confidence that Jesus could heal the sick slave without coming under his roof.

Day 2
Reconciliation

Read Galatians 2:1-16 about Jew-Gentile tensions in the early church.

1. What does the centurion story tell us about possible good relations between Jews and Gentiles in pre-Christian settings? What was the basis of good will between the soldier and Jews of Capernaum?

2. What is to be the basis for respect among races

Comparing Jesus' authority from God to his own authority over soldiers, he said that a mere word from Jesus could heal his servant. "Lord, don't trouble yourself, for I do not deserve to have you come under my roof," he said. "But say the word, and my servant will be healed."

For one of only two times in the Gospels (cf. Mark 6:6), Jesus is said to have been "amazed." The faith of this non-Israelite astonished Jesus and caused him to say to the crowd of people with him: "I tell you, I have not found such great faith even in Israel." What kind of faith is genuine? What constitutes digging down to build one's life on a solid rock? What sort of faith do kingdom people display? Luke's answer is to offer us a model of authentic faith in this humble centurion who was willing to trust in the power of God as exhibited in the words spoken by Jesus.

Just as he always does, Jesus honored authentic faith in this man's heart. By virtue of his compassionate response to the centurion's request, Jesus healed his slave without seeing or touching him. By simply speaking the word, Jesus made him well. Before the centurion's messengers could deliver his communication and get back into the house, the servant was healed.

By such an intriguing story, Luke has communicated several things to his readers. First, he has given more of Jesus' credentials as Messiah and Lord. Second, he has supplied an example of faith that puts flesh to the concept of good trees bearing good fruit and wise builders laying a solid foundation for living. Third, he has communicated that Jesus is interested in Gentiles as well as Jews. Fourth, he has cited a case study that proves Jews and Gentiles can respect each other and work together for a common goal.

in Christ? How can we best communicate this?

3. Describe any problems you have had with racial prejudice or other types of alienation from people.

4. Can you recall a church situation where you saw reconciliation take place in the body? If so, how did the Spirit of Christ bring it about?

5. Does disunity in the church concern you? Are there things you would recommend that believers or churches could do to promote reconciliation?

Day 3
True Faith

Read James 2:14-26 about the nature of saving faith.

1. The centurion was not a Jew. Why does this make his faith all the more remarkable?

2. Is there someone who has served as a particularly important model of true faith for you? If so, describe that person.

3. If "very weak" is 1 and "very strong" is 10, how do you rate your faith today? Why?

4. What spiritual exercises strengthen faith? How many of these are part of your regular routine?

5. When someone's faith

is weak, what helps him or her to get through? Do you know of someone who is struggling? Can you do some helpful things for that person today?

**Day 4
Compassion**

Read Psalm 86 and reflect on the nature of God.

1. Jesus raised the widow's son out of compassion, not compulsion. Which of these motives leads you to help persons in need?

2. Who has been the most compassionate person in your life? How has it affected you?

j. Raising the widow's son. 7:11-17.

Shortly after the episode at Capernaum, Jesus and his disciples — with a large crowd following them now — went to a little town near Nazareth called Nain. There Jesus performed his most astounding miracle to date in Luke's Gospel by raising someone from the dead. It gives another group of people the opportunity to consider his claims and to respond to him in faith. It also provides important background to the reply that he will later make to John the Baptist's messengers about his identity as the Messiah (v. 22).

Jewish burials did not include embalming and typically took place within a few hours of a person's death. The body would be washed, anointed with aromatic spices and/or perfume, wrapped in burial cloths, and carried to the burial ground on an open stretcher. As Jesus approached the town gate of Nain, he met a procession of mourners on the way to the cemetery. This was a particularly sad funeral, for it was of a man who was "the only son of his mother, and she was a widow." The poor woman had lost her only child and henceforth would have no male to protect and provide for her. Furthermore, the family name would end with the burial of her son.

As Jesus met the procession, "his heart went out to" the grieving woman. Three astounding things then happened. First, he made what must have appeared to be a preposterous statement to a woman consumed with grief. "Don't cry," he told her. Second, he approached the corpse and "touched the coffin [stretcher, bier]" — an action that would have made him ceremonially defiled. Third, he spoke to the dead body lying on the stretcher in front of him and said, "Young man, I say to you, get up!"

One can only guess the stunned reaction of the pallbearers and mourners who had witnessed this

80

sequence of events. Did they think Jesus was mad? Were some about to confront him and drive him away? Did the people accompanying Jesus believe the widow's son really would come back to life on Jesus' word?

Regardless of their thoughts or expectations, the authoritative and powerful word from Jesus — Luke calls Jesus "the Lord" for the first time in his narrative at 7:13 — had its effect. "The dead man sat up and began to talk, and Jesus gave him back to his mother."

Three significant things happened as a direct result of this astonishing miracle. First, the people who witnessed it were "filled with awe and praised God." Whether by virtue of their own spiritual discernment or on the basis of some word from Jesus, the people gave their praise to God and his divine power — not to the man Jesus. Like Nicodemus, perhaps, they knew that a man is able to do such great signs only when God is with him (John 3:2b).

Second, like Nicodemus, the crowd knew that God's power at work through Jesus signified something important about him and his ministry. Nicodemus said, "Rabbi, we know you are a teacher come from God" (John 3:2a). These people proclaimed him a "great prophet" and exclaimed, "God has come to help his people." The acknowledgment of Jesus as a "great prophet" likely reflects the people's recollection of similar feats of raising the dead by two Old Testament prophets. Both Elijah (1 Kgs. 17:17-24) and Elisha (2 Kgs. 4:32-37) had raised young men and given them back to their mothers, so these precedents would be the biblical background to affirming that Jesus belonged in the ranks of such great men of God himself. Though correct in their judgment about him, their view of his status was incomplete. Perhaps, however, we need to be cautioned against faulting them. They

3. Do you think people see you as a compassionate person? Why?
4. Do you see yourself as a compassionate person? Why? Write a prayer asking God to enlarge your compassion.

Day 5
God's Nearness

Read Psalm 71:1-12 for a tribute to God's nearness to his people.

1. When Jesus raised the boy, people exclaimed, "God has come to help his people!" What did they mean?
2. Have you ever witnessed something so moving that you expressed the confidence that God was near? If so, what was it? Why did it affect you so?
3. Do you live with a constant sense of God's nearness? What difference do you think this makes in your spiritual life?

4. Have you ever felt that God was far away from you? What created that feeling? How did you deal with it?

5. Do you know someone who is struggling with the sense that God is far away or that God has abandoned him or her? Are there things you can do to help?

made a correct judgment on the basis of what they knew and would need more evidence still to confess Jesus as the Messiah and Son of God. And in their use of the exclamation "God has come to help his people," they were using an Old Testament expression that honored God for some great blessing to his people (Ruth 1:6, et al.; cf. Luke 1:68,78; 19:41-44; Acts 15:14).

Third, word about this miracle "spread throughout Judea and the surrounding country." The fame of Jesus could not be contained in light of events so spectacular as this one. Such publicity was both a blessing and a curse. It was a blessing in that more people sought him out and would therefore be exposed to his teaching. Yet it was a curse in that more and more people would seek him only for the sake of getting to witness or to benefit from one of his signs.

Week Twelve

Luke 7:18-35 (IV A 4 k in Outline)

k. His estimation of John the Baptist. 7:18-35.

By this point in Jesus' ministry, John the Baptist was no longer a public figure preaching on the banks of the Jordan River. He was a prisoner in Herod's jail (cf. 3:19-20). [Note: For details on the reason for John's arrest and his ultimate fate at the hands of Herod, see Mark 6:14ff.] From his prison, he had been hearing reports through his disciples about the ministry of the man he had pointed out as the Lamb of God and Messiah. He sent two of them to Jesus to ask, "Are you the one who was to come, or should we expect someone else?"

This question tends to unsettle some of us and has generated some creative comments. Against the natural reading of the text that John had moments of doubt concerning Jesus, some have suggested that John sent these two disciples with this question for their sakes. The idea is that John had no doubts about Jesus' identity but sent them in the expectation that Jesus would convince them as well. Such an explanation seems contrived and appears to have risen from the assumption that a person so central to God's purposes as John could not experience uncertainty in his spiritual life.

It is *not* unthinkable that John asked this question for himself, for many believers have had to deal with crisis times in their faith. Disease, disaster, death — this 3-D combination has caused more than a few Christians to face psychological despair and spiritual uncertainty. Perhaps John's less-than-pleasant experiences in prison had thrown him into such dejection and melancholy that he questioned what Jesus

Day 1
The Work of John the Baptist

Read another Gospel account of the ministry of John from Matthew 3.

1. John and Jesus were very different. Did their ministries reflect their different personalities? How?
2. How might John's personality have created incorrect expectations of the Messiah in John?
3. Did John's misgivings change Jesus' opinion of him and his work? Are people generally this gracious in spirit? Explain your answer.
4. Reflect on John's *courage* and *humility*. Which of these virtues is more natural to you? How have you learned to balance it with the other?

was doing. Hadn't Jesus read an Old Testament prophecy about "freedom for the prisoners" and claimed its fulfillment in himself? (4:18). Then why was John being left to languish in prison? Or, perhaps more likely, the things John had been hearing about Jesus' ministry didn't fit his image of messianic activity. After all, John had prophesied that the Messiah would "clear his threshing floor and . . . burn up the chaff with unquenchable fire" (3:17). Given John's passionate nature, it is not unlikely that he expected Jesus to be as confrontational as he had been and to bring an immediate fiery judgment against the Romans and the complacent religionists among his own nation. But what had John been hearing about Jesus? He was not doing works of judgment, but mercy! Perhaps it was not John's *faith* that was wavering, but his *patience*.

Confronted with John's question, Jesus pointed the men who had brought it to the things he had been doing and that they could witness for themselves. In fulfillment of predictions such as Isaiah 35:5-6, the blind, deaf, lame, and dumb were being made whole. Dead persons were being raised to life! And, in fulfillment of Isaiah 61:1, "the good news is preached to the poor." Such deeds were offered by Jesus as his credentials and confirmation from above. "John's doubts would not have been removed by Jesus' simply saying emphatically, 'Yes, of course, I am the Messiah!' By healing the sick, the blind, and the deaf and by preaching God's Word to them, Jesus was fulfilling some very specific messianic prophecies. The fulfillment of those Scriptures would have had a comforting and encouraging effect on the despondent John. The best way to remove doubts is not by pretending that they do not exist but rather by exposing them to the truth of God." [Paul Benware, *Luke: The Gospel of the Son of Man* (Chicago: Moody Press, 1985), pp. 63-64.]

To the evidence he offered John, Jesus added the following challenge: "Blessed is the man who does not fall away on account of me." The verb translated "fall away" comes from a word that originally referred to trapping small animals and birds. In effect, then, Jesus was warning John and others against getting trapped by their own expectations of how the Messiah would minister. What they expected and what God chose to do through him might not be the same, and it would be a terrible tragedy to reject God because of one's own preconceptions. "We are not to be offended by Jesus, not taken aback by the unusual nature of his ministry. It might not be what we expected, but it is what God promised. Do not worry; the time of fulfillment comes with him." [Bock, *Luke*, p. 138.]

Many of our own times of crisis in faith are caused by the same problem of mistaken preconceptions. "If God is a loving Father, there should be no hungry people anywhere in the world," says one. "If I am a Christian, life shouldn't be so hard!" cries another. "If my child can still get sick and die," demands someone else, "there is no reason to believe or pray." Some of these notions have been brought to the life of faith by people who then fell away when life worked differently for them than they thought — perhaps *demanded* — it should. The essence of personal faith is *trust* in God when things work differently from our expectations. God is sovereign and has created this world out of his wisdom. It functions according to his purposes and to his ends. For us to reject his wisdom, purposes, and ends on the basis of our expectations is roughly comparable to listening to a member of the Flat Earth Society explain how everyone has been hoodwinked by NASA's claims of shuttle travel and moon landings.

This sort of response to John was less a rebuke than a call for trust in God during a dark time. It is

Day 2
Confronting Doubt

Read Hebrews 11 for a biblical list of people with great faith.

1. John had been a bold prophet. Explain how he might have come to have doubts about Jesus as the Messiah.
2. Are there people in Hebrews 11 whose life story in Scripture includes episodes of doubt? Personal failure? Sin?
3. Can you recall a time of doubt and uncertainty in your faith? What caused it? How did God enable you to deal with it?
4. What advice would you give someone who is experiencing a time of spiritual uncertainty?
5. What things can one do to help another who is experiencing a faith crisis? Do you know anyone who needs your help today?

the same call that concludes the book of Job. And it is the call that comes to each of us during our times of confusion and doubt.

After Jesus sent John's messengers back with his answer, he took advantage of an opportunity to speak to the crowd about John and the significance of his work. "What did you go out into the desert to see?" he asked. The first two answers he offered were obviously to be rejected. John was certainly no wind-blown reed reflecting popular sentiment; his unyielding message of repentance made him the exact opposite of such a caricature. Neither was he a soft and effeminate man dressed in fine clothes; he lived a rugged lifestyle in a forbidding and difficult environment. It was his third answer to his own question that Jesus affirmed. John was a spokesman for God. "A prophet?" he said. "Yes, I tell you, and more than a prophet." Quoting from Malachi 3:1, Jesus simultaneously endorsed John as the one Yahweh promised to send before the Messiah and claimed that his own ministry was the fulfillment of all the prophetic anticipation.

Then comes one of the most interesting statements in Scripture: "I tell you, among those born of women there is no one greater than John; yet the one who is least in the kingdom of God is greater than he." Do you sometimes wish you could have lived in the times of Moses or David? Have you ever wondered what it would have been like to share in the ministry of one of the prophets? Or have you ever longed to have the miraculous gifts of some of the Bible's ancient heroes? According to Jesus, you and I are better off than any of those people! To know the identity of the Messiah, to share in his salvation, and to participate in his kingdom rule gives one a status greater than history's greatest prophet! "John belonged to the time of promise. The least in the kingdom is *greater*, not because of any personal

Day 3
God's Kingdom

Read Matthew 13:36-52 for a series of parables about the kingdom.

1. Jesus said the "least in the kingdom" was greater than John. What did he mean?
2. Define the terms *kingdom of God* and *church*. What is the relationship of the two?
3. What did Jesus mean by saying, "The kingdom of God is within you?" (Luke 17:21).
4. What evidence would you offer to prove this statement: "I am a citizen of the kingdom of God"?
5. Which is easier to do: be a church member *or* be a kingdom person? Explain your answer.

qualities he may have, but because he belongs to the time of fulfillment. Jesus is not minimizing the importance of John. He is putting membership in the kingdom into its proper perspective." [Morris, *Luke*, p. 143.]

Reactions to Jesus' preaching and his estimation of John's work before him fell along rather clear lines of distinction. Those we might call "average Joes" and outcasts such as the tax collectors responded positively to what Jesus said. In affirming his preaching, they had in effect "acknowledged that God's way was right" (i.e., willing to submit themselves to God's way revealed in Christ) and had given public evidence of that acknowledgment by submitting to John's baptism. But the Pharisees and official teachers of the Law of Moses "rejected God's purpose for themselves" (i.e., saw themselves as having no need to repent and certainly believed they were above learning from a young Galilean rabbi) and likewise had refused to submit to the baptism of repentance John preached. Another way of expressing this contrast is to notice a pattern that recurs across time. People with no vested interest but to receive the truth can hear new things, gain insight, and adjust their lives to the will of God; people who have position and power to maintain are unwilling to consider anything that would require change.

Jesus then proceeded to characterize "this generation" to which he and John had preached. He gave his characterization by quoting what may have been a child's ditty from the time. As used by children, it was likely either a petulant or mocking couplet that challenged their peers who sat on the sidelines while they played their games. On the one hand, they would neither play happy games and "dance" with their playmates; on the other, they were equally distant and disengaged if their friends were sad enough to be moved to "cry." In other words, the children's

Day 4
Acknowledging God's Ways

Read Isaiah 55 and notice what is said about God's ways and man's ways.

1. How had "all the people" acknowledged that "God's way was right" in connection with John's ministry?
2. How do we acknowledge God in our lives? How can we repudiate him?
3. Is obedience to God only a *duty* to you, or can you honestly say it is the *desire* of your heart? How may one move from the former state to the latter?
4. How does obedience relate to *grace*? Does one eliminate the other? Does either include the other?
5. How will you acknowledge that God's way is right for you today?

Day 5
The Character of a Generation

Read Genesis 6:1-8 about the character of Noah's generation.

1. Do you agree that different generations have a "character" of their own? Explain your answer.
2. Characterize your parents' generation. Your own generation.

3. Did generational differences create any problems for communication between you and your parents? Cite a specific example.
4. What is the character of this generation? What challenges does this create for us?
5. Does Christian ministry have to take a generation's unique features into account? How have we done so in this generation? Failed to do so?

verse rebukes those who can never be satisfied. What an apt way to describe the adult religious leaders who knew of John the Baptist and Jesus!

As different as John and Jesus were, neither was acceptable to the Jewish establishment. What was wrong with John? He was too strange, austere, and ascetic for them. So they said he was possessed by a demon. Then perhaps they would respond to the more gregarious and sociable Jesus? Hardly. With his nonascetic manner and normal habits of eating and drinking, he was judged too cheerful. "Here is a glutton and a drunkard," they said of him. Not only did they not approve of his altogether normal lifestyle, but they also thought it shameful that he ran with the wrong crowd. They intended it as an insult to point out that he made himself "a friend of tax collectors and 'sinners.' "

Returning to the issue of the nature of true faith that was discussed in Jesus' great kingdom sermon (6:20-49) and which is being illustrated now by case studies chosen by Luke, this sequence of exchanges certainly fits. Genuine faith such as John had is honest with its times of doubt and seeks answers from appropriate sources; it acknowledges that God's way is right and submits to his commandments; it is willing to receive the truth from any messenger God sends, even if that person's lifestyle and manner of presentation are different from one's own.

Jesus' concluding words here form an excellent summary of this entire section: "Wisdom is proved right by all her children." That is, wise persons will not be critical of God's ways, means, and messengers. They will look beyond God's surprising methods to receive the life-changing truth he is revealing to them.

Week Thirteen

Luke 7:36-50 (IV A 4 l in Outline)

l. A sinful woman forgiven. 7:36-50.

The final example of true, saving faith in this series is the story that pulls together several of the themes Luke has been developing. It not only illustrates authentic faith but again shows that the world's expectations run counter to kingdom experiences and that Jesus consistently claimed to be divine.

This episode is frequently taken to be Luke's recounting of an anointing episode that appears in the other Synoptics at Matthew 26:6-13 and Mark 14:3-9 and in the Gospel of John at 12:1-8. But this seems clearly to be a story unique to Luke. The other accounts are of an event in the last week of Jesus' life, but this narrative comes much earlier in his ministry. Furthermore, Matthew and Mark say the event they relate took place in the house of a leper, a place where a scrupulous-about-uncleanness Pharisee would never go. Finally, both details of the scene itself and the topic of the conversation following it in the other Gospels are different from Luke's account.

Jesus was not a respecter of persons. While it is true that he associated with outcasts and was called "friend of sinners," he was also willing to accept the invitation of a Pharisee to dine at his house. His host had the common Jewish name "Simon" and cannot be identified beyond this event.

The purpose of the dinner may well have been to honor Jesus. As a teacher of some renown who had come to Simon's hometown, it would not have been unlikely that a man of his stature would invite him to

Day 1
Status and Need

Read Romans 3:9-26 about the common need of all humankind.

1. A respectable Pharisee and a prostitute were at the same dinner party. How did that come about?

2. What *assumptions* do people tend to make about preachers? People in jail? Bankers? Sunday School teachers? Alcoholics?

3. Are assumptions about others always correct? Cite an instance where your assumption about someone was terribly wrong.

4. Regardless of social status, what spiritual need do all people share in common?

5. If you had been at Simon's party, who would you have *assumed* to have the greater spiritual need? Might we make the same mistake today?

his home and engage him in discussion of the Law and traditions. Such a dinner-discussion would have been public to the extent that people could come in and observe the evening — perhaps even engage in the conversation.

One person who came to Simon's house that evening appears to have come with a mission. An unnamed "woman who had lived a sinful life" (i.e., probably a prostitute) found out that Jesus was eating at Simon's house. She came and "brought an alabaster jar of perfume" with the clear intention of anointing Jesus with the expensive ointment. Many perfume jars — small glass flasks with long necks that were sometimes worn on strings much like a necklace — have been excavated at archaeological sites around Israel. The perfume was likely a fragrant oil that represented considerable expense.

From what follows in the story, it appears that the woman had either heard and/or met Jesus during his teaching tour in the city. The experience had moved her deeply and caused her to turn from her sinful life. So she had sought him out, brought a flask of perfume, and meant to honor Jesus by anointing his feet.

The typical eating arrangement at the time was very different from ours. Rather than eating in chairs with their feet under a table, people "reclined at the table" on low couches or mats. Resting on the left arm and with his head toward the table, Jesus' body extended toward the edge of the room. His sandals would have been removed upon arrival. The woman who had come with the purpose of anointing his feet with perfume took a position in the shadows and moved toward him. Overcome now with emotion and paying no attention to anyone else's opinion of her, she began to weep. As the woman "stood behind him at his feet weeping, she began to wet his feet with her tears."

Day 2
Affirming Others

Read Acts 9:23-31 and note how Barnabas "vouched for" Paul.

1. What risk did the woman take who showed up at Simon's dinner party for Jesus?
2. What is the most awkward situation you ever faced? What happened? Did anyone help you through it?
3. Who believed in you and gave you confidence — perhaps before you believed in yourself? A parent? Teacher? Coach? What difference did that make in your life?
4. Jesus saw something beautiful and good in a

The scene that followed was one of total abandon on the woman's part. As her tears fell, she "wiped them with her hair, kissed them and poured perfume on them." It was also one of incredible sensitivity on Jesus' part. Regardless of the embarrassment he might have felt, he neither refused her attention nor made her feel foolish for offering it.

At this point in the narrative, the attention shifts from the woman to Simon. Seeing what had happened between the woman and Jesus, his own theological biases and assumptions kicked in. For one thing, he assumed — as the Pharisees all did — that righteous people should desire to keep distance between themselves and the "unclean." Thus it followed (for Simon!) that Jesus could not really be a prophet. Otherwise he would have known what a "sinner" the woman was and put a stop to her display over him.

Knowing what Simon was thinking about both him and the woman, Jesus said he had something to say. This might have signified the start of the evening's conversation for which Simon had been waiting. He certainly did not know at this point that Jesus could read his mind and was about to reply to his thoughts! In a rather disinterested response, Simon said, "Tell me, teacher." At best it was a polite signal to begin the discussion. He had no idea how personal and intense it would be.

Jesus told a simple story about "two men who owed money" to someone. One owed him 500 denarii, and the other owed 50. Since a denarius was a full day's wage for the time (cf. Matt. 20:2), the two debts were remarkably different. Whereas the latter represented a couple of months' work, the former owed what amounted to the total wages one could earn in a year and a half. Both debtors were unable to pay what they owed, so the lender "canceled the debts" of both men. Then came Jesus'

woman that Simon did not see. Explain why.
5. Is there someone you are taking pains to affirm? Build her self-esteem? Help him believe in himself? Summarize what you have learned from Jesus in this story that can help you.

Day 3
Parables

Read the disarming parable of 2 Samuel 12:1-9.

1. What was the story Jesus told Simon? With what question did he end the story?
2. How did Jesus apply the story? What was his conclusion?
3. Why are stories such excellent teaching devices?
4. What is your favorite biblical allegory? What lesson does it teach?
5. What is your favorite nonbiblical parable? What is its point?

question for Simon: "Now which of them will love him more?"

The Pharisee gives the same answer anyone would to such a question: "I suppose the one who had the bigger debt canceled." The point here is not a lesson in economics, but theology. The story is clearly one of God's grace. Like empty-handed debtors before him, each of us is unable to satisfy the debt he or she owes. What shall we do about it?

Returning to the story, Jesus told Simon that he had "judged correctly." Of course the man forgiven the ten-times-greater debt would be the more grateful to have his debt canceled. Now it was time to apply the story to the real issue of grace and forgiveness. In relative terms, Simon probably did have a shorter list of moral offenses against God than the town prostitute had. And that was both his blessing and his curse. He was certainly better off not to have done the harm and created the bitter memories that such sins would have generated; this was his blessing. Yet he had been led to feel smug and superior because of his moral uprightness; this was his curse. He had not found the motivation for humility and love over the course of a lifetime that a sinful woman had found in her very recent encounter with Jesus!

Jesus did not leave Simon to draw conclusions from the story he had told. He was pointed and direct. Simon had not offered Jesus the minimal courtesy of water for his feet, a kiss of greeting, or an inexpensive touch of olive oil for his head. Yet a woman Simon despised had washed Jesus' feet with her tears, kissed not his cheek but his feet, and had poured expensive perfume over them as well.

How shall we explain the thoughtlessness of the one and the extravagance of the other? Simon saw no need for grace in his life, but a woman with a horrible past sensed her need acutely. "We don't know how Simon reacted, but he is exposed. He

Day 4
Self-Righteousness

Read Jesus' rebuke of Pharisaic attitudes at Matthew 23:1-12.

1. What does the term *self-righteous* mean to you? Recall an example of what you regarded as self-righteous behavior.

2. Why are humans tempted to act in self-righteous ways? What does it take to break that pattern in a life?

knew everything about religion, liturgy, theology, ethics, temple worship, and the law. He knew all about the things of God, but somehow he missed the essence of it all, which this woman captured. The woman knew how sinful she was. Simon's problem was that he thought he was better than he was and he misunderstood the nature of God who is the giver of unconditional love." [Bruce Larson, *The Communicator's Commentary: Luke* (Waco, TX: Word Books, 1983), p. 139.]

One must be careful in reading the words of Jesus about forgiveness here. "Therefore, I tell you, her many sins have been forgiven — for she loved much. But he who has been forgiven little loves little." He did not make the woman's loving behavior the ground of her pardon. As she stood before Jesus and Simon, her sins had already been forgiven. To the contrary, God's acceptance and grace to her through Christ had motivated her to works of love that were beyond Simon. Her loving deeds had been a response to forgiveness received from Jesus. The same phenomenon of service in proportion to one's awareness of God's mercy can be observed in our own experience.

As a final act of assurance to a woman who must have been made to feel self-conscious and uncomfortable by the night's proceedings, Jesus said, "Your sins are forgiven." Yet what was offered her as assurance of pardon became a provocation not only to Simon but to the other guests at his house. "Who is this who even forgives sin?" they asked. For a second time in the Gospel of Luke (cf. 5:21), the issue of Jesus' right to forgive sins comes to the fore. Since only God can pardon sins and since Jesus granted pardon, there can be no doubt that he was affirming his deity in the strongest possible terms here.

Still concerned about the woman rather than defensive of himself, Jesus let his statement about

3. Why were Jesus and the Pharisees always at odds with each other?

4. Have you ever caught yourself feeling or behaving self-righteously? If so, how did you feel when you realized what you were doing?

5. Unbelievers sometimes label all Christians "self-righteous hypocrites." How would you respond to someone leveling such a charge?

Day 5
Son of God

Read how Jesus witnessed to his deity in John 5:30-47.

1. Jesus told the woman, "Your sins are forgiven." What was the reaction of the other dinner guests?

2. What claim is implied in granting forgiveness of sins? Where have we run into this already in Luke's Gospel?

3. Did Jesus disclaim the implication of deity?

Correct his hearers' natural assumption? Explain the significance of his silence.

4. Why is the confession that Jesus is the *Son of God* Christianity's central issue? In what ways do you confess this truth in your ordinary experiences?

forgiveness stand without further comment. He turned instead to the woman and said, "Your faith has saved you; go in peace." This is the habitual practice of Jesus in this Gospel. He turns no one away. He leaves no one else to bear the brunt of hostility over his statements and actions. He offers grace and peace to all who have faith in him.

Perhaps more fully in this section of text than in any so far in his Gospel, Luke gives us an insight into his own heart. Why had he fallen in love with Jesus? Why could he offer Jesus to Theophilus without reservation? It is because Jesus makes those who have customarily been made to feel shut out feel included and welcome. And he looks with compassion and forgiveness on those who have only been glared at with stern and condescending looks before. Yes, a penitent prostitute would appreciate this very different treatment from Jesus. So would a Gentile who heard her story and took heart from its message. And so may we!

Week Fourteen

Luke 8:1-21 (IV B 1 to IV B 2 b in Outline)

B. A Later Ministry in Galilee. 8:1-56.

Following the events we have traced from 4:14 to this point, Luke relates a preaching tour as "Jesus traveled about from one town and village to another, proclaiming the good news of the kingdom of God." Although Jesus attracted large crowds during this time (cf. 8:4,19,40,45), there is a noticeable absence of references to synagogue visits. This may be accounted for in the fact that he had generated such hostility among the people who were typically synagogue leaders. This escalating tension may have driven him to open-air gatherings as he moved through Galilee.

1. Women in ministry to Jesus. 8:1-3.

In case you have ever wondered how Jesus lived when he was not being hosted by Lazarus at Bethany or by some other sympathetic host, Luke provides the answer here. He and his apostles received generous support from several women who sponsored them with their resources.

Luke tells more stories of women and their association with Jesus than the other Gospels combined. This is consistent with his pattern of showing that Jesus included people that others had worked systematically to exclude. Rabbis of his time would not teach women and typically regarded them as spiritual inferiors to males. Jesus, by contrast, taught women, worked miracles for women, affirmed the worth and dignity of women, and accepted their ministry on his behalf. There is no record in the Gospels of any women setting themselves as Jesus'

Day 1
Jesus and Women

Read John 4:1-27 about Jesus and a woman from Samaria.

1. How were women generally treated in Jesus' culture? How did his practice differ from the norm?
2. Recall specific accounts of Jesus' respectful dealings with women.
3. What is "sexism"? How has it been practiced in our culture? In our churches?
4. Why do you think Luke makes such a point of the importance of women in his Gospel?
5. What assumptions does our culture typically make about women?

Day 2
Women and Ministry

Read Romans 16:1-16 and count the female names among Paul's co-workers.

1. What liberties for Christian service do you see for women in the NT? What restrictions?

2. Why do we tend to focus on the (b) part of question 1?

3. Who was/is the most gifted and effective female Christian you know? On what do you base your opinion?

4. In what areas is the church's ministry particularly hindered if women's gifts are not sought and used?

enemies to act against him. It should not be overlooked that Luke's summary statement about women helping in his ministry comes immediately on the heels of the story of a woman's lavish anointing of him at Simon's dinner party.

Three women are named here, with the statement that "many others" also participated in "helping to support [Jesus and the Twelve] out of their own means." What they all had in common was that they "had been cured of evil spirits and diseases" by a compassionate Christ.

Christian tradition has represented Mary Magdalene as a beautiful but immoral woman whom Jesus rescued from a wicked lifestyle. Thus the musical *Jesus Christ Superstar* has her sing "I Don't Know How to Love Him" to Jesus, and some commentaries identify her with the woman in Luke 7. All of this supposition is completely without textual merit. She had indeed suffered from demon possession, but there is nothing that suggests she was a prostitute. She is identified as Magdalene (i.e., from the town of Magdala) to distinguish her from Jesus' mother, Mary of Bethany, and other women with this very common name.

Joanna is mentioned not only here but also at 24:10. Since she was the "wife of Cuza, the manager of Herod's household," we may assume at least two things about her. First, she and her husband were people of considerable wealth and likely of some social standing. Second, the identification of herself with Jesus would surely have subjected both her and her husband to suspicion and criticism in the Herodian household. Since her husband is not mentioned anywhere else in the Gospels, we do not know whether he was also a believer or perhaps opposed to his wife's involvement with the teacher from Galilee. The later reference to Joanna in the Gospel of Luke lets us know that she was present at Jesus' crucifixion. Unlike even the apostles, she did not flee when things reached their crescendo for the Lord.

We know nothing about Susanna beyond the listing of her name here. We may allow her to represent those godly women across the centuries who have used their skills and financial resources to promote the things of God's kingdom. Although they are not memorialized and have not had their stories told to the masses, their quiet, faithful ministry has made possible the more visible ministries of public figures.

2. The activity of his ministry. 8:4-56.

In describing the work of Jesus in Galilee, Luke records both his teachings and his miracles. His words are backed by actions. Men could know he was speaking with divine authority because of the things he did among them (cf. John 3:2).

a. Two kingdom parables. 8:4-18.

Jesus was being followed by a "large crowd" at this point. Yet he was discerning enough to realize that the group was hardly homogeneous in nature. Indeed, Luke tells us that it had assembled "from town after town" in the region. Teaching in the open air — perhaps beside a field being plowed and prepared for planting — Jesus knew that the hearts of the people listening to him were as diverse as the kinds of soil in such a field. So he gave two related parables about hearing the Word of God.

The first is his famous Parable of the Soils (8:4-15), and it describes the various types of reaction his preaching would get. The second is the Parable of the Lamp (8:16-18). Its focus shifts from the hearers of the gospel to its heralds; it challenges his disciples to boldness in proclaiming what Jesus has revealed to them.

As a teaching medium, Jesus did not invent the *parable* (cf. 2 Sam. 12:1ff). He did, however, raise this ancient form of instruction to its most masterful level. Anyone who has studied the teachings of Jesus

Day 3
Parable of the Soils

Read 1 Corinthians 1:18-31 about varied reactions to the gospel.

1. What is the focus of this parable? Define the four "soils."

2. Why did Jesus use such a simple story to teach this lesson?

3. What sort of soil was your heart when you first became a Christian? Illustrate your answer.

4. Can soil types change? Explain your answer.

5. What sort of soil is your heart today? Illustrate your answer.

comes away amazed at his skill in communicating so much by means of such simple stories. At v. 10, he even explained to his disciples why he preferred to use this method so frequently. His twofold reason for teaching in parables still makes sense to us: these easy-to-remember stories would allow the serious and attentive student to remember his teachings easily, while hostile or indifferent hearers would dismiss them as "silly little stories" without significance. From our point of view, it is important to note that this explanation Jesus gave was not about the *intent* of his parables but their *result*. He always spoke to reveal God, but the condition of the hearer's heart would determine what could be heard.

As Jesus taught on any given day, his "seed" was always the Word of God. The fruitfulness of that seed would vary, though, because people made a variety of responses to what they heard. The hearts of some who heard him were like the trampled "path" bordering or cutting across a field (vv. 5,12). Because a path is hard and impenetrable, seed falling on it cannot get beneath the surface, take root, get nourishment, and grow; instead, the seed is either "trampled" or "birds of the air" see it, swoop down, and feast. These are unbelieving hearts that have been made hard by self-centeredness and preoccupation with the world; the Word of God does not penetrate such hearts and "the devil comes and takes away the word from their hearts" by the confusion and falsehood he offers those who are not set on knowing the truth (2 Cor. 4:4).

Jesus likened other hearts to that which has only a thin layer of soil spread over a ledge of "rock" (vv. 6,13). Because of its deposit in such soil, the seed is warmed both from above and beneath and germinates quickly. It springs up, but it quickly exhausts the moisture and nutrients available to it; it cannot send its roots beneath the rocky ledge below.

In a similar way, there are always people who "receive the word with joy" but who cannot endure the blast of trials and temptations Satan sends against every believer. They fall away "because they have no root."

The third soil is one in which "seed fell among thorns, which grew up with it and choked the plants" (vv. 7,14). Again, the problem was not with the good seed. In this case, neither was it the nature of the soil. Although the soil was fertile enough to allow the good seed to spring to life, it was cluttered with noxious seeds that also sprouted, grew, and "choked" what could have become fruitful plants. These are human hearts cluttered with "life's worries, riches and pleasures." People whose hearts are so divided "do not mature" in their spiritual lives.

Finally, however, Jesus pointed to "good soil" capable of producing "a hundred times more than was sown" (vv. 8a,15). These are genuine believers who display a "noble and good heart, who hear the word, retain it, and by persevering, produce a crop." The point of the parable is difficult to miss: Hearing the Word of God is not only a great privilege and joy; it is also a great responsibility.

In the Parable of the Lamp, Jesus spoke not of the larger multitude but to his disciples directly. By means of this figure, he reminded them that the knowledge they were receiving from him was not for their sakes alone but for others. They were to share what they had been given. As surely as a lamp is made to give light, people who know the Lord are meant to light the way for others to know him. People who keep the knowledge of Christ "hidden" or "concealed" do a great disservice to others — and will be exposed for their failure (i.e., "brought out into the open") at Judgment.

Verse 18 holds out the frightening prospect that people who fail to couple their *hearing* of the Good

Day 4
Parable of the Lamp

Read 1 Timothy 4:6-16 for instructions to teachers.

1. What is the focus of this parable? Tell how it differs from the Parable of the Soils.
2. What "frightening prospect" is found at v. 18?
3. How do you see yourself *sharing* the Word of God? How effective are your efforts?
4. Who taught you about

Christ? How was it done?

5. Write a prayer for God to make you more effective in communicating the gospel.

Day 5
Jesus' Family

Read Colossians 3:1-17 about life with Christ.

1. What did Jesus teach us about his concept of family?
2. What does his teaching imply about our concept of the church as spiritual family?
3. What was the greatest blessing of growing up in your family? The greatest challenge?
4. Describe the blessing of having one's natural family as spiritual family also.
5. What is your greatest wish for your family?

News with an eager *sharing* of it will thereby diminish their personal capacity for receiving and applying the truth to their own lives. For those who couple receiving with giving, however, their joy in the Word of God increases as the Holy Spirit makes them even more adept with and responsive to the truth in their personal discipleship experience.

b. Kinship with Jesus. 8:19-21.

On the heels of two parables about hearing and receiving the Word of God, Luke relates an incident involving Jesus' earthly family. It illustrates the point of the parables beautifully by affirming that faith in and obedience to him creates a relationship between a disciple and the Lord that is more precious than that of blood relationship.

On a day when "Jesus' mother and brothers came to see him," some in his audience apparently expected him either to stop his teaching and pay attention to them or to give them a place of honor while he continued to teach. He did neither. He used the situation to teach that spiritual kinship comes only to "those who hear God's word and put it into practice." Since his own brothers were still in disbelief at his claims when he said this (cf. John 7:50), a word of rebuke and challenge for them is to be heard here. But clearly the primary message to be heard is the positive prospect held out to his original hearers — and to us as well — that none who want to know Christ will be turned away or treated as unworthy. The relationship to God that is offered through Jesus is the holiest and nearest that anyone can have, and it was offered to Gentiles such as Luke, first-century women who had been neglected by the religious establishment, or you. Anyone who hears God's word and puts it into practice will be received by Christ (cf. Acts 10:35).

No wonder Luke fell in love with Jesus. Wouldn't anyone who knows his story fall in love with him?

100

Week Fifteen

Luke 8:22-56 (IV B 2 c in Outline)

c. Miracles establishing his kingdom authority. 8:22-56.

Luke tends to intersperse accounts of Jesus' teachings with narratives of events that illustrate just how powerful his presence and words were. There is an obvious point to such a procedure. The Lord's miracles establish both his concern for people and his power to meet their needs; his teachings extend his powerful words to those who did not experience his physical presence and touch. After all, those of us who have never seen Jesus but nevertheless believe in his word have the power of his presence with us (cf. John 20:29). In this section of text, a series of miracles exhibits the dramatic and mighty power of the Son of Man.

In turn, these miracles demonstrate the power of Jesus over nature (calming a storm, 8:22-25), evil spirits (casting out a demon, 8:26-39), and disease and death (healing a hemorrhaging woman in the context of raising Jairus' daughter, 8:40-56).

After the day of teaching in which he had told the Parable of the Soils (cf. Mark 4:35), Jesus called his disciples to accompany him across the Sea of Galilee. [Note: Although named the *Sea* of Galilee, a glimpse at a topographical map will let you see it is really only a small inland lake.] As they made the crossing, a very human Jesus lay down in the boat to rest from the strenuous day he had put in with the multitude. He must have been fatigued from an intense day's work. He was sleeping so soundly that it did not wake him up when a "squall" arose.

It is common for quick storms to come up on the Sea of Galilee. Some 700 feet below sea level along-

Day 1
Miracles

Read John 20:19-31 and try to visualize the scene.

1. What is the dual message of Jesus' miracles?
2. Do you think your faith would be stronger if you had seen Jesus work miracles? Explain your answer.
3. How do the miracles recorded in the Gospels affect your faith?
4. What sort of miracle would you most like to see Jesus perform today? Why?

side a mountainous region, cooler air from the surrounding heights can funnel down and turn the placid surface of the water into a foaming cauldron. But was this an ordinary storm? The fishermen-disciples with him were familiar with Galilee's storms and how to navigate them, but this one seems to have been particularly fierce. Because the verb translated "rebuked" in v. 24 calls to mind Jesus' practice in casting out demons, some have speculated that this storm was initiated satanically to try to destroy the boat's occupants and keep them from the demon-possessed man on the opposite shore.

Faced with a storm threatening to take them under, the disciples woke Jesus with a frantic cry, "Master, Master, we're going to drown!" At his word of rebuke, the wind and waters immediately subsided "and all was calm." He then turned to the disciples and asked, "Where is your faith?" The rebuke here was not that they had awakened him or asked for his help; it was that they were so panic-stricken when he was so close.

In our own experience, we should not be shocked at encountering "storms" of temptation, stress, and peril. Being a traveling companion with Jesus does not exempt one from turbulence. We are not told to get through these difficult times under our own power, for that would be impossible. Call on Jesus. Ask for his deliverance. But do so in full trust. Then, when deliverance comes, you will not react with surprise but with gratitude!

Jesus' disciples in the boat that day still had a way to go in the formation of their faith. This is evident from their reaction to the miracle they had witnessed. They were dumbstruck with "fear and amazement." They asked each other, "Who is this?" Although they were on the road to full and confident faith in him, they had hardly arrived there yet.

When Jesus and his awed companions reached

Day 2
When Storms Strike

Read Jonah 2:1-10 for another story of peril and rescue.

1. Review the story of the storm. How does it parallel the life experience of many who have never been in a boat?
2. What does this story tell about Jesus' humanity? His deity?
3. Why did Jesus rebuke his disciples for their fear?
4. What is the greatest fear you feel today? How do you account for its presence?
5. How will you deal with your fear?

the other side of the lake, they were met by a demon-possessed man. The description of his physical circumstances (i.e., naked, living in tombs, screaming, violent) is both touching and frightening. These details of the way he lived underscore the anguish of his daily life. He was under the control of powers diametrically opposed to God. "Righteousness, peace and joy in the Holy Spirit" are the hallmarks of a life under God's sovereignty (Rom. 14:17), but this man's life exhibited only negations of these beautiful traits.

Modern readers of the Bible are tempted to read accounts of demon possession and translate them into ancient accounts of severe mental illness. While certain aspects of bizarre behavior may incline us to equate the two, it is a mistake to do so. Luke clearly distinguishes between sickness and demon possession (cf. 4:40-41), and so should we. While the latter sometimes expressed itself with physical symptoms, it was a real phenomenon in which a human personality was subdued and controlled by an evil spirit or demon. Jesus' ministry built toward the claim that "all authority in heaven and on earth has been given to me" (Matt. 28:18). In order to prove his claim, it was necessary that he exhibit power adequate to control not only nature, disease, and death but also the spirit world. Thus, encounters of this sort were necessary.

When the demon-possessed man "fell at [Jesus'] feet," it was not on account of a worshipful spirit but out of stark terror. Specifically, the demons — for there were many who had taken possession of the man (v. 30) — "begged him repeatedly not to order them to go into the Abyss" (v. 31). The Abyss is the place of confinement for evil spirits, including Satan (Rev. 20:1-3; cf. Matt. 25:41). The demons who had been permitted to leave that awful place of confinement to spend a brief period on earth had no desire to go home! So they begged to be allowed to enter a

Day 3
A Demon-Possessed Man

Read Ephesians 6:10-20 about our fight against "spiritual forces of evil."

1. If you had seen this man, would you have felt sympathy or fear? Why?
2. Where do you see satanic powers at work in the world today?
3. What evidence was there that Jesus had successfully cast out the demons?
4. Is there always evidence to see when Jesus triumphs over some satanic work? Explain your answer.
5. Why did Jesus refuse to let the man go with him? What lesson do you see for yourself in this exchange?

herd of pigs that was nearby. That permission was granted, but it spared them nothing. The pigs, once possessed by the evil spirits, acted as unpredictably as the poor man had earlier. So the whole herd rushed down a steep bank into the lake and was drowned.

It seems to bother many who read this text that Jesus permitted pigs to be killed as a result of his miraculous rescue of the possessed man. How shall we respond to that concern? For one thing, surely the rescue of a human from so terrible a fate as he was suffering is more important than the fate of pigs. Also, one may point to the fact that the demons affected the pigs only by permission from Jesus and not by his original intent or design (v. 32); we thus have a small-scale version of the problem of evil on our hands. But perhaps the fundamental response is to ask why these animals — "unclean" under Old Testament regulations — were present in the first place.

At the end of this episode, the people of the region missed the greatest opportunity of their lives. Instead of welcoming, acclaiming, and following Jesus because of the miracle he had worked, they asked him to leave. The dominant reaction was neither curiosity nor faith, but "fear." Because he never forces his presence on anyone, Jesus got into the boat and went away.

As Jesus was leaving, the man who had been freed from the demons found him "and begged to go with him." His natural impulse was to be near and to serve the one who had blessed him with freedom and wholeness. But Jesus had other plans for him. He told the man to stay among his own people in order to bear witness to them of God's grace. At the start of this story, Jesus neither wanted nor accepted the unsolicited confession of the demons (v. 28). At the end, he commanded the liberated man to bear witness to the one who had expelled the demons from him. Perhaps this fact should tell each of us something: "It is ever the desire of the Master that the testimony of those who have known his power should be given first to those by whom they are best known." [Erdman, *Luke*, p. 101.]

When Jesus and his disciples came back from their eventful trip across the Sea of Galilee, a crowd of people not only "welcomed" him but "were all expecting him." This is Luke's way of saying how popular Jesus had become and what constant demands were now being placed on him. In the account that follows, Luke relates the intertwined story of Jairus [Jī´-rəs] and his daughter and a sick woman. In this account of a "miracle within a miracle," Jesus deals with situations that have the ironic twist of being rooted twelve years earlier.

Jairus was an important man in the Jewish community. A "ruler of the synagogue" arranged the details of synagogue assemblies, choosing the persons who would read Scripture, teach, and pray. His precious only child, a daughter, was twelve years old. More urgently important, she was dying. Laying aside his high position in the community, Jairus "fell at Jesus' feet" and begged Jesus to come to her aid.

As Jesus was walking to Jairus's house, the crowd around him was so large and the people were so raucous that he was "almost crushed" in the jostling going on. One of the women in the crowd had been ill for twelve years with a constant discharge of blood. This not only had physical implications, but social-spiritual as well. Her problem made her ceremonially unclean and unable to participate in temple worship, synagogue assemblies, and other events within her community (Lev. 15:25-33). Mark tells us that she had "spent all she had" on doctors who had only made her worse by their ineffective treatments (Mark 5:26). Luke, perhaps because he was a physician himself, chooses to omit this detail.

Day 4
Chronic Illness

Read Matthew 25:31-46 about ministering to people in need.

1. Describe the plight of the woman Jesus encountered while on his way to Jairus's house.

2. Have you ever known someone who had to deal with a chronic illness for 12 years? What effect did it have on that person's faith?

3. What would you need people to do for you, if you were chronically ill? Why?

4. Is there someone who needs these things from you today?

5. It is easy to overlook and forget chronically ill, handicapped, or shut-in persons. Pray for God to make you more sensitive to them.

The woman's faith could be seen as ill-formed and wrong-headed. It might have been more superstition than anything else, focusing as it did on touching the rabbi's clothing. Or, giving her the benefit of the doubt, since only God knows her heart, it might have been a last desperate attempt to get as near as possible to a healer she believed in, without calling attention to herself. Either way, true to her plan, she got near enough to touch him. She did so, sensed she was healed, and was ready to slip away unnoticed. Always aware of what was going on around him, Jesus would not let the matter end there. He asked, "Who touched my clothes?" His intent was not to embarrass her. It was to affirm her faith for her sake and to let the crowd know that her impurity and isolation were no longer necessary.

Does faith have to be perfectly informed and expressed to save? This story seems to be one of several in Scripture designed to demolish such a foolish idea. The power of faith is not so much in the person who has it as in its object. Even a weak and imperfect faith in Jesus has great power.

Day 5
Jairus' Daughter

Read Psalm 116 about God's gracious response to human need.

1. Jairus was an important man. How does that make his humility more impressive?

2. Describe how you think Jairus felt when the messenger arrived to say his daughter had died.

3. What was Jesus' reaction to the news? His counsel to Jairus?

4. How does the story end? What "strange"

Meanwhile, a messenger came from Jairus' house to update the synagogue ruler on his daughter's condition. "Your daughter is dead," he said. "Don't bother the teacher anymore." Jesus immediately reassured Jairus and bolstered his imperfect faith. For, though he certainly appears to have had a more informed faith than the woman just healed, he nevertheless had not demonstrated as much faith as the centurion who had disclaimed the need for Jesus to come under his roof to heal his servant (cf. 7:1ff). "Don't be afraid," Jesus told him. "Just believe, and she will be healed."

When Jesus and his party arrived at Jairus' house, they encountered a large group of mourners. He sent everyone except Peter, James, John, and the girl's parents outside the house. Turning then to the crowd before entering the house himself, he said, "She is not dead but asleep." As the people "laughed at him" — for they knew she was in fact dead — he went inside, took her by the hand, and said, "My child, get up!" By telling us the girl's "spirit returned," the text lets us know that the crowd had indeed been correct about her having been dead. An awe-inspiring miracle had just taken place.

What should one do after a moment of incredible triumph that draws attention to oneself? Jesus' answer was to turn the focus away from himself and back to the little girl, telling her parents to "give her something to eat" and "not to tell anyone what had happened." Strange as the latter command may sound to us, Jesus did not need more clamor and excitement than was already around him (cf. v. 42b). The crowd outside — still laughing at him, we may presume — would know soon enough what had happened. And there would be time later for Peter, James, and John to relate this story to others of us who would need to know it. It would be one of many such accounts establishing the kingdom authority of Jesus and causing people of all subsequent generations to fall in love with him.

twist do you find in Jesus' behavior?

5. For whose sake do you need to make a Jairus-like appeal to Christ today?

Week Sixteen

Luke 9:1-27 (IV C 1 to IV C 3 in Outline)

Day 1
Acting under Authority

Read Matthew 10:1-20 for another account of the apostles' first commission.

1. What does the word "apostle" mean? (See p. 47.) How does the term imply being under another's authority?

2. Why is it so important for persons to respect and live under appropriate authority?

3. The apostles were also *given* authority. What was its nature? How was it to be used?

4. How do you see yourself living and acting under Christ's authority?

5. What *power* and *authority* come to you when you honor his authority over you? Explain.

C. An Expanded Ministry with the Twelve. 9:1-50.

The time Jesus had spent in Galilee was almost at an end. He would soon begin his movements toward Jerusalem, the final conflicts of his ministry, and his Passion. Prior to leaving the northernmost region of Palestine, he gathered and commissioned the Twelve he had chosen earlier (6:12-19) for a preaching mission. Their work and the events immediately following it are critical to the narrative Luke is developing.

1. The mission of the Twelve. 9:1-9.

That Jesus "called the Twelve together" may mean nothing more than that he separated them from the larger group with him. It may mean, however, that our commonplace notion of twelve men leaving home, family, and all other responsibilities for the three years of Jesus' public ministry is mistaken. "We should not exaggerate the amount of time the apostles spent together. Some of them had homes and families in Capernaum and we need not doubt that they spent some of the time at their homes." [Morris, *Luke*, p. 163.] Also, remember that Judas was a full-fledged participant in these early events of preaching and working miracles in Galilee.

To this point in their association with Jesus, the apostles had been observers and students. Now they were to be called to take up their duties as authoritative representatives of the Son of Man. It was on-the-job training while he was still available to instruct and help them. Later, when he was gone from their company, they would have this experience as background to their larger ministry in establishing churches. So he "gave them power and authority to drive out all demons and to cure diseases, and he sent them out to preach the kingdom of God and to heal the sick." It would have been both unfair and unrealistic to send them out to preach without somehow equipping them for what lay ahead. Jesus therefore gave them power (*dynamis*=divine energy) and authority (*exousia*=the right to act in his name). This sort of credentialing would be particularly important for the confrontations they would have with demons (4:34,41; 8:28; cf. Acts 19:13-16).

Having equipped them for their work, he then commissioned them to do two things. First, they were to "preach the kingdom of God." Second, they were to "heal the sick." Even though their first priority was preaching, they were not to neglect the immediate physical needs of the people they met along the way. In recent times, conservative churches have tended to emphasize preaching to the neglect of people's need for food, shelter, and emotional support; liberal churches, on the other hand, have majored in the latter while forgetting to preach the kingdom message of repentance and salvation. We would be wise to restore the balance Jesus intended.

The Twelve were required to travel light (i.e., "no staff, no bread, no money, no extra tunic") and to accept whatever hospitality was offered them. They were even told not to move from one house to another in a given town. The point of all this was to establish among these men a sense of trust in God's ability to provide for them. In the statement of v. 5, Jesus also prepared them for the inevitable rejection they would face in some settings. To "shake the dust off your feet" was an action symbolizing a separation between themselves and anyone who rejected their Master (cf. Acts 13:51).

Day 2
Living by Faith

Read 2 Corinthians 11:16-33 for insight into one apostle's experience.

1. What demands did Jesus make of the apostles as they went out?

2. Which requirement do you find most challenging? Why?

3. What demand does Christ make of you that challenges your faith? Explain.

4. Describe the results of the apostles' ministry. How do you relate this to their faith-obedience?

5. What happens in your life when you truly live by faith? Cite an example.

This initial ministry of the Twelve apparently had great success. So great was its success, in fact, that it attracted the attention of Herod the tetrarch. Although he had imprisoned and beheaded John the Baptist, this superstitious man feared that he had come back to life. His desire to "see" Jesus for himself and to settle the matter of his possible identity with John would be satisfied only in the closing hours of Jesus' life as he was shuttled from one official to another in Jerusalem (23:6-12).

2. Feeding a great multitude. 9:10-17.

When the apostles returned from their preaching tour, there must have been great excitement as they reported on what had happened. Their "testimonies" likely became competitive with one another, given their immature faith at this point (cf. 9:46ff). So Jesus sought to pull them aside for a more private time of debriefing and instruction at Bethsaida. When the people seeking first Jesus and now the apostles learned where they were, they pursued the little band and took away the option of privacy for the teacher and his pupils. Rather than register displeasure or banish them, however, Jesus "welcomed" them and met their needs with teaching and healing.

As the day was about to end, the apostles suggested that Jesus dismiss the people to find food and lodging for themselves. The Lord responded to them with a suggestion of his own: feed the people before they leave. In a scene that is actual and symbolic at the same time, they confessed that their limited resources could not meet the needs of so many. Following this exchange, Luke gives his account of the only miracle (other than the resurrection) that is recorded in all four Gospels.

Jesus took the five loaves of bread (i.e., similar to our biscuits) and two fish and proceeded to feed a multitude of "about 5,000 men" (*andres*=males), in

---

Day 3
Feeding 5,000

Read John 6:1-13 for a parallel account of this miracle.

1. Why do you think this miracle is found in all four Gospels? Why is it so impressive?
2. How do you show your concern for homeless, poor, and hungry people?
3. Have you ever seen God "multiply resources" for people helping the poor? If so, when and how?
4. What barriers and excuses keep us from helping needy people?

addition to whatever women and children may have been there. The meal they ate was not merely a symbolic one in which each took a small amount, but "all ate and were satisfied." Although there was abundance, there was to be no waste. Fully twelve baskets of leftovers were picked up after the meal.

3. The prediction of his death. 9:18-27.

Do you not wonder what effect such a miracle had on the people who witnessed it? More particularly still, have you not been curious as to its impact on the apostles who knew the full details of it? By now, in fact, the apostles had seen, heard, and done (under commission from Jesus) enough that they should be drawing some conclusions about their leader. Indeed, the time had come for Jesus to draw them out.

On a day when he was apparently alone with them, Jesus began a conversation with the Twelve by asking them what they were hearing about him. "Who do the crowds say I am?" he began. In an early version of our modern polling technique, they began relating the things they had heard — John the Baptist, Elijah, a prophet come back to life. The common theme of all they reported was that the people had no doubt that Jesus was acting for Yahweh and in the prophetic tradition.

Then Jesus came to the real point of his inquiry. "But what about you? Who do you say I am?" His questions were not for the sake of information. They were to give the apostles a chance to articulate what they had come to believe about him. On the foundation of that faith, Jesus could reveal still more to them.

In what the Gospels clearly intend for readers to see as a watershed moment, Peter confessed for himself and the group their considered conviction that Jesus was the "Christ of God." The Greek term "Christ" has for its Hebrew equivalent "Messiah."

Day 4
Jesus' Cross

Read Isaiah 53 for an Old Testament prediction of the death of Christ.

1. What circumstance called forth Peter's confession?
2. Is there any doubt that Jesus knew what lay ahead for him? Explain.
3. Why was it important for Jesus to tell his disciples in advance about his death?
4. How do you think they reacted to this news? See Matt. 16:21-23.
5. How do you think you would have reacted? Why?

111

The term signified to the Jews of Jesus' day the anointed deliverer for whom the covenant community of Israel had been waiting. Yet it is clear from the Gospels that the expectation of Yahweh's Messiah was mistaken in many respects. The most glaring flaw in the popular mind was the notion that he would function principally as a military-political redeemer whose mission would be to expel the Romans, reestablish the Davidic dynasty in Jerusalem, and lead the Jews to unprecedented prosperity.

Peter's confession — given in abbreviated form here and in a fuller version at Matthew 16:13ff — was correct but confused. Yes, Jesus had come as the "Messiah." But, no, he was not on a mission to establish an earthly kingdom whose principal features would be peace and wealth. So Jesus startled the apostles by telling them that the role of the Messiah involved suffering and death. "The Son of Man must suffer many things and be rejected by the elders, chief priests and teachers of the law, and he must be killed and on the third day be raised to life."

Although there are earlier hints of Jesus' fate in Luke (2:35; 5:35), these words constitute the first explicit prediction of suffering and death for Jesus in this Gospel. What would it mean for Jesus to fill the role of Messiah? It was important that the apostles be prepared to see it unfold. To be sure, this single statement did not fix the matter in their minds. Even when the crucifixion takes place, they will be caught off guard by it. But without this background instruction that would come to their minds after the fact, they might never have accepted so radically different a definition of what God's anointed one was to be and do.

That "Jesus strictly warned them not to tell this to anyone" should not shock us. The apostles had no business trying to explain to others the meaning of something they did not know themselves. Only when the events of the cross were behind Jesus could they speak of it with correct understanding.

With his shocking statement about a cross in prospect for himself on the floor, Jesus proceeded to speak of still another cross with his disciples. "Then he said to them all: 'If anyone would come after me, he must deny himself and take up his cross daily and follow me.'" While Christianity knows only *one cross where atonement can be made*, the realistic and regular demands of commitment to Jesus require a *discipleship cross* for every genuine follower of the Son of God.

For one of us to "take up his cross" means far more than identifying with the shame and suffering of Jesus. And it certainly means more than to bear one's daily infirmities with some measure of dignity (e.g., "This arthritis is just my cross to bear, I suppose!"). A cross meant only one thing to the original hearers of Jesus' words. It signified *death*. As Christians, we are called to die to our own egos, wills, and desires so we can embrace Christ's agenda for a human life.

For someone to "deny himself" is to renounce the creed of our own generation about self-determination. "It's my life, so I'll do as I please!," goes the chant. No Christian can join such a chorus, for we have made a vow to give the control of heart and life to Jesus. No one ever understood or expressed this commitment better than Paul: "I have been crucified with Christ and I no longer live, but Christ lives in me. The life I live in the body, I live by faith in the Son of God, who loved me and gave himself for me" (Gal. 2:20; cf. 2 Cor. 4:10-11).

In the voluntary surrender of one's life to Christ, he or she "loses" it insofar as the right to choose its focus or outcome; on the other hand, to "save" one's life for his or her own purposes is to forfeit the

Day 5
My Cross

Read 2 Corinthians 6:3-13 for more information on Paul's suffering for Christ.

1. What distinction do you see in the two crosses of this section? What connection?
2. To confess Jesus is to invite suffering for his sake. How ready are you for that role?
3. How does one "save his life"? "Lose his life" for Jesus?
4. What means more to you than anything else? How will you prove it today?
5. Write a prayer based or Galatians 2:20.

meaning and destiny of life as it was intended by its Creator. In what one writer has termed a "magnificent hyperbole," Jesus laid out the alternatives for us: "What good is it for a man to gain the whole world, and yet lose or forfeit his very self?"

When would these things become clear? How could the apostles understand such depths of truth for themselves — much less make them clear to others? Jesus promised that all would become clear for them within their lifetime. "Some who are standing here [though not himself and Judas, the remainder of the Twelve?] will not taste death before they see the kingdom of God." In his death, resurrection, ascension, and sending of the Holy Spirit, the sovereign reign of God would become a reality for them.

Week Seventeen

Luke 9:28-50 (IV C 4 to IV C 6 in Outline)

4. *The Transfiguration. 9:28-36.*

With the first explicit mention of Jesus' death on record at 9:22, more and more of the events and discussions in the Gospel of Luke focus on his Passion. Hardly any event in that sequence has the significance of his Transfiguration.

Approximately a week after the events that called forth Peter's confession of Jesus as the Christ and the latter's response to clarify the meaning of his role, Jesus withdrew to a mountain for prayer. He took Peter, James, and John with him, and what they saw made a most remarkable impression on them. Peter was writing about it more than thirty years after the fact. Contrasting "cleverly devised fables" with things known to "eyewitnesses," he clearly had this day in mind at 2 Peter 1:16-18. There he spoke of the "honor and glory from God the Father" bestowed on Jesus when he was with him "on the sacred mountain."

While Jesus was praying, his physical features changed and his very clothing became "as bright as a flash of lightning." What is more important, Moses and Elijah appeared with him and discussed what lay ahead in Jerusalem. Luke writes: "They spoke about his departure." It is significant that the word translated "departure" is the Greek term *exodus*. Just as the Jews were delivered from their captivity in Egypt by heaven's appointed agent, Moses, so would Jesus act on heaven's behalf to deliver all mankind from bondage to sin.

In addition to the parallelism between Moses and Jesus just mentioned (cf. Deut. 18:15), one can think

Day 1
Powerful Memories

Read 2 Peter 1:16-18 for Peter's memories of the Transfiguration.

1. Why do you think this experience was shared with only three apostles?
2. Who appeared and talked with Jesus? Why are they such pivotal figures in the Bible?
3. What was the topic of their discussion? What was the purpose of it?
4. Do you understand Peter's desire to "capture the moment" he had witnessed? Explain.
5. From 2 Peter 1, what effect do you think this event had on the long-term development of Peter's faith?

of other reasons for Moses and Elijah being chosen as the representatives of the ages to have this conversation with the Son of Man. For one, Moses represented the Law and Elijah the prophets, and both pointed forward to Jesus. Also, both of them had experienced rejection and suffering at the hands of unbelieving men, so they could encourage Jesus for what lay before him. Finally, it would be a final, dramatic witness for them to bear to Christ before Peter, James, and John.

We must remind ourselves that Jesus "shared in [our] humanity" in fact and not merely in appearance (Heb. 2:14). Just as he would later recoil in horror in Gethsemane over the prospect of what lay ahead for him and need the ministry of angels (22:43), so he apparently needed clarification and encouragement as he was closing his ministry in Galilee and about to make his way to Jerusalem.

Day 2
Knowing What to Say

Read Proverbs 10:11-21 for wisdom about the tongue.

1. What suggestion did Peter make at the Transfiguration? What did Luke write of that statement?

2. Recall a time when you were in a situation and didn't know what to say. How did you handle it?

3. What answer/rebuke did Peter receive to his suggestion? Explain its meaning.

4. What proverb from Proverbs 10 fits this situation best? Why?

5. What was Jesus' personal reaction to Peter's foolish statement?

As they had accompanied Jesus to his place of prayer that day, Peter, James, and John were "very sleepy." But the radical changes in Jesus' appearance, the arrival of Moses and Elijah, and their overhearing of the conversation among those three glorious figures brought them wide awake. What should they do? Was it appropriate to speak or ask questions? Could they touch Moses and Elijah? While thoughts such as these may have been darting through their consciousness, the discussion was obviously about to end and Jesus' two colleagues in revelation were about to leave. Still unsure as to what they should do, Peter could not let the moment pass. He wanted to preserve the moment by doing something to commemorate it. Thus he blurted out a totally inappropriate remark to Jesus about building three "shelters," perhaps similar to the sort Jews customarily built for the annual Feast of Tabernacles.

In retrospect, Luke excuses Peter by writing: "He did not know what he was saying." Indeed, he did not know what to say at that point in his own faith development. It was not yet clear to him just how inappropriate it was to suggest three presumably either rest shelters or shelter-monuments that would have implied equality among Moses, Elijah, and Jesus. As he was speaking up with his proposal about shelters, a "cloud" surrounded the three apostles and their Master and the Father's voice spoke to say, "This is my Son, whom I have chosen; listen to him."

There was no need for Moses and Elijah to stay. The disciples had Jesus with them, and they needed no more. "Listen to *him*" was a command that corrected Peter's naive suggestion of parity among the three he had just witnessed. Coupled with the identification of Jesus as "my Son" by the voice they heard, Peter, James, and John were then in position to know precisely why he was superior to the men who had testified about him beforehand. Although this was an astounding event, they would talk about frequently later on (cf. Peter's comments in 2 Pet. 1:16ff), "the disciples kept this to themselves, and told no one at that time what they had seen." It would take events that had not yet happened to make it intelligible to them. Only then could they relate it to others in a meaningful way.

5. Healing a demon-possessed boy. 9:37-45.

No matter what mountain-top experiences anyone has in his Christian experience, there comes a time when he must return to the routine. A two-week mission trip comes to an end. A weekend retreat gives way to Monday morning work. So the disciples' experience on the Mount of Transfiguration had to give way to the realities of their still-immature faith.

On the very next day, a large crowd met Jesus as he came down from the mountain. One man was aggressive enough in that crowd to get the Lord's attention for the sake of his only child, a son pos-

Day 3
A Difficult Case

Read another account of this event from Matthew 17:14-21.

1. What effect does failure have in your life?
2. How do you think the apostles felt about their failure here? Explain.
3. Explain your understanding of Jesus' statement at v. 41.
4. From Luke and Matthew, what was lacking in the disciples at this point?

sessed by an evil spirit. The physical symptoms associated with his condition were clearly frightening. As his father summarized the progression of what had been happening to the boy, "[the demon] scarcely ever leaves him and is destroying him."

Captured as his own mind must have been with the conversation he had had with Moses and Elijah about his impending death, Jesus turned immediately from any self-absorption to sensitive awareness of the demon-possessed boy. It must have increased his anguish considerably to hear the man close his tale of woe with these words: "I begged your disciples to drive it out, but they could not." In spite of the fact that Jesus had given them both the power and authority to "drive out *all demons*," they had somehow been unable to prevail in this particular contest with evil. The reason for their failure will shortly become apparent.

Although Jesus' statement in response to this situation is clear enough, the objects of that statement are not clear from the text. He said, "O unbelieving and perverse generation, how long shall I stay with you and put up with you? Bring your son here." It seems absurd to think the first part of the statement is directed to the father of the possessed boy, for he had retained faith in Jesus in spite of the failure of the disciples to help his son. It is possible that the objects of Jesus' rebuke were the apostles who had failed to cast out the demon. Others think it was a statement directed to both the apostles and the curious bystanders who were gawking to see if Jesus himself might meet his match in this particular case.

Jesus' confident use of power is evident in Luke's narrative. Although the demon made a final frantic attempt to destroy the boy and to thwart faith in God's power, the authoritative Son of God simply "rebuked the evil spirit, healed the boy and gave him back to his father." While this miracle caused every-

Day 4
Faith and Prayer

Read Psalm 91 about trust in the Lord.

1. Jesus attributed the failure of his disciples to a lack of faith. Explain.

one who witnessed it to be "amazed at the greatness of God," Jesus was clearly still distressed over the fact that his disciples had been stalemated in this situation. Their weak faith in his promises made to them earlier had kept them from providing the blessing they should have been able to give the possessed boy.

In another Gospel account of this same event, the detail is given that the disciples later requested a private explanation of why they had tried and failed to cast out the demon. Here was Jesus' answer: "Because you have so little faith. I tell you the truth, if you have faith as small as a mustard seed, you can say to this mountain, 'Move from here to there' and it will move. Nothing will be impossible for you" (Matt. 17:20). Their failure that day is an all-too-common situation among today's disciples. Our lack of faith in Jesus' promises keeps us from bringing the kingdom's liberation and joy to those who need it.

While everyone was rejoicing over the healing of the demon-possessed boy, Jesus' mind turned back to the matter that had been on his mind as he came down the mountain that day and before the boy's father approached him. "Listen carefully to what I am about to tell you," he told his apostles. Then he told them for a second time in Luke's Gospel that he was going to fall into the hands of his enemies. This time, he added the fact that his enemies would take him because of a betrayal. They neither understood the meaning of what he said nor pressed for more information. Like so many things in his ministry, this would become clear in hindsight.

6. A rebuke of pride and intolerance. 9:46-50.

What happens next is simply unthinkable. The disciples who had just failed to cast out a demon and who had been rebuked for their faithlessness got into an argument among themselves about "which of them would be the greatest" in heaven's kingdom! Of all the times when they should have been feeling

2. Could some of our failures be explained the same way?

3. Is there a situation of frustration in your life today that traces to a lack of faith?

4. How is faith made stronger? What are you doing to strengthen your faith?

5. How does the discipline of prayer relate to faith?

Day 5
Pride and Intolerance

Read Luke 22:24-30 to see that this issue was not settled easily.

1. What issue was being debated among the

disciples? How do you react to this?

2. What object lesson did Jesus use to reply to their dispute?

3. How should adult believers be like children?

4. Why had the disciples rebuked a man who was casting out demons? What was Jesus' response to what they had done?

5. By what inappropriate standards do we sometimes exclude others? How can we overcome this tendency?

humble and needy, they were thinking about rank and pecking order in the nation-state they envisioned (cf. Acts 1:6). Who will be Prime Minister? Who will be Secretary of State? Who will be Treasury Chairman? What absurd presumption on their part!

Jesus rebuked their pride by calling a child to stand beside him. He told the disciples — perhaps thinking specifically of the little boy whose pain they had addressed so ineffectually — to "welcome" little children in his name. He coupled that object lesson with the call for them to seek greatness through humble service.

Before we are too hard on the Twelve, we should think of our own experience. They were not the last whose pride caused them to worry about position for themselves rather than following Jesus' example of identifying with those who had no position. In God's kingdom, those who understand its nature identify with the neglected and powerless in order to invite them to the Messiah's banquet table.

Then, as if to shift attention away from the rebuke of their pride, John apparently sought to put himself and his friends in a better light by telling of an incident in which they had forbidden a man who was "driving out demons in [Jesus'] name." The basis of their having put a stop to his work was simply that "he is not one of us."

While there was a trace of something admirable in what John did (i.e., a passionate regard for his colleagues and their close relationship to Christ), there is a larger issue of the bigotry it betrayed. After all, the man was casting out demons and doing it in the name of Jesus. "But for these disciples it was not enough that he should be able to do in the name of Jesus what they had so recently and so conspicuously failed to do. He had to follow with them. This has been the error of Christians in every age and it is interesting to see it in the very first generation of Jesus' followers." [Morris, *Luke*, pp. 176-177.]

While it is encouraging to see people exhibit loyalty to their church or fellowship, it is still disheartening to witness the bigoted rivalry of sectarianism within the body of Christ. Anyone who sees another believer doing good works and giving the glory to Jesus must recall the Lord's words: "Whoever is not against you is for you." At the very least, we must be on guard against the tendency to sectarian bigotry that has divided believers so often across the centuries.

Week Eighteen

Luke 9:51–10:42 (IV D 1 a to IV D 1 e in Outline)

Day 1
Rejection

Read Isaiah 53 for a prediction that Jesus would be rejected.

1. Why did the Samaritans react negatively to Jesus?
2. How did James and John react to this slight? How would you have reacted?
3. Have you ever experienced *rejection*? Relate the experience. Describe your feelings.
4. How have you allowed God to get you past that experience?

D. Ministry on the Way to Jerusalem. 9:51–19:28.

At this point in Luke's Gospel, there is a noticeable shift of focus and attention. From this point forward, Jesus' intent is to go to Jerusalem and there to bring his mission to completion. Interestingly, Luke introduces this section by speaking not of the cross or resurrection but the ascension. Before writing the painful details of the Savior's passion, he looks beyond it to his heavenly coronation.

In this section is found much that is unique to this Gospel. Many parables and sayings of Christ recorded here are not found anywhere else in the Word of God.

1. The first phase of the journey. 9:51–13:21.

The early stages of this trip to Jerusalem are set in the Trans-Jordan region. Leaving Galilee and passing through a portion of Samaria, Jesus and his disciples crossed the Jordan River and moved south through Perea.

a. Rejection by a Samaritan village. 9:51-56.

The first event on the journey took place in an unnamed Samaritan village. Several disciples went ahead of the larger group to prepare things for Jesus and his followers. They were apparently treated rudely by the Samaritans. The villagers "did not welcome him, because he was heading for Jerusalem." This could mean either that they were insulted because Jesus was not planning to spend time teaching among them or that they were simply unwilling to be hospitable to anyone headed for the city that was a rival worship center to their own Mount Gerizim [Gĕ´-rĭ-zĭm] (cf. John 4:20ff).

The Samaritans were a mixed race whose existence traced to the fall of the northern kingdom to Assyria. The Assyrian conquerors deported Israel's leading citizens and repopulated the area with foreigners (2 Kgs. 17:6, 24-26). Intermarriage between the Jews still in the region and the new pagan settlers produced both a new racial and a new religious group. Unwelcome at Jerusalem because of their mixed blood, the people of Samaria built their own worship site at Gerizim, delimited their canon of Scripture, and evolved an identity separate from the Jews. The prejudice and hostility between the two groups is reflected in the New Testament literature.

Faced with this rudeness, James and John raised the possibility with Jesus of calling down "fire from heaven to destroy" the Samaritans. While we may feel some sympathy for their defensive attitude toward their Lord, Jesus let these brothers know that his disciples were not to respond in kind to insults. He "rebuked" them and simply moved on to another village. "There may be place for righteous indignation, but there is no place among the followers of Christ for anger, for intolerance, or for revenge. This is not a time of judgment, but of grace. It is not for us to attempt to administer vengeance, but to preach the gospel of love." [Erdman, *Luke*, p. 118.]

b. A rebuke of halfhearted discipleship. 9:57-62.

As the group continued to move along the road, three individuals who met Jesus learned just how radical it would be to be numbered among his followers. The first apparently volunteered to follow Jesus "wherever you go." If he entertained illusions that discipleship would be an exciting and pleasant experience, Jesus challenged him to realize that it

**Day 2
Commitment**

Read Galatians 1:11-24 for an account of one man's commitment.

1. Which of the three men had the best excuse for delay?

2. Why was Jesus so unyielding with each of them?
3. Describe a "golden moment" that you let slip away.
4. Is there a golden-moment challenge facing you today? If so, what will you do with it?
5. On a scale of one to ten, what is your *commitment level* to Christ?

would mean sacrifice. "Foxes have holes and birds of the air have nests, but the Son of Man has no place to lay his head." What an insight into the nature of life on Planet Earth for its creator! The God who had created the world claimed no part of it for his personal comfort while here. Far from wanting to discourage the man, Jesus simply wanted him to make an informed commitment — to count the cost.

The second man did not offer himself but was challenged to join with Jesus and his disciples. But he was reluctant to follow immediately in view of a family crisis. His father had died, and it was a son's duty to see that his father got a decent burial. (Others have suggested the father was still alive, and this man wanted to wait until after he had died.) The strong response Jesus made to him probably takes into account his knowledge of the man's heart. He was apparently using his family duty as an excuse for postponing something even more important. "Let the dead bury their own dead, but you go and proclaim the kingdom of God." Jesus was passing through this man's region (and life!) for the final time, and nothing was so important as the commitment Jesus was asking him to make. All else must wait when we are called to obedience by the Lord.

The third man offered to join Jesus as soon as he had gone to say his farewells to family. Again, however, Jesus called for more than had been offered. There can be no hesitancy when the Son of God is near and calling. Indecision misses the opportunity of a lifetime. "No one who puts his hand to the plow and looks back is fit for service in the kingdom of God."

Jesus knew the hearts of these men. If they did not drop everything else then and there to follow him, they would never give themselves to the kingdom of God. So he offered each of them a golden moment of opportunity that one could ill afford to miss. We are left to wonder what each did with his once-in-a-lifetime challenge. Perhaps Luke leaves each story unfinished for the sake of inviting his readers into self-examination about our own situation before God. "Golden moments of opportunity" come to each of us, and too many slip through our fingers unclaimed and unused.

c. The mission of the seventy. 10:1-24.

With so much yet to be done and time running out quickly, Jesus did a prudent thing in delegating the work of preaching the kingdom to others. Luke alone tells of this occasion when seventy [or, in some manuscripts, "seventy-two"] disciples were sent to preach for him. It is interesting that this story is told right on the heels of the challenge to wholehearted discipleship. Indeed, these men were sent out "like lambs among wolves" and with minimal provisions.

With a plentiful harvest available and although the number of workers was limited, Jesus nevertheless did not send these seventy men out alone. They were sent "two by two." Not only did this satisfy the Old Testament ideal of confirmed witness (cf. Deut. 17:6), but it also met the practical need of each disciple for protection and encouragement. It is still wise for every believer to have at least one dear friend and confidant in the gospel. Grand worship experiences with hundreds or thousands lift the spirit. But there also comes a time when one needs to know and be known at a personal and intimate level.

As workers in God's kingdom, the seventy were to offer a blessing (i.e., "Peace to this house") wherever they went and to accept whatever hospitality was offered to them. But they were not to be pushy or go where they were unwelcome.

If these disciples encountered opposition to their ministry of preaching and healing, they were to go through the symbolic act of wiping the dust from their feet as a warning against deliberate rejection of the truth. Such arrogance against God would turn

**Day 3
Delegation**

Read Exodus 18 for Jethro's advice to Moses about shared responsibility.

1. What was the mission of the seventy? Why were they sent out in pairs?
2. Do you have a safe place for sharing hurts and joys? Sharing prayer needs? Getting encouragement?
3. How does sharing/delegating responsibility achieve greater good?
4. Why do most people find it hard to share/delegate?
5. Pray for your church leaders to know how and when to share/delegate responsibility.

out to be self-judgment. Even the people of Sodom would be better off before God's judgment than such persons. Apparently Jesus had experienced a particularly arrogant repudiation in the cities of Korazin [Khō-rā́-zĭn] and Bethsaida [Bĕth-sā́-ĭ-də] — towns likely located in the vicinity of Capernaum, the city that served as Jesus' base of operations during his ministry in Galilee.

Likely at some prearranged time and place, the seventy "returned with joy" from their ministry tour. They were especially thrilled that even demonic forces were powerless before the authority Christ had given them. Indeed, Jesus affirmed their work and said, "I saw Satan fall like lightning from heaven." This should not be taken as a comment on the origin of Satan and the demons but as a summary of the ministry just completed. Satan had been routed by the power of God as the message of the kingdom had been shared. As impressive as this was, however, Jesus tried to help these exhilarated men from taking pride in their accomplishments. "However, do not rejoice that the spirits submit to you," he told them, "but rejoice that your names are recorded in heaven." The ultimate honor that comes to any man or woman is to have his or her name known in heaven, and that is a gift of grace. Yet he shared fully in the joy of the events they had experienced.

d. The Parable of the Good Samaritan. 10:25-37.

As Jesus was teaching one day, a man with impure intent asked him about the requirement for inheriting eternal life. The question set off a discussion about loving one's "neighbor." By means of one of the best-known stories in the Bible, Jesus taught that a neighbor is not just the person who lives nearby but anyone in need. In this story, a man of a different race and religion acted heroically by showing love. It is our duty to imitate such unselfish love to all. "Go and do likewise."

**Day 4
Compassion**

Read Psalm 112 for God's view of compassionate persons.

1. What factors weighed against the Samaritan's actions? What overcame those negatives?
2. Could those same factors keep you from showing compassion?
3. What commandment was Jesus illustrating by this story?
4. Why was the question about the identity of one's "neighbor" asked?
5. Do you have a neighbor in need today? What will you do about it?

e. A visit with Martha and Mary. 10:38-42.

At the home of two sisters in Bethany (cf. John 11:1), Jesus reinforced a basic lesson about discipleship. Practical life concerns of the sort that Martha was preoccupied with satisfying are important. After all, hasn't the Good Samaritan been commended for taking care of needs? But some things are even more important than a neat house or hot meal. Sometimes a parent is wise enough to hold a child or read with him rather than do housework. Sometimes a disciple is wise enough to worship and hear Jesus rather than meet another hectic deadline.

"Jesus noted that Martha was pulled in several directions at once and her service was characterized by anxiety and stress. He noted that life has very few necessities, but one of those is communion with Him. Worship is not an option for quality living but is a cornerstone for healthy, spiritual living. Mary was commended for her wise choice." [Benware, *Luke*, p. 89.] In order to fall in love with Jesus, one must spend time with him.

Read Philippians 3:1-14 about Christian priorities.

1. Try to describe the personalities of Mary and Martha based on this scene.
2. Is your nature more like Mary's or Martha's?
3. How does stress affect your spiritual life? How does God help you deal with it?
4. Does worship affect your stress level? If so, how?
5. Pray for God to help you define your priorities and to live in peace.

Week Nineteen

Luke 11:1–12:12 (IV D 1 f to IV D 1 i in Outline)

Day 1
Prayer

Read Daniel 6:1-23 for a glimpse into one man's prayer life.

1. Define in your own words the three *fundamental elements of prayer* seen in the Lord's Prayer.
2. What value and/or danger do you see in memorized prayers? Impromptu prayers? Written prayers?
3. What has been your most helpful insight into meaningful prayer?
4. What did Jesus teach about *persistence* in prayer?
5. Jesus' personal example of prayerfulness prompted his disciples to want a deeper prayer life. Who could be your model and teacher in prayer? Whom are you influencing to be more prayerful?

f. Teaching about prayer. 11:1-13.

The men who spent time with Jesus were greatly impressed by his prayer life. Luke has repeatedly called our attention to his prayerful lifestyle (cf. 3:21; 6:12; 9:28). We deceive ourselves if we think we can follow the model of our Lord's life without embracing his regular involvement with prayer.

One day the disciples came to him during his prayers and asked, "Lord, teach us to pray, just as John taught his disciples." In response to their request, he called them back to a form of the prayer he had already taught them in the Sermon on the Mount (Matt. 6:9-13). Although the prayer is valuable when memorized and repeated as it stands, it is still more valuable when viewed as a type or style of prayer.

Many ways of analyzing this prayer have been offered across the centuries. At least three things are critical. First, prayer grows out of a *relationship*. Thus we pray, "Father." The sense of being a member of God's spiritual family gives assurance to the youngest, most timid, and weakest of his children. Because we have been born anew, we are his children and can pray without fear of being rejected. Second, prayer is *praise*. God's name is to be "hallowed" in all things. That is, he is worthy of worship because of his very nature. Thus our desire must be for his will to be sovereign in all things (i.e., "your kingdom come"). God alone deserves so exalted a place in human thought, desire, and behavior. Third, prayer is *confession*. We confess our absolute dependence on him by acknowledging that our "daily bread" is from him; we confess our spiritual brokenness by asking that God "forgive us our sins"; we confess our inability to choose our own path by praying, "And lead us not into temptation."

These three fundamental elements to meaningful prayer must always be present. Apart from a relationship with God, there is no purpose to prayer. Without praise for him, we show that we have no genuine appreciation for the relationship he has given us through Christ. Failing to confess our own weakness, we deny ourselves the opportunity to experience his power.

Another important issue relative to prayer is not only its form, but our persistence and boldness. So Jesus gave a brief parable about a man caught without supplies when a friend comes to his home. Late at night, the man goes to another's house, knocks on his door, and asks him to share his bread. The first answer he got was that his neighbor was already in bed with his family and could not get up to help him. Rather than go away embarrassed and empty handed, however, he continued to knock and ask. Finally, because of the man's "persistence," his neighbor gets up and gives him "as much as he needs."

Every parable has one central point and must be read for that thesis, without pressing the details. Is the point of this parable that God is reluctant to share his limitless resources? Is the point that the supplicant should have been better prepared for unexpected guests? No, the point is that prayer's real power lies not in some rigid form of words but in the passionate boldness of the petitioner. "So I say to you: Ask and it will be given to you; seek and you will find; knock and the door will be opened to you. For everyone who asks receives; he who seeks finds; and to him who knocks, the door will be opened."

Lest anyone miss the point of this parable and see God as a grudging dispenser of grace, Jesus follows it up with a reminder of his first point about the essentials of prayer. Prayer grows out of a relationship with God as "Father." Do we humans understand how a good father treats his children? Would such a father give a snake to a son asking him for a fish? Would he give a scorpion when asked for an egg? Knowing the answer to these rhetorical questions, Jesus draws the following conclusion for us: "If you then, though you are evil, know how to give good gifts to your children, how much more will your Father in heaven give the Holy Spirit to those who ask him!"

Luke has a demonstrable interest in the Holy Spirit. Here he sees the Holy Spirit being given by God as his supreme gift to man. If he gives so great a spiritual gift, what else would he withhold? It follows, then, that our faithlessness in prayer rather than God's hesitancy in giving good gifts is the explanation for our spiritual poverty.

g. Rebuking blasphemy and unbelief. 11:14-36.

One day Jesus was "driving out a demon that was mute." The fulness of his power over demons was evident when the man who had been possessed spoke. This public verification of his power to set people free of demonic possession had its effect on the crowd of witnesses who saw what he had done, and they were "amazed." Yet there were enemies of Jesus in the same crowd. With their hearts fully hardened and set against him, they could not allow themselves to draw the conclusion that his works were divine confirmation of his claims.

But how could Jesus' critics respond to what had happened in public view? Since they could not deny that a miracle had occurred, their tactic was to attribute the miracle not to God but to "Beelzebub, the prince of demons." Still others simply taunted

Day 2
Signs

Read John 20:19-31 about the impact of signs on others.

1. Why were Jesus' critics so eager to "explain away" what he had done?
2. Have you ever known someone so blinded by prejudice that he/she could not see the truth? If so, describe the situation.
3. How did Jesus respond to this attack on himself?
4. What is the ultimate "sign" Christianity offers the world?
5. What did Jesus say about one's reaction to the resurrection?

him "by asking for a sign" — apparently a sign so impressive that it would compel belief in him. Jesus responded to the charge that he was in league with the demons and the taunt for a still greater sign in turn.

First, Jesus responded to the blasphemous suggestion that he was somehow in league with Satan in his ministry. Although they had not made their charge publicly, he "knew their thoughts" and brought it out into the open. His response was to say that it was absurd to think that Satan ["Beelzebub" appears to have been a common name given him by Jews of that time] was working against himself. Beelzebub was giving Jesus the power to drive out demons? That would be an instance of a "kingdom divided against itself," something that Satan and human leaders know to be a suicidal act. Furthermore, Jesus offered a brilliant dilemma to his critics, neither horn of which they were anxious to grasp. On the one hand, if casting out demons signals that one is in league with the devil, these Jewish opinion leaders would have to indict their own followers — some of whom were alleged to cast out demonic spirits — with the same charge. On the other hand, if the ability to cast out demons means that one is functioning with heaven's blessing and approval — which, of course, was the claim of the Jewish exorcists — then they would be forced to admit that the "kingdom of God has come to you" in Jesus' presence. The logical force of this dilemma apparently put one segment of the critics to silence.

With his opponents on the run before his argument, Jesus pressed his point still further. He insisted that his ability to cast out demons ought to be interpreted as meaning that "someone stronger" than Satan was on the scene to overpower him, take away his weapons, and take the spoils of war from him. This strength is exactly what Jesus' ministry had

Day 3
Overcoming Evil

Read Colossians 3:1-17 for a listing of put-off and put-on behaviors for Christians.

1. What is the point of Jesus' story about the demon-possessed man who was eventually overtaken by a group of demons?

2. Have you ever tried to root out an evil without replacing its void with something positive and spiritual? How successful were you?

3. Is there any issue in your life now to which this story is relevant?

4. How does v. 28 summarize the point of this story?

131

been about. In his teaching and works, evil was being destroyed. As he brought in the kingdom of God, Satan was unable to stop him and was being routed. At the cross and in his resurrection, Jesus would win the final battle over him and rob him of his power to hold men and women as his "spoils" any longer (Col. 2:15).

In this high moment of tension with Jewish leaders, Jesus threw down his challenge in unambiguous terms. They would either stand with him for the sake of the kingdom of God or stand against him and "scatter" God's flock; they would either stand with him to overcome evil or stand against him and become part of the evil strategy of Satan.

Jesus pressed the options before his hearers further by the illustration of a man set free from demon possession. Because the man did not fill his heart with righteousness, the evil spirit who once inhabited that heart as his house brought "seven other spirits more wicked than itself" and they reestablished possession of that man. This parable may be read as a commentary either on Israel or a given individual. It is not enough to renounce evil and repudiate Satan. The kingdom of God does not exist in a vacuum but in the fulness of righteousness. Neither a nation nor a given individual can conquer evil until unbelief is replaced with faith and evil behavior with good. Salvation is not a matter of tidying up someone's past life but of giving a new, positive way of life. The kingdom is for "those who hear the word of God and obey it."

Second, to the demand for a "miraculous sign," Jesus said that one indeed would be given his "wicked generation." The sign would be his resurrection from the dead. Anyone who rejected it would stand under judgment. It was therefore critical that one's "eye" (i.e., entrance for light and, in this metaphor, understanding) be healthy enough to see Jesus, come to faith in him, and be "full of light." The willful blindness of critics such as these would condemn them to perpetual "darkness."

h. Rebuking hypocrisy. 11:37-54.

Invited to eat at the house of a Pharisee, Jesus accepted the invitation but offended his host by not first washing his hands in the ceremonial, ritualistic fashion that pharisaic tradition prescribed. Jesus' response to the man's displeasure was to deliver a scathing rebuke to the spirit of hypocrisy that puts ritual above authentic spirituality. The essence of his message here was that God values the heart (i.e., inner state) above ceremonies (i.e., public display). While not going so far as to condemn religious rituals (cf. v. 42b), he clearly did condemn the substitution of ceremonies for repentance and renewal. To be concerned more for public appearance than for one's kingdom relationship with God is to be a "hypocrite" (i.e., actor) and to come under condemnation. A series of six "woes" against such a spirit was delivered with such passion that "the Pharisees and the teachers of the law began to oppose [Jesus] fiercely and to besiege him with questions, waiting to catch him in something he might say."

i. Encouraging the disciples to boldness. 12:1-12.

With the conflict between Jesus and the religious establishment of his day in bold relief now, Jesus turned his attention to the emboldening of his own disciples. With the crowd following him growing into a group of "many thousands," he publicly warned against the "yeast of the Pharisees, which is hypocrisy" and called instead for integrity of the sort that would allow even their secret conversations to be broadcast in public places.

Speaking of what would be "proclaimed from housetops" became Jesus' bridge for calling these disciples to boldness in their witness to him. Because

Day 4
Hypocrisy

Read Mark 7:1-23 for Jesus' teaching about heart versus ritual.

1. Why did Jesus' host take offense at his behavior?
2. Which of the *six woes* in Jesus' response sounds most frightening to you? Most familiar?
3. What is *hypocrisy*? Why is religion vulnerable to this hateful behavior?
4. How do we sometimes get tangled up over *form* and *content*?
5. How did this episode end? Explain why.

Day 5
Boldness

Read Paul's appeal for boldness in Ephesians 6:10-20.

1. What jeopardy were his disciples in on account of Jesus?
2. Can one ever follow Jesus without peril? Explain.
3. When are you most challenged or intimidated about your Christian identity? How do you handle it?

4. In what area of your life do you need more spiritual boldness?
5. How is the Holy Spirit related to Christian boldness?

"fear" often keeps people silent or forces them to act hypocritically, he specifically warned them against fear, intimidation, and denial. To bear faithful witness to Christ will bring opposition. But heaven's promise is that the needs of his faithful witnesses will always be known and met by the Holy Spirit. This promise is still true today and will be validated whenever you stand firm in your integrity and daily confession of Christ.

Week Twenty

Luke 12:13–13:21 (IV D 1 j to IV D 1 o in Outline)

j. Warning against covetousness. 12:13-21.

An interruption from someone in the crowd seems to inject an abrupt change of subject matter into the flow of Luke's text. A man spoke up and asked Jesus to mediate between him and his brother over the dividing of an inheritance. But maybe there is nothing terribly "abrupt" about the flow of events here. How many people sit in worship on any given Sunday today with hearts preoccupied by money-related issues? From people worried about being able to pay their bills to others who are greedy schemers, money can be a serious obstacle to spiritual focus for one's life.

Rabbis were sometimes asked to help settle ethical disputes or to mediate within families. So someone called out to Jesus, "Teacher, tell my brother to divide the inheritance with me." Perhaps his brother was in the crowd with him. His hope may have been to embarrass him and to force some sort of settlement on the spot. At any rate, Jesus refused to step into their conflict. Instead he warned both of them to "be on your guard against all kinds of greed" and to realize that "a man's life does not consist in the abundance of his possessions."

Materialism is such an enemy to godliness that Jesus turned from the single questioner to the larger crowd to tell them a parable about how greed can distract a person from the true meaning of life. In his story, a successful farmer-businessman becomes so obsessed with making money, expanding his operation, and saving up for the future that he forgets what matters most in a human life. Caught up

Day 1
Greed

Read 1 Timothy 6:6-19 about a Christian's attitude toward money.

1. What event is behind the Parable of the Rich Fool?
2. Is wealth sinful? Is poverty spiritual? Explain.
3. What was this rich man's real problem?
4. Is money a spiritual snare to you? Explain.
5. How are you using your possessions to be "rich toward God"?

in thoughts about "my crops," "my barns," and "my goods," the man obviously thought the future was under *his* control. So he planned his investments and retirement years without concern for God. Then God — the one who *really* controls the future — looked at him and called him a fool. "This very night your life will be demanded from you. Then who will get what you have prepared for yourself?"

Human life is incredibly fragile, and there are no assurances about the future except the ones God gives to his own people. So two brothers, a crowd of first-century hearers, and we should take care not to confuse our priorities. The ultimate goal of a life should be to be "rich toward God" (i.e., invest in eternity) rather than to accumulate the perishable things of this world.

k. Warning against anxiety. 12:22-34.

As Jesus refocused his attention from the crowd to his disciples, he gave still another challenge with regard to human life, wealth, and anxiety. Not only should Christ's disciples not be greedy, but we must also guard against being too concerned even about the daily necessities of life. Preoccupation with this world can distract the average person as well as the wealthy man or woman. "Do not worry about your life, what you will eat; or about your body, what you will wear. Life is more than food, and the body more than clothes."

Of course Christians who are able must work and pay a reasonable amount of attention to meeting the customary needs of human life (2 Thess. 3:6). Irresponsibility is a wicked attitude that seeks to impose on others. Even so, life is not about the things of the five senses. It is about the kingdom of God and his righteousness (Matt. 6:33).

To buttress his point, Jesus appealed to God's provisions for the "ravens" (i.e., crows = unclean birds, Lev. 11:15) and "lilies" (i.e., wildflowers of the

**Day 2
Anxiety**

Read Psalm 54 to hear David's prayer for God's help.

1. What sorts of things cause you anxiety?
2. How does anxiety affect your health? Relationships? Spiritual life?
3. What *positive* benefits can you attribute to worry? Explain.
4. How does *faith* relate to *anxiety*?
5. Write a prayer that is specific about your anxieties.

region). If God feeds unclean animals and gives beauty to wildflowers, shouldn't the creatures made in his own image believe that he knows our needs? Should we not trust him to see that our basic needs are met so long as we are faithful to his agenda for human living? We must not behave like pagans and act as if this world is the defining reason for our existence. The lesson is obvious — but so difficult to live!

God is generous and giving in his nature. Indeed, "your Father has been pleased to give you the kingdom." In order to be like him, his disciples must learn to be generous and giving as well. We must hold whatever we have here with a light touch and be ready to use it for God's purposes. Only "treasure in heaven" is secure against exhaustion, theft, or corruption. Only those hearts fixed on heavenly treasure can know peace and security.

l. A call to watchfulness. 12:35-48.

What will be the best safeguard against greed and preoccupation with the things of this world? Jesus' answer seems to be that watchfulness for his coming is the surest safeguard of a heart. "As to the events preceding this return, as to its circumstances and results, he taught them more definitely just before his death; here he simply enjoined upon them the attitude of watchfulness, implying that if his coming was occupying their thoughts, they would be kept at once from worldliness and from worry and would be diligent in serving him." [Erdman, *Luke*, pp. 144-145.]

Two parables reinforce Jesus' point here. The first is about a master who was attending a wedding banquet and whose servants are waiting for his return. They are alert for his arrival, dressed appropriately, and have his meal prepared. Even though he arrives in the wee hours of the morning, all is in readiness. He is so pleased by their competence that he invites them to sit at his banquet table and enjoy

**Day 3
Watchfulness**

Read 2 Peter 3:1-13 about the Day of the Lord.

1. How is *watchfulness* a safeguard against greed and worldliness?
2. Explain the point of the two parables Jesus gave here.
3. How are knowledge, opportunity, and responsibility related?
4. What degree of responsibility do you believe God will hold you to in Judgment? Why?

the feast prepared for him. The second parable is about the ways of a thief. Since such characters don't announce their arrival in advance, the only preparation against their plundering is to be on guard at all times. Similarly, the only way to be ready for the appearing of Christ is to be faithful to him at all times and under all circumstances. "You also must be ready, because the Son of Man will come at an hour when you do not expect him."

At this point, Peter asked a question about the nature of responsibility for himself and his apostle-colleagues. Does the duty of watchfulness apply equally to all? Or do leaders and teachers have a special degree of responsibility? In a teaching that we sometimes ignore, Jesus responded by saying that there are degrees of accountability in spiritual things. When one thinks about it, though, his statement seems to summarize what everyone would know to be fair and just. The person who has more opportunity to know the teachings of Christ has greater responsibility than the person with limited opportunity. "From everyone who has been given much, much will be demanded; and from the one who has been entrusted with much, much more will be asked." There will be degrees of reward and punishment in the end (cf. James 3:1; 1 Cor. 3:10-15).

m. The divisive influence of the Savior. 12:49-59.

Although the second coming of Jesus will bring his disciples together for a great banquet (cf. 12:37) and lead to the reward of his faithful servants (cf. 12:47-49), his first coming had introduced strife and division. The ultimate Prince of Peace divided friends and family along the lines of faith in him.

The "fire on the earth" in this paragraph is not a reference to something to follow his second coming and Judgment. This is the fire of judgment and purification brought by his personal ministry and subsequent establishment of the church. He has rebuked sin, and lines of division mark those who heed it from those who do not. His call to purification and spiritual renewal also divides people from one another. There can be no other way until he returns.

In our own situation, it is the cross that divides humankind. It is true enough that all who have come to God through Jesus' death have been reconciled both to God and one another by that cross (Eph. 2:11ff). But the cross divides all who are under its shadow from all who trust anyone or anything else to give meaning to their lives and hope for their futures.

n. A call to repentance. 13:1-9.

To illustrate both his lessons about constant readiness (12:37,40,48) and the need for repentance (12:49), Jesus made an appeal to current events. By the same reference, he also warned against judging the spiritual state of people based on their immediate circumstances. Pilate had apparently slaughtered some Galileans recently under conditions otherwise unknown to us, and there had also been a widely reported construction accident when a tower near the Pool of Siloam collapsed. Jesus did not share the common belief of ancient and modern times that tragedy was punishment for sin (cf. John 9:1ff). The dead Galileans and workmen were not "worse sinners" than the rest of their contemporaries. As a matter of fact, *all* are sinners and have the same need for repentance. Without repentance, no one will be able to stand before a Holy God in the last day.

What was true of individuals was also true of the entire nation of Israel. Using imagery borrowed from Micah 7, Jesus compared Israel to a "fig tree" that had been planted, tended, and inspected for fruitfulness. In the absence of fruit after a reasonable time, no one could blame the owner of a vineyard for cutting down such a tree. An additional

Day 4
Repentance

Read Romans 2:1-16 for an apostle's teaching about repentance.

1. Does suffering in someone's life always mean God is punishing him? Explain.
2. What was Jesus' point about the two tragedies in Jerusalem?
3. How does *grace* relate to repentance? Is God's grace without limits?
4. What has been the primary cause of repentance in your experience? The primary fruit?
5. Where does repentance belong in your schedule of events for today?

year of grace is given in the parable for tending and fertilizing, but even grace has its limits. Beyond the additional year, the tree would be cut down if it continued without fruit. In the same way, Israel was about to miss its final opportunity to accept Jesus as Messiah. He would offer himself again at Jerusalem, and Israel's faithlessness would squander God's grace.

Day 5
Hatred

Read 1 Corinthians 13 to find the alternative to hatred.

1. Why was Jesus criticized so harshly for healing a crippled woman on the Sabbath?
2. What do you think of Jesus' sharp reply to the criticism? Why was he so indignant?
3. Why did his critics feel "humiliated" by these exchanges?
4. Have you ever witnessed an instance of hatred growing into unreasoning opposition? How was it like this episode in Jesus' life? How different?
5. How do you guard your heart against hatred toward others?

o. Conflict on the Sabbath. 13:10-21.

In Israel's ultimate rejection of Jesus, the Sabbath question played a major role. It was another of the fault lines along which division was created by his presence and teaching.

Once Jesus healed a woman whose eighteen-year suffering as a cripple was somehow tied to a "spirit" (i.e., demon) who had bound her. "She was bent over and could not straighten up at all." Jesus' sympathy moved him to say, "Woman, you are set free from your infirmity." He then "put his hands on her" and she was cured. The "synagogue ruler" rebuked Jesus for violating the Sabbath rule against work by what he had just done. Without patience and giving no quarter, Jesus turned on him and his allies to rebuke a petty spirit that would permit someone to care for his animals on the Sabbath but prohibit showing mercy to a suffering human being. Although the people who witnessed this miracle were generally "delighted with all the wonderful things he was doing," his action and response to the synagogue ruler "humiliated" his opponents and surely made them even more determined to destroy him (cf. 11:53-54).

140

Week Twenty-One

Luke 13:22–14:35 (IV D 2 a to IV D 2 d in Outline)

2. The second phase. 13:22–17:10.

Because Luke is tracing Jesus' trip toward Jerusalem in something of a travel narrative, we enter the "second phase" of the narrative at 13:22 (cf. 9:51). With the observation that these things happened as Jesus "made his way to Jerusalem," Luke reminds us again of the divine purpose that was attached to everything Jesus did.

a. The "narrow door" of the kingdom. 13:22-30.

The first incident in this new series came about in response to a question put to Jesus by someone in his large entourage: "Lord, are only a few people going to be saved?" In his reply, Jesus turned the question away from quantitative analysis to qualitative concerns about participation in the kingdom of God. He was less concerned about *how many* would be saved than about *who* could be saved. Whether many or few entered the kingdom, the concern of each person should be to "make every effort" to be in that number.

From the way the narrative develops, it seems that the point of Jesus' oblique answer was to counter the widely held notion among the Jews that everyone descended from Abraham was automatically entitled to expect to share in the messianic feast. To the contrary, Jesus said the door to that great feast was "narrow" and would go unused by many. Although the banquet hall was spacious and the invitation to share in it went out to many, the would-be participants sought to find their own way to enter it. As a matter of fact, Jesus is himself the

Day 1
Who Will Be Saved?

Read Philippians 3:1-11 about the true hope for salvation.

1. What do you think was behind the question about "only a few" being saved? How did Jesus shift the question?
2. What was the gist of the answer he gave?
3. What is the "narrow door" of which he spoke? Why would it exclude many?
4. What did his answer imply about God's patience with Israel?
5. What does his answer mean to people living today?

141

"gate" (cf. John 10:9) and the exclusive "way" (cf. John 14:6) to salvation. Anyone who refuses to repent and turn to him excludes himself from admission to the great kingdom feast.

The point in this illustration about a time when "the owner of the house gets up and closes the door" echoes what was noted at 12:56 and 13:8-9. As Jesus neared Jerusalem for the final time in his earthly ministry, he warned the Jewish people that their opportunity for turning to God through him was slipping away. When the people in the story proceeded then to bang on the door and ask admission, the owner disclaims knowing them. Their reply at that point only makes their guilt greater. "We ate and drank with you," they call out, "and you taught in our streets." Then why had they not listened to his message? Why had they not come through the door he had opened for them? So they are turned away with the rebuke, "Away from me, all you evildoers!"

The grief that will come to those persons is the grief of those who will know it could have been otherwise. They will see Abraham, Isaac, Jacob, and the prophets inside the banquet hall to participate in the feast. Their descendants and intended hearers will have been "thrown out" because of their unbelief. What is more, Gentiles will have come from the four corners of the earth to "take their places at the feast in the kingdom of God." So not only was Jesus telling the Jews that their ethnic heritage was not enough to insure entrance into the kingdom, but he also served notice that Gentiles who entered by the narrow door of faith in him would be granted kingdom privileges. "Indeed there are those who are last who will be first, and first who will be last."

Day 2
Grieving over
Jerusalem

Read Psalm 137 for a lament over Jerusalem by a captive in Babylon.

b. *The message to Herod and a lament over Jerusalem. 13:31-35.*

At that point, some Pharisees brought a message to Jesus that Herod (the tetrarch, cf. 3:19-20) was hatching a plot to kill him. By bringing him such a warning, it seems unlikely that these men were among the number of Pharisees and teachers who were themselves already implacably hostile to Jesus (11:53-54). At any rate, Jesus was hardly intimidated by the news. In effect, he told them they could report back to Herod that he was going about his ministry as usual and would see it through to the end. Though Jesus knew that his mission would end in death, he also knew that all things were under his Father's control and not Herod's.

In response to the word about Herod's plot, Jesus made two interesting and revealing statements. First, he called Herod a "fox." Thinking in Hebraic rather than English categories, the point here is to identify Herod as nothing more than a petty nuisance (cf. Song of Songs 2:15) or insignificancy (cf. Matt. 8:20). Second, he sounds a note of indignant irony over Jerusalem. Far from being inclined to flee Herod, Jesus would make his way directly to the Holy City. After all, in view of that city's history with divine messengers (cf. 2 Kgs. 21:16, et al.), "surely no prophet can die outside Jerusalem!"

That the statement about Jerusalem was prophetic irony rather than personal animosity is clear from what follows. A passionate lament over the city comes from the Lord's mouth. Though he had offered himself and his salvation to that city already, it had resisted and rejected him. Although he had been as tender as a mother hen trying to protect her chicks from harm, he had been rebuffed. Even so, he took no delight in the prospect that the ancient Holy City — along with the nation for which it served as the chief city — would soon be "desolate."

c. Jesus as a Pharisee's guest. 14:1-24.

On a certain Sabbath, Jesus accepted an invitation to eat in the home of a "prominent Pharisee." Whether his host was personally sympathetic or hos-

1. Why was Jesus grieving over Jerusalem? Why was that city so important to him?
2. Have you ever felt genuine grief of this sort for a nation? City? Family? Explain.
3. What positive impact is your church having on its larger environment?
4. Describe the greatest threat you see to your city. What can you do to help with the situation?
5. Write a prayer for your city.

Day 3
Humility

Read the call to Christian humility that is found in Philippians 2:1-11.

1. What scene prompted Jesus to say what he did about humility? Have you ever witnessed a similar situation?
2. Define *humility*.
3. Is it egotistical to think you are humble? Explain your answer.
4. How does one learn humility? Exhibit it? Teach it?
5. How did Jesus broaden his comments to include *charity* and *grace* in this teaching? What would be an equivalent situation for you?

tile, the fact remains that Jesus "was being carefully watched" by the larger group of his kind. He put those watchdogs of orthodoxy on the defensive by calling their attention to a man afflicted with "dropsy" (i.e., swelling and distention from excess fluid) and asking, "Is it lawful to heal on the Sabbath or not?" He knew they would find fault with whatever he did with this man. If he healed him, they would ask why he had done it on the Sabbath. If he ignored him, they would accuse him of a lack of sympathy. One wonders if the man might have been placed before Jesus as part of a plot to find fault with him. When the Pharisees and experts in the Law refused to answer, Jesus proceeded to heal the sick man. He then cited the provision in the Law allowing merciful acts on the Sabbath and essentially dared them to fault what he had done.

With this episode finished, the guests headed toward the choice seats at the banquet. These would have been the ones at the head table, nearest the host. One can easily visualize the scuffle. Jesus saw in their behavior a wicked form of pride and gave a parable to rebuke that ugly spirit. The parable was about the humiliation that would come to someone who went to a position of honor at a wedding feast only to be asked to move for the sake of a more honored person. How much better it would be to take a lowly seat and to be elevated to a better one.

The point of this parable was not to teach table manners or to enjoin some sort of false modesty that draws attention to oneself. It was to point out the tendency of religious leaders to take (or demand) deference for themselves rather than to model the authentic humility that comes of knowing God (cf. 1:48). "For everyone who exalts himself will be humbled, and he who humbles himself will be exalted."

Turning then from the guests to his host, Jesus taught a lesson about charity and grace. One should not only invite "your friends, your brothers or relatives, or your rich neighbors" to social occasions but also "the poor, the crippled, the lame, the blind" as well. The point of this saying is not that it is wrong to have kindnesses reciprocated. The point is, instead, that unselfishness must guide and inform our kindnesses. If one learns to think in terms of a calculus of possible returns to charity shown, he abandons God's way of thinking. The divine method is to bestow kindness and benefit wherever possible — even on the "undeserving" and to those who will never be able to return it in kind. In its nature, such magnanimity is an act of grace; done without condescension, it is true charity. Although such deeds cannot be repaid by their immediate recipients, they will be rewarded "at the resurrection of the righteous."

At the mention of the resurrection, one of the dinner guests appears to have tried to break the tension by offering what he must have thought would be a noncontroversial statement: "Blessed is the man who will eat at the feast in the kingdom of God." Noncontroversial? That was the critical issue at hand! Who is going to be saved? (13:23). Who will enter the "narrow door"? (13:24).

Jesus immediately gave the Parable of the Great Banquet in which he told of a man preparing a great feast and sending an initial announcement to "many guests." With the banquet prepared, he sent notice to all who had been invited originally to come and share his bounty. But everyone "began to make excuses." Angered at this rebuff, the man sent his servants out to "bring in the poor, the crippled, the blind and the lame" (i.e., all who would respond to God's grace, cf. 14:13). With room still left, he sent his servants out yet again to "the roads and country lanes" to find those at the greatest distance from himself. We are expected to hear another warning to the Jewish people when the story ends with the fill-

Day 4
Excuse-Making

Read Romans 10 for Paul's perspective on the plight of his fellow-Jews.

1. The Parable of the Great Banquet is about Judaism's rejection of Yahweh. What is its central point?

2. What sorts of excuses were made by those invited to the great banquet? Do any of them sound familiar?

3. What tendency do you see in yourself to make excuses rather than accept personal responsibility?

4. Have you ever caught yourself making excuses to God? If so, what about?

5. How can one overcome the tendency to make

145

excuses rather than act in times of personal responsibility?

Day 5
A Hard Saying

Read Mark 9:42-50 for more hyperbole about Christian discipleship.

1. In what sense would it ever be right for a Christian to "hate" significant people in his or her life?

2. What is *hyperbole*? Why is it an effective teaching tool?

3. Cite some other examples of hyperbole in Scripture.

4. Do you know anyone who has had to make the choice between family and Jesus? If so, what happened?

ing of the banquet hall without those who had been invited first.

d. The cost of discipleship. 14:25-35.

In spite of the "large crowds" following Jesus at this point in his ministry, he was interested in something much more important than numbers. He was concerned to generate a level of commitment that would see his disciples through the impending crisis of faith they could encounter in connection with his death, the beginning of the church, and the eventual persecution they would face for his sake. "The people imagined that he was about to establish a kingdom in pomp and splendor and power, and in these glories they expected to share. To remove the misunderstanding, Jesus turned to declare the true conditions of discipleship. His followers must expect sacrifice and suffering and be willing to part with all they possessed, even with life itself." [Erdman, *Luke*, p. 159.]

One of Jesus' several "hard sayings" comes at this point: "If anyone comes to me and does not hate his father and mother, his wife and children, his brothers and sisters — yes, even his own life — he cannot be my disciple. And anyone who does not carry his cross and follow me cannot be my disciple." Unless Jesus means everything to you, he means nothing. Until one dies to himself and is willing to suffer rejection for Jesus' sake, he cannot have eternal life. Discipleship is not something to take lightly.

To clarify his meaning, Jesus used two illustrations. One involved a financial calculation about building a tower, and the other a life-or-death calculation about going to war. So must would-be disciples count the cost of following Jesus. Anyone unwilling to pay the price would be better advised never to begin the journey. Indeed, like salt that "loses its saltiness," a disciple who does not have a depth of commitment that will sustain him during trials is useless for heaven's purposes and will be "thrown out." Such a person can have no part in God's kingdom business. To be a descendant of Abraham in the flesh was an accident of birth, and to be a church member is sometimes little more than an empty formality. But to be a *disciple* is understood as serious business. So, even today, "He who has ears to hear, let him hear."

5. How do you think you would handle such a situation? Why?

Week Twenty-Two

Luke 15:1-32 (IV D 2 e in Outline)

Day 1
Lostness

Read Jonah 2 for one man's expression of anguish over being lost from God.

1. Have you ever been *lost* from your family? On the highway? In a mall? Describe the feelings you had.
2. How different were the circumstances under which something got lost in each of these parables?
3. Can you describe a life situation that corresponds to these three different circumstances?
4. How do these different situations call for different approaches in presenting the gospel message?
5. What occurs in heaven whenever some lost person is found? Explain.

e. Parables about lost things. 15:1-32.

The fifteenth chapter of Luke is justifiably one of the best-known and best-loved chapters of the Bible. It affirms God's passionate love for the lost. It contrasts the generous and seeking spirit of Jesus with the critical and closed spirit of the religious establishment of his time. In fact, this chapter begins a larger block of material essentially unique to the third Gospel. Chapters 15–19 reveal what Manson calls the "Gospel of the Outcast" and repeatedly shows Jesus' concern for the religious and social outcasts of his time.

The three parables are about a lost sheep (15:1-7), a lost coin (15:8-10), and a lost son (15:11-32). Though they have essentially the same message (i.e., God's joy over one sinner's repentance), there are also slight differences that may have significance. A sheep gets lost because of its own carelessness in wandering away from safety, a coin gets lost because of someone's carelessness in handling it, and a son gets lost because he chooses to rebel against his father. Our own experience teaches us as much about human lostness. Some people may simply be lacking in spiritual sensitivity, while others have been brutalized by life; many more simply do not want to live under the restraints of another's authority. No matter the cause for anyone's lostness, God is thrilled when any *one* of his beloved creatures is found. More than that, he goes out to seek for them in person.

Omitting the chapter break inserted long after Luke's writing, there is a note of irony that introduces these stories. Jesus has just called for committed discipleship. "He who has ears to *hear*," he said, "let him *hear*." And who were the most responsive people to that call? Luke's report is this: "Now the tax collectors and 'sinners' were all gathering around to hear him." In other words, those who were giving positive attention to Jesus' call to discipleship were disreputable and immoral folk. The Pharisees and experts in the Law of Moses were listening to Jesus only to find fault (cf. 11:54; 14:1); social and religious outcasts, however, were hearing a message of hope from him and were lining up to follow him. The former were not pleased at the response of the latter. They "muttered" about it and faulted Jesus that he not only permitted such lowlife to travel with him but actually seemed pleased about their presence. "This man welcomes sinners and eats with them," they complained.

With his critics as his primary target audience, Jesus began his first parable with a question to draw them in. "Suppose one of you has a hundred sheep and loses one of them," he began. "Does he not leave the ninety-nine in the open country and go after the lost sheep until he finds it?" Sheep are rather helpless and defenseless animals. For one of them to be outside a shepherd's attentive care even for a night could mean his death. In this parable, the shepherd who discovered that one of his sheep was missing immediately went in search of it. How long does he search? "Until he finds it." Then, having found the wayward sheep, he neither curses nor strikes it. To the contrary, "he joyfully puts it on his shoulders and goes home." What is more, upon arriving at home, he calls together his friends and neighbors to celebrate finding his once-lost sheep.

The point of this parable is not that ninety-nine sheep in a fold need no attention. Neither is Jesus' point that God takes no delight in his sheep that stay in the fold, obedient and faithful. His point is that

Day 2
The Lost Sheep

Read Psalm 23 for a glimpse into God's concern for his sheep.

1. Ninety-nine sheep were safe in the fold. Does God neglect the "found"? Does he love the *church* less than the *world*? Explain.

2. What sort of things should a church do to strengthen itself and encourage its members to faithfulness?

3. Could a church "get carried away" tending to itself and forget to seek the lost? Have you ever seen that happen?

4. What is your church's most effective outreach to the lost? How does it work?

5. To what degree do *you* share God's passionate concern for the lost?

God delights in the reclamation of his wayward sheep — and so should those who are already in his fold. Thus the application of the story at hand is clear: God takes greater delight in a penitent soul who appreciates his grace to the wayward than in a proud and critical religionist, no matter how exemplary his moral conduct may be. "Edersheim quotes a Jewish saying, 'There is joy before God when those who provoke Him perish from the world.' But Jesus has a very different concept of God. He rejoices over the returning penitent more than over many safely in the fold." [Morris, *Luke*, p. 238.]

Without pausing for a response, Jesus moved directly to his second story about a woman with ten silver coins who loses one of them. Realizing that one of the coins is missing, the woman cannot bring herself to wait for the light of day. "Does she not light a lamp, sweep the house and search carefully until she finds it?" Each silver coin was a day's wage for the time (cf. NIV marginal note), and the woman's urgency about losing one indicates something of her own life situation. If a young woman, the coins may have been her dowry; if an elderly woman, they may have been the savings of a lifetime. In either case, ten percent of one's total estate could not be taken lightly.

The reward of her careful search comes in finding it. With great excitement, she calls her friends and neighbors together to celebrate with her. As with the shepherd in the first parable, her great joy must be shared with people who are important to her. Similarly, God's delight over "one sinner who repents" is meant to be shared not only with the angels in heaven but with righteous and compassionate persons on earth. But where were such people in Jesus' day? Could the people regarded as religious leaders only criticize Jesus for finding some who had been lost?

Day 3
The Lost Coin

Read Hosea 11 and sense Yahweh's anguished concern over lost Israel.

1. This parable can be seen as pointing out that some are lost because of the carelessness of others. Explain.
2. How might these childhood experiences cause one to be a lost adult: parental neglect? abuse? lack of spiritual training?
3. How might these adult experiences cause one to be lost: bad experience with a church? failed marriage? financial crisis?
4. What is your church doing to help people from such backgrounds? Are there other things you would suggest trying?

Again without pausing for a response, Jesus moved to the third parable about lost things. Not only is it the longest and most detailed of the three, but it is also one of the most famous stories in all literature. It sets forth the love of God in language that can be appreciated by almost every person, whether by association with the love remembered from an affectionate and devoted father or in connection with what deprived children know instinctively that a father's love should be like. It has communicated with many a tender-but-burdened heart at just the right moment to speak of God's mercy to sinners.

The story tells of a man with two sons. The younger son made a rude demand of his father, asking for "my share of the estate." This would have amounted to one-third of his father's wealth, for Hebrew law provided that a double portion (i.e., twice the amount of any other son) should go to the oldest male heir. The incredible rudeness of this request is seen when one realizes that it really reduces to a lament on the boy's part that his father was still alive and in control of what he had accumulated. When the division of property had been made, the intent of the rash young son became clear. He "got together all he had, set off for a distant country and there squandered his wealth in wild living." Having turned his back on his father, the rebellious son lost no time in embracing a lifestyle among pagans that never would have been allowed at home. The disgrace that such behavior would have brought to a family of that time and place is probably beyond the imaginative powers of anyone in the western world of modern times.

The boy was impoverished after a while. Not only had he "spent everything" from his father's bequest, but a "severe famine" came over the country he had chosen for his new home. His position in that pagan

Day 4
The Lost Boy

Read Psalm 32 to find a prayer David prayed after a "prodigal" time in his life.

1. Explain why a boy with such a good father might want to leave home. What does this say about the boy?
2. Do you fault the father for permitting him to leave home? Explain.
3. Describe the boy's fate after he left home. What does this represent?
4. What motivated the lost boy to go home?
5. Explain the father's treatment of his returned son.

151

(i.e., Gentile) territory ultimately became so destitute that he accepted employment from a man "who sent him to his fields to feed pigs." For a Jewish boy to come to such an end was unthinkable. His job was to tend unclean animals, thus he remained perpetually unclean and unpresentable to the Lord. What a picture of sin's ability to reduce someone to nothing!

It appears to have been the pain associated with his circumstances that brought the prodigal son back to his father. Hungry enough that he "longed to fill his stomach with the pods (i.e., berries of the wild carob tree) that the pigs were eating," he felt the physical pain that often accompanies a dissolute lifestyle; abandoned so that "no one gave him anything," he also felt the emotional-spiritual pain that always comes with a godless life. These circumstances humbled the boy, and he "came to his senses." This expression in context is surely to be taken as the equivalent of "repented." In addition to repentance produced by his anguish (cf. 2 Cor. 7:8ff), the prodigal son formed and acted on a holy resolve. "I will set out and go back to my father . . . ."

As to what would happen upon his arrival, the wayward son envisioned making a full confession of his sinfulness. He would acknowledge that he had sinned not only against his father but "against heaven" (i.e., God). After his confession, he intended to make the following plea: "I am no longer worthy to be called your son; make me like one of your hired men."

At this point in the story, the true hero of the parable emerges. It is a loving father who rises above the sorry details of his prodigal son's behavior to receive him home graciously. He saw his son "while he was still a long way off" and was "filled with compassion for him." He acted on his sentiment by running to the boy, embracing him while he still had his unclean and smelling-of-pigs clothing on, and kissing him. As the son began his penitent speech, the father appears to interrupt and cut it off with orders to his servants. "Quick! Bring the best robe and put it on him," said the boy's father. "Put a ring on his finger and sandals on his feet. Bring the fattened calf and kill it. Let's have a feast and celebrate."

The sweetest words to the boy's ears were yet to come. He heard his father say to his servants, "For *this son of mine* was dead and is alive again; he was lost and is found." The picture is one of complete forgiveness and total restoration. This is an assurance to every lost soul that his or her turn to God will not be rejected. No one goes too far or sinks too low to be received back. And what a reception it is!

If the story ended here, it would be only half-told. Its original point, after all, was to challenge the smugness of the Pharisees and teachers of the Law who questioned the appropriateness of Jesus' receiving and eating with sinners. Having set the stage for representing their attitude toward him and those he was drawing to himself, Jesus brings them into the scene in the character of the father's older son. As he made his way to the house on that eventful day, "he heard music and dancing." Asking a servant what it meant, he was informed, "*Your brother* has come." One can almost see his face flush at the use of the term. He had long since repudiated him as a "brother" and washed his hands of any responsibility for him. He had surely hoped never to see him again. In a later conversation with his father, he would only refer to him as "this son of yours" — not "my brother."

The father should have been able to rejoice that his family was whole again. Instead, he had to go out and plead with his older son to join the celebration. It was then that the older son's wicked spirit was

Day 5
The Older Brother

Read Matthew 23:1-15 to get a characterization of many Pharisees in Jesus' time.

1. The real point of this parable was to rebuke some people. Who? Why?

2. Why could the older brother not share his father's happiness?

3. Explain the attitude he had toward his younger brother.

4. Have you ever had difficulty receiving someone back from a prodigal experience? If so, how did you deal with it?

5. Write an alternative "happy ending" to this parable.

revealed. He is shown to be wicked, small-souled, and selfish. In his complaint that he had been "slaving for" his father and had "never disobeyed" him, one detects resentment rather than appreciation; in his recitation of his brother's sins, one senses suppressed longings of his own. The religion of the people for whose sake this story was originally told were joyless, burdened, and unfulfilled by their rituals. Performing their duties had given them neither satisfaction nor freedom.

The abrupt ending of the story (i.e., we never learn the outcome of the father's plea to his older son) leaves each of us to question himself or herself about the nature of religious experience. Is it the joyous, celebrative experience of God's grace? Or is it the performance of burdensome duties?

Week Twenty-Three

Luke 16:1–17:10 (IV D 2 f to IV D 2 i in Outline)

f. The Parable of the Shrewd Manager. 16:1-13.

This parable is notorious for its difficulty, and a glance at any good commentary will list the principal issues that create problems for the interpreter. The central problem for even the most casual reader, of course, is that someone who has been dishonest winds up being praised. But perhaps some of the difficulty with this story can be cleared up by putting it in the larger flow of Luke's intent.

Two themes seem to be intertwined here. The first and more encompassing theme is *discipleship*. The entirety of the so-called "travel narrative" that begins at 9:51 and reaches its crescendo with an account of Jesus' triumphal entry (19:29ff) can be read as an extended dialogue on the meaning of discipleship. Not only are there explicit comments about the demands of following Christ (cf. 9:57ff; 12:49ff; 14:25ff, et al.), practically every interspersed section of dialogue among these comments may be read as a warning about some obstacle to whole-hearted discipleship. This very parable ends with a warning against trying to "serve two masters" (v. 13). The second theme at work through the entire chapter in which the parable occurs is the *perspective on wealth* a disciple should take.

On the assumption that this story is being told to somehow reinforce a healthy attitude toward material possessions, it may not be quite so difficult to interpret. It turns out that the point of commendation for the steward is neither his dishonesty nor his cleverness but his foresight in using the temporary wealth at his disposition for the sake of his long-term security.

Day 1
Whole-Hearted
Discipleship

Read Hebrews 11:1-19 to be reminded of some who gave all to God.

1. Explain how the difficult parable of the unjust steward can be interpreted as a perspective on wealth.
2. How can money be an obstacle to following Christ with one's whole heart?
3. Has money ever been an obstacle to your discipleship? Explain.
4. How do you know that your *whole heart* belongs to God?
5. Write a prayer for God to help you choose him daily as the only master for your life.

155

Day 2
Treasure in Heaven

Read Matthew 6:19-24 for more insight on this subject.

1. How did the unjust steward manage to provide for his future? What was Jesus' application of his story?
2. What are some ways to "use worldly wealth to gain friends"?
3. Why are heavenly treasures safer than earthly ones? Better investments?
4. Explain the meaning of Luke 16:10-11.
5. What specific methods are you using to store up treasure in heaven?

A certain rich man discovered that his estate manager was "wasting his possessions." This meant, of course, that the man would be fired. So he was ordered to "give an account of your management" (i.e., close out the books) prior to his dismissal. Reasoning that he was "not strong enough to dig" and was "ashamed to beg," the manager looked into the future and tried to think of a way to provide for his long-term benefit. "I know what I'll do so that, when I lose my job here, people will welcome me into their houses."

The plan he formulated had him calling in "each one of his master's debtors" and reducing their outstanding bills. Thus someone who owed 800 gallons of olive oil was allowed to repay only 400, a man who owed 1,000 bushels of wheat settled for 800, and so on. Did he simply cheat his master by this process? Or had his master inflated the debt by hiding interest in the outstanding bill? (cf. Exod. 22:25). Or was he eliminating the commission he had built into each transaction for himself? No firm answer can be given to these questions.

Whatever the explanation, the result of his action is clear. He endeared himself to a great many people by using his temporary oversight of another's funds shrewdly and thereby made sure that they would receive him warmly when they next met. So this was Jesus' summary and application of the story for his disciples: "I tell you, use worldly wealth to gain friends for yourselves, so that when it is gone, you will be welcomed into eternal dwellings."

The only way a Christian can use money to its ultimate benefit is to invest it in kingdom projects. More particularly still, using one's possessions to benefit the poor and needy is to bestow kindness on Jesus himself (Matt. 25:31-46). Since the wealth of this world will someday be gone, only what is "laid up in heaven" by virtue of its use in spreading the gospel, helping the weak, and otherwise promoting the interests of God will have been saved for eternity (Matt. 6:19-21). "Money cannot come with us to heaven. Its value is limited when it comes to everlasting life. So recognize its limits and use it for others, not selfishly. To *gain friends* by means of mammon is to use money in such a way that others appreciate you for your exercise of stewardship, your kindness and generosity." [Bock, *Luke*, p. 266.]

Money and material possessions have spiritual implications. Anyone who cannot be trusted to handle the "very little" value represented by "worldly wealth" certainly cannot be entrusted with the "much" of God's "true (i.e., spiritual) riches." Thus the parable ends with the discipleship challenge already noted: "No servant can serve two masters. . . . You cannot serve both God and Money."

g. Replying to the Pharisees' reaction. 16:14-18.

The Pharisees who heard Jesus make the unequivocal demand that one choose between God and wealth "were sneering at Jesus." The reason for their derision was both theological and practical. They had worked out a theology, supported by case studies such as Abraham, that one's material prosperity was a true indicator of his spiritual status with God. Wealth was therefore always good and constituted a sign of divine approval, whereas poverty — perhaps of the sort Jesus experienced (cf. Matt. 8:20) — meant that God was against the unfortunate person. And at a purely practical level, these particular Pharisees "loved money."

Jesus replied to their contemptuous sneers with a restatement of the biblical truth that external circumstances cannot be considered a true index to one's character and relationship with God. Outward displays of piety by the Pharisees were their attempts to "justify [them]selves in the eyes of men"; such displays, though "highly valued" by men, were never-

Day 3
Self-Justification

Read Philippians 3:1-11 to see why one man gave up self-justification.

1. Why did the Pharisees feel a need to "justify themselves"?

2. How successful were they? Explain.

3. Do you think others see you as *defensive* and prone to *self-justification*? Is their opinion correct?

4. How does James 5:16 relate to this subject?

5. How does one avoid defensiveness and self-justification?

theless "detestable in God's sight" — for "God knows your hearts."

At this point, Jesus made a most significant statement about the new departure in spiritual matters that had begun with John the Baptist. His ministry constituted a dividing line between the old way of pharisaical intimidation with Scripture and the new way of kingdom preaching that John had initiated. "The Law and the Prophets were proclaimed (*by the Pharisees*) until John. Since that time, the good news of the kingdom of God is being preached (*first by John and later by Jesus*) . . . ." The former had called for outward display and encouraged hypocrisy; the latter called for genuine repentance and the surrender of one's very heart to God. Whereas the former had driven people away, the latter had created such enthusiasm — for even the poor, outcasts, and non-establishment persons could come to God under its conditions — that people were "forcing" (i.e., eagerly pushing) their way into the kingdom as if they were shoppers elbowing their way to the counter where once-unavailable items were now within their reach.

The new beginning made with John and Jesus certainly was not to be seen as a repudiation of the Law and the Prophets. To the contrary, both John and Jesus honored and taught them. More than that, they both *fulfilled* (i.e., brought to their fullest significance) them. Indeed, "heaven and earth" would both "disappear" before the Holy Scripture given through Moses and other Spirit-guided men could be revoked. Even its most minute details (i.e., "the least stroke of a pen") would be fulfilled.

To illustrate his high regard for the Law as compared to pharisaic gamesmanship with it, Jesus cited the seventh commandment. "Adultery" had not lost its sinful and hateful character to God because of the lax theory and practice the Pharisees had come up with to circumvent the Decalogue's attempt to protect marriage. Divorce was still hateful to God in spite of the flimsy pretexts upon which the Pharisees had come to approve divorce and remarriage (cf. Matt. 19:1-9).

h. The rich man and Lazarus. 16:19-31.

Although interesting in its own right for what it reveals about the state of the dead, the primary point of the story about an otherwise unidentified "rich man" and a "beggar named Lazarus" is its contextual meaning. Jesus had just argued that wealth and poverty could not be counted on as indicators of spiritual standing with God (v. 15). To illustrate his point, he cited an incident that would be judged altogether differently on the basis of outward appearances known to men versus God's awareness of men's hearts. [Note: Although some scholars consider this to be a parable, it seems more likely that it is a narrative about real persons. For one thing, it is not called a parable. For another, if this *is* a parable, it is unique among all the others in the New Testament in that it assigns names to some of its characters. Since parables are true-to-life stories, nothing of its doctrinal content is altered if one chooses to consider it one.]

By all outward appearances, the rich man would have been taken to be favored of God. He "lived in luxury every day." On the other hand, Lazarus' condition might have caused people passing by to wonder what sin he had committed to be under such a weight of suffering (cf. John 9:1ff). But outward appearances are often misleading! Indeed, when these two men died, their circumstances were immediately and totally reversed. The rich man "was in torment," but "angels carried [Lazarus] to Abraham's side." One who does not use whatever wealth he may have in order to make provision for eternity will suffer total loss (cf. vv. 8-9).

Reminded again that the primary point of this

Day 4
Life after Death

Read Revelation 22:1-6 for a glimpse at the ultimate destiny of the redeemed.

1. How can we be sure this story speaks of life *after* death but *before* Judgment Day?
2. Will we know each other after death? Remember life on Earth? Support your answers from this text.
3. What does this story lead you to think about communication between the dead and people still alive on Earth?
4. If people know their destinies immediately after death, why does there need to be a Judgment Day?

story is about the right use of money, we cannot leave it without pointing out its implications for our knowledge of the state of the dead. "Some of the details might be debated, but the story does teach that there is conscious life immediately after death, that the saved and the lost are eternally separated, and that the lost carry with them some memories of their earthly experiences." [Benware, *Luke*, p.112.] To this one could also add that contact between the dead and those still on earth is not allowed and that one's status as saved or lost is irreversible after this life.

Day 5
"We Have Only Done Our Duty"

Read Psalm 1 about those who delight in God's will.

1. What called forth the appeal of verse 5? Explain Jesus' response.
2. What do you understand verse 10 to mean?
3. Is God ever under obligation to his servants? Explain.
4. Contrast the spirit taught here with Luke 18:11-12.
5. How has God taught you *humility*?

i. Warnings to the disciples. 17:1-10.

Having been in conversation with the Pharisees since 16:14, Jesus turns his attention back to his disciples. Against the backdrop of his stern warnings to the Pharisees about their love of money, his purpose seems to be to warn his own followers that their lack of wealth did not exempt them from spiritual peril. Luke records a series of non-thematic warnings for them.

Had the Pharisees been the source of "things that cause people to sin"? Indeed, and others who were willing to twist the Word of God to their own purposes were "bound to come." But Jesus called his disciples to take heed to themselves and their teaching (cf. 1 Tim. 4:16) lest they be responsible for misleading "one of these little ones (i.e., innocent, trusting souls) to sin."

As to their own internal relationships, Jesus required that his disciples take sin seriously but stand ready to forgive freely. When they saw sin, they were to "rebuke" the offender; when that offender repented, they were to "forgive him" — even if that person repeated his offense "seven times in a day" and repented equally often. Challenged by this particular demand and surely feeling the weight of responsibility that was beginning to be passed to them, the apostles replied, "Increase our faith!"

Jesus' enigmatic response seems to be an effort to shift their thinking away from themselves (i.e., that their faith had to be incredibly great) and to the Almighty God in whom their faith was placed. So "faith as small as a mustard seed" was promised a mighty result whenever it is exercised within the scope of God's will.

The final warning in this sequence of sayings is about the nature of servanthood that has been his constant theme with them for so long. In a short parable that reflects the master-servant relationship from that historical period, he reminded his followers in every age that faithfulness under difficult circumstances (e.g., Lazarus) is not more than should be asked of us. To the contrary, proper humility would require that those who managed to do "everything you were told to do" — a contrary-to-fact hypothesis! — should still say, "We are unworthy servants; we have only done our duty."

No one's salvation will ever be on the basis of his or her having "done enough." It will be on the basis of God's amazing grace. Thus, without fearing that we have done too little, we reject the notion that we could ever do enough! To serve so generous a master makes us want to give our all to honor him. One who understands this great truth of the Christian faith could not help falling in love with Jesus.

Week Twenty-Four

Luke 17:11-37 (IV D 3 a and IV D 3 b in Outline)

Day 1
Racism

Read Ephesians 2:11-22 about Christ's plan to unite all races by the cross.

1. Have you noticed things in this Gospel that signal Luke's Gentile perspective? Cite a few specific instances.
2. Where have you observed Christ's power to unite people who are typically kept separate in society?
3. What are some of the most urgent concerns of this sort that Christians need to address today?
4. What is your church doing to combat racism?
5. What are *you* doing about racism?

3. The third phase. 17:11–19:28.

With the words "on his way to Jerusalem" (cf. 9:51; 13:22), Luke moves to the so-called "third phase" of his travel narrative. These words remind us again of Jesus' deliberate movement toward his purpose for coming into the world. He has come to seek and to save the lost, but that mission can only be fulfilled by way of the cross.

a. The Samaritan leper. 17:11-19.

As Jesus approached an unnamed village near the "border between Samaria and Galilee," an incident occurred that would have had particular significance to Luke. As a Gentile, Luke was quick to notice interactions between Jesus and non-Jews. That Jesus not only healed but paid a special compliment to a "foreigner" (v. 18b) would have been important to him. It attested to the fact that Jesus saved all people, not merely those of his own Jewish race.

"Ten men who had leprosy" appear to have become a community in exile. Their disease would have made it impossible for them to live with their families or in a village of healthy people (Num. 5:2-3). Both for the sake of protection and in order to meet their common needs, they were banded together as a group of social and religious outcasts. It also seems likely that both Jews and Samaritans were in the group, for otherwise why would it have been noteworthy that the one person among the ten who returned to thank Jesus was a "Samaritan" and "foreigner"? The divisions that otherwise would have been so important for them to maintain in better times appear to have gone by the board in their distress.

In keeping with the requirement of the Torah — the only part of our Old Testament that Jews and Samaritans *both* recognized to be binding — the ten men "stood at a distance" from healthy people (Lev. 13:45). Instead of crying out merely as a warning for Jesus and his group to avoid them, they "called out in a loud voice, 'Jesus, Master, have pity on us!'" His response to their appeal was a command that they present themselves to a priest for inspection, again according to the provision of the Law of Moses for someone either suspected of being infected with leprosy or believing himself to be cured from this terrible disease.

It is interesting that Jesus required the men to act on the presumption of being cured before pronouncing them healed and without letting his traveling companions witness their healing. This was clearly a test of their faith. Would they protest that there was no need to see a priest since nothing was changed about their condition? Or would they do what he had said simply on his command? True faith always acts in obedience to the revealed will of God, while a professed faith that refuses to obey is exposed by that refusal to be unauthentic. "Faith by itself, if it is not accompanied by action, is dead" (James 2:18).

As the men obeyed Jesus and started in the direction of a priest, they were all made well. "And as they went, they were cleansed." The promise implied in Christ's command to them was kept in the process of their obedience. What excitement and joy must have swept over the little group! There may have been a simultaneous sense of confusion and frustration. Should they continue to the priest, as Jesus had ordered? Should they first go back and thank Jesus before seeking a priest? Apparently only

**Day 2
Gratitude**

Read Psalm 100, a psalm of gratitude to the Lord.

1. Explain Jesus' disappointment in the failure of the other nine lepers who had been healed.

2. Do you ever "take things for granted" with God? With family? With friends?

3. What are some of the most appropriate ways of showing gratitude to others?

4. Have you ever caught someone off guard by expressing gratitude? Recall the incident.

5. Write a note of gratitude today to someone who has blessed your life.

"one of them, when he saw he was healed, came back" to Jesus. If others followed his lead or sought Jesus out later, it is never told to us in the text.

When the healed leper returned to Jesus, he was "praising God in a loud voice." He knew that a power great enough to cure something so terrible as leprosy could only come from God, so it was God's name that was on his lips as he came back. As to his attitude toward Jesus, the man "threw himself at Jesus' feet and thanked him." Whether this man yet honored Jesus as divine is doubtful. His *praise* was given to God, and his *gratitude to Jesus* was that God had exercised his power through him (cf. John 3:2). This is not to fault the healed leper for distinguishing between God and his instrument-prophet at this point. To the contrary, it is simply to acknowledge that the information he had available to him at this stage had brought him near enough to God to be healed. Whole now and allowed to join in the larger community of disciples making the trip with Jesus to Jerusalem — where he could find a priest! — the man could learn more and come to fuller faith.

The Lord was clearly disappointed with the thanklessness of the rest of the men who had been healed. "Were not all ten cleansed?" he asked. "Where are the other nine?" Perhaps they were so caught up in their new status as healthy people and so anxious to rejoin their own family circles that they could not bring themselves to take out time to return and thank Jesus. While this may be understandable to us, it is still wrong and should serve as a warning. Praise to God for his mercies is not only the polite and considerate response but the *right* one. "Give thanks in all circumstances, for this is God's will for you in Christ Jesus" (1 Thess. 5:18). The fact that the man who returned was a Samaritan must have startled some who were with Jesus, but it obviously pleased Luke and helps account for his decision to include this otherwise unrecorded episode for Theophilus and his other readers.

Jesus' response to the man who had come back was to bless him a second time. "Rise and go," he said to him. "Your faith has made you well." Some commentators believe this means that his faith had secured the salvation of his soul as well as the cleansing of his body. "It may be that Jesus recognized in this man the attitude that brings salvation and sent him off with the assurance that it was well with his soul as it was with his body. Full restoration means a saved soul as well as a sound body." [Morris, *Luke*, p. 259.] Whether this is reading too much into these words or not, his return certainly gave him the opportunity to learn that Jesus was not only a *healer* but also the *redeemer*.

Are nine out of every ten people ingrates? Do you allow nine of every ten blessings from God to go unacknowledged? Ingratitude is clearly a hateful offense to God that cuts off further blessings to the one who refuses to acknowledge the divine hand in his good fortune.

b. The coming of the kingdom. 17:20-37.

Along the way to Jerusalem, some Pharisees asked Jesus "when the kingdom of God would come." His initial response to their question was to indicate that the kingdom was something different from what his questioners were expecting. They thought of God's kingdom in terms of geography, government offices, and armies. The kingdom Jesus would someday usher in could not be located on a map by even the most "careful observation." It would not take a form comparable to the Roman Empire so that someone could point it out on a map. Rather, "the kingdom of God is within you." The Greek phrase here (*entos hymon*) is difficult to translate and unclear in meaning. Does it mean "within you," "among you," "within your grasp," or

Day 3
The Kingdom of God

Read 1 Peter 1:13–2:12 for one description of a kingdom lifestyle.

1. What do you think Jesus meant by his comment about the kingdom being "within you," "among you," etc.?
2. What do you understand the Kingdom of God to be?
3. How do the *kingdom* and *church* relate to each other? Is every church member a kingdom person?

4. In what sense is the kingdom a present reality? In what sense do we still pray, "Your kingdom come"?

5. What was the basic misunderstanding of Jesus' contemporaries about the kingdom? Is that point of view still with us?

Day 4
Too Busy for God?

Read Matthew 19:16-29 to find a man who was too preoccupied with this world.

1. How will Jesus' return resemble the days of Noah and Lot?

2. Will there be a specific sign to announce that Jesus' coming is near? If not, why do you think so many people speculate about "signs of the return"?

3. Does your life ever get so busy that you neglect God? Be specific.

"in your midst"? It seems unlikely that Jesus would tell a group of hostile and unbelieving Pharisees that the kingdom was "within" their hearts. On the other hand, since Jesus has already claimed that the kingdom "has come to you" in his own person and ministry (11:20), one of the latter possibilities seems more likely.

God's kingdom (*basileia*) is not a location or institution; it is his *sovereign reign in the lives of his people.* In the person and activities of Jesus, that sovereignty was seen in perfect form. For the remainder of us, we must wait for the fullness of that experience until Christ's "appearing and kingdom" (cf. 2 Tim. 4:1) at the end of time. In the meanwhile, we live in the creative tension between what has already happened once in Christ and what will someday happen when he is united with "all who have longed for his appearing" (cf. 2 Tim. 4:8). As the center of God's kingdom activity on earth, the church serves as the herald of the kingdom, calls people out of Satan's reign into Christ's, and waits for his *parousia* (i.e., presence) with eager anticipation.

Anticipating his return to the Father, Jesus told his disciples that they would "long to see one of the days of the Son of Man, but you will not see it." In their longing for him, they would be liable to deception by false prophets. Thus they were warned against false claims about his return (cf. 2 Thess. 2:2) and told, "Do not go running off after them." The return of Christ will not be secretive and known only to a select few. His "day" will instead be "like the lightning, which flashes and lights up the sky from one end to the other." It will be visible and known to all.

Furthermore, the fullness of his kingdom would not come until certain preconditions had been satisfied. Certainly he would first "suffer many things" in connection with his crucifixion. Furthermore, he would be "rejected by this generation." When the time for his return does come, the vast majority of people will be caught unexpecting and unprepared. Just as people "in the days of Noah" and "in the days of Lot" were going about their everyday routines and were destroyed in the great catastrophes associated with those biblical figures, so will people be off their guard at Jesus' coming. "It will be just like this on the day the Son of Man is revealed."

The point here seems to be the same one made several times already in the Gospel of Luke. It is not enough to keep ourselves free of evil. We must also guard against getting so busy with the routines of a normal and upright life that we forget life's most urgent business — preparation for the coming of the Son of Man. Thus we must guard against letting the good seed of the kingdom get "choked by life's worries, riches and pleasures" (8:14), stay constantly prepared "because the Son of Man will come at an hour when you do not expect him" (12:40), and remember the people of Noah's and Lot's time. But so consumed are some people with the things of this world that their first thoughts when Christ appears will not be of him but of whether there is time for them to rush down from their roof to gather up their "goods inside" or to dash in from the field to "go back" for something precious. What a tragedy that will be, for anyone so attached to this life will lose eternal life.

When Jesus appears, there will be a sudden (and final) separation of those who have kingdom hearts from those who are too attached to this world. Two persons in the same bed may well be separated, with one "taken (into eternal life) and the other left (unto judgment)." Two women may be "grinding grain together; one will be taken (to be with Christ) and the other left (for judgment)."

With the thought of separation and judgment introduced, the disciples shifted their concern from the original question asked by the Pharisees about

4. How can you prevent getting too caught up in this world to the neglect of the one to come? Be specific.

Day 5
Christ's Return

Read 2 Peter 3 about The Day of the Lord.

1. Judging from the New Testament, first-century believers appear to have thought about Jesus' return often. Do you?
2. When someone mentions the second coming of Christ, what thoughts

167

come to your mind?
What visual images?

3. When you think about Christ's return, does the thought frighten you? Comfort you? Leave you unaffected?

4. If you were convinced Jesus would return within a month, what sorts of things would you do today?

5. Since you don't know that Jesus *won't* return today, which things named in response to the previous question are you going to do today?

"when" the kingdom would come to "Where, Lord?" In other words, where will such judgment come against men? Among the pagans? Among the Jews? Among the whole of humanity? Jesus' answer was in the form of a grim image that said, in effect, judgment will come wherever corruption is found among humankind. "Where there is a dead body, there the vultures will gather."

Teachings such as these served to keep the earliest generations of the church watching the heavens and anticipating Christ's return at any moment. With nearly two millennia now gone by, a clear danger for today's church is that we are likely to forget this promise or even to think that it has no relevance to our faith. What a mistake that will be for the generation alive when his sure and certain coming takes place! (2 Pet. 3:1ff).

Week Twenty-Five

Luke 18:1-34 (IV D 3 c to IV D 3 g in Outline)

c. The unrighteous judge. 18:1-8.

This parable ties directly to the things Jesus has just said about his second coming. In the interval between the cross and his return, he knew his followers would face weariness and perhaps even some of the same opposition he had faced in his own ministry. The point of his teaching here is to remind his followers "that they should always pray and not give up" during those difficult times.

Jesus certainly does not compare God to an unjust judge in this parable. Rather, it is a particular variety of parable that Jesus used elsewhere (cf. Matt. 7:11). It takes the form "If so-and-so is true, *how much more* is this true." If you can imagine that an unjust judge who has no regard for piety or public opinion would finally hear the petition of an otherwise powerless widow lest she "wear me out" by her persistence, then *how much more* should we believe that our just God will respond to the requests of his people whose prayers have been made powerful by the name of Christ.

In the previous chapter, Jesus described the general condition he would find on earth at his return. People will be going about their everyday routine, with no concern about the possibility of his appearance. Unbelievers will be caught as unprepared as were the people of Noah's generation for the flood or the population of Sodom for the destruction God rained down from heaven. "However, when the Son of Man comes, will he find faith on the earth?" is a question designed to call the church to watchfulness over against the world's general disregard for that day.

Day 1
Prayer

Read Psalm 86 about God's willingness to hear prayers.

1. What is the point of the parable about an unjust judge?
2. Under what circumstances are people more likely to be prayerful? Why?
3. What period of your life has made you most prayerful? Explain.
4. How much time do you plan to spend in prayer today?
5. What do your current prayer habits say about your faith? Explain.

In times of persecution for its allegiance to Christ, the church is more likely to be constantly prayerful and longing for Jesus' return. In times when God's people are so bland that they face no opposition, they are more likely to pray with less urgency and less frequency. Although the specific application of this parable is to those who experience opposition in the Christian Age, it is certainly true that believers under whatever circumstances need to be encouraged to persistent prayer.

Day 2
Good Works

Read Ephesians 2:1-10 and notice the role of good works in a Christian's life.

1. What do you find unusual about this Pharisee's prayer?
2. Have you ever heard a prayer like this one? Ever prayed one?
3. Is there any reason to think the Pharisee was lying about his deeds? What use was he trying to make of them?
4. What is the place of good works in authentic Christian experience?
5. How are *grace* and *good works* related?

d. A Pharisee and a publican. 18:9-14.

Although the parable about a Pharisee and publican has both of them in prayer, it is not really a continuation of Jesus' call for his followers to pray. While it teaches that we should be humble in our prayers, this story is ultimately about justification. What is the nature of righteousness? Who will be declared righteous in the eyes of God?

The parable was not so much addressed to the Pharisees of that time as to those with what we have come to call a "pharisaical spirit" in any generation. The target audience for this story were "some who were confident of their own righteousness and looked down on everybody else." Experience teaches us that these are more likely church members and church leaders than the "sinners" who show up at church in search of God. One writer has called this the story of "The Churchman and the Politician."

The Pharisee's prayer is notable for the fact that it was "about himself." Although he opened it with the name of God, its content was self-congratulation. He declared himself thankful "that I am not like other men — robbers, evildoers, adulterers — or even like this tax collector." Did he really think that everyone but himself was evil? Was he really so insensitive that he would publicly single out a tax collector and applaud himself for being different? People who are close to God see their own unworthiness all too clearly (cf. Isa. 6:1ff), but those at great distance from him tend to look at themselves only in relation to other people. But the churchman wasn't through yet.

In terms of his good works, the Pharisee reminded God that he fasted "twice a week" and was scrupulous to "give a tenth of all I get." The Law of Moses has only one mandatory fast per year, and it is on the Day of Atonement. The ultra-pious Jews of Jesus' day had gone farther than God to require Monday and Thursday fasting every week. They had also required more than God in the matter of tithing. The Law required that certain crops be tithed, but they had required "a tenth of *all* I get" — down to the tiniest garden herbs (Matt. 23:23). These legalists monitored each other's devotion to God in terms of strict adherence to *their* system of righteousness.

In stark contrast to the Pharisee, the tax collector "stood at a distance" from the Temple and its masses. He did not want to call attention to himself and "would not even look up to heaven." Instead, he "beat his breast" (i.e., a sign of remorse) and prayed, "God, have mercy on me, a sinner." Translated literally, he did not call himself "*a* sinner" but "*the* sinner." He had nothing to offer God comparable to the Pharisee's do-and-don't list. He simply threw himself on the mercy of God and acknowledged his sinfulness.

The Pharisee's loud public prayer may well have justified him in the eyes of his own kind and before the crowd who heard him boast of his own obnoxious goodness; it did nothing for him in the eyes of God. Instead, it was the tax collector who "went home justified before God." The Pharisee had offered God his good deeds and isolation from others, while the tax collector had offered only his penitence. God honored only the latter gift.

In our post-Calvary setting, this parable makes us think of the familiar old hymn: "Nothing in my hands I bring; simply to Thy cross I cling." Right standing with God does not come through our good works but through Christ (Rom. 10:1-4). "For everyone who exalts himself will be humbled, and he who humbles himself will be exalted."

Day 3
Little Children

Read Deuteronomy 6:1-12 about teaching children about God.

1. Why do you think people were bringing their children to Jesus? Might you have done the same thing?
2. What importance did the culture of Jesus' time give children? What about our culture?
3. Why do you think the disciples reacted as they did?
4. What do Jesus' actions say about his evaluation of children?
5. What is the best advice you could give the parents of young children?

e. Jesus and the little children. 18:15-17.

As if to reinforce the lesson just offered about humility before God, Luke immediately tells us that people were "bringing babies to Jesus to have him touch them." Either in an overly zealous effort to protect their Lord or with certain assumptions about the unimportance of little children, his disciples "rebuked" those who were bringing them. When Jesus saw what they were doing, he "called the children" to himself and made this statement to the larger crowd of adults: "Let the little children come to me, and do not hinder them, for the kingdom of God belongs to such as these. I tell you the truth, anyone who will not receive the kingdom of God like a little child will never enter it."

At least two things should be noted from this text. First, it confirms the spiritual status of infants. The kingdom belongs to them. In their innocence and trust, they model the traits that adults need most to learn. Consistent with Luke's habit of showing that people who had been thought to be of little significance were important to God, this episode affirms little children — and those who train, nurture, and protect them. Second, it underscores the hatefulness of the pharisaical spirit that boasts about human achievement and righteousness. Little children are notoriously unimpressed with such arrogance. It is typically not children who need to be rebuked or warned against a holier-than-thou spirit; it is adults who more often need to be called to the trust and simplicity of little children.

f. Encountering a rich young ruler. 18:18-30.

Again reinforcing the spirit one must have to receive God's grace, Luke next includes a case study of someone very different from the penitent tax collector and trusting little children. Although Matthew (19:16-29) and Mark (10:17-30) both tell the story of this wealthy young man's encounter with Jesus, only Luke identifies him as a "ruler." He presented himself to Jesus and asked, "Good teacher, what must I do to inherit eternal life?"

The stark and confrontational manner of Jesus' reply indicates from the start that this is an unpromising encounter. He was always gentle and patient with those who came to him as sincere seekers. When encountering someone whose heart was hard and reluctant, however, he tended to adopt an unyielding posture. "Why do you call me good?" was his first question to the man. Was this mere flattery? Or had he come to join the other disciples' in a confession of Jesus' deity? "No one is good — except God alone." This was in no way a disclaimer of goodness or deity for himself on Jesus' part. It was an invitation for the young ruler to confess him. At the least, it was a call for him to reflect on the possibility of his deity.

Turning to his question, Jesus said, "You know the commandments." He then cited the final five of the Ten Commandments, those that focus on loving one's neighbor. If the young man had no conviction about Jesus' deity, what conviction did he have of himself before God? Did he see himself as the tax collector had — a sinner in need of grace? Hardly! "All these I have kept since I was a boy," he responded. One need not see this as a claim to perfection. More likely, it was a reflection of the legalistic righteousness of that time which held that one who acknowledged the commandments and offered the appropriate ritual sacrifice upon breaking one

Day 4
A Rich Young Ruler

Read Matthew 19:16-29 for a parallel account of this episode.

1. What does this man's question reflect about his sense of need for God?

2. Why did Jesus answer him as he did?

3. What is *universal* about Jesus' command here? What is *particular* to this man?

4. What was the reaction of Jesus to the man's departure? Explain it.

5. What is your most valued treasure? Could you give it up for Jesus?

of them was considered "faultless" (cf. Phil. 3:6b). In other words, this rich young ruler saw nothing compelling in either the teaching or person of Jesus. He therefore probably expected Jesus to offer a rabbinic blessing on his commitment to the Law of Moses and to assure him that continued observance of its requirements would result in eternal life. One cannot "do" enough to deserve eternal life; he can only acknowledge Jesus and receive it as a free gift (cf. Phil. 3:7ff).

This man understood neither Jesus nor the commandments. So, in order to jolt him awake to his need for the tax collector's humility and the little children's trust, Jesus continued, "You still lack one thing. Sell everything you have and give to the poor, and you will have treasure in heaven. Then come, follow me." Could this man "hate" his wealth for Jesus' sake? (cf. 14:26). Would he leave everything for the sake of the kingdom of God? "When he heard this, he became very sad." He chose to hold to this life's treasures, thereby abandoning those of the world to come (cf. 9:24). Although the commandment to sell all his possessions was particular to this man, the requirement that one must give up whatever is most precious to him for the sake of Christ is universal (14:26-27; cf. Gen. 22:1ff).

Jesus used the young man's departure as the occasion for reminding his disciples about the treachery of wealth. "How hard it is for the rich to enter the kingdom of God! Indeed it is easier for a camel to go through the eye of a needle than for a rich man to enter the kingdom of God." Money can buy neither happiness nor heaven, but it can easily blind one to his spiritual needs. Anyone with an attachment to wealth comparable to this young man's has no hope of eternal life. Camels will jump through suturing needles before such people enter the kingdom of God!

The disciples were startled by this exchange, for they shared the prevailing view that wealth implied divine approval of one's life. So they asked, "Who then can be saved?" Jesus answered by telling them salvation is totally of God's doing and is possible for anyone, whether rich or poor, who demonstrates his trust in God. When Peter offered the commitment of those disciples who had indeed left everything for his sake as a counter-example to the rich young ruler's decision, Jesus reassured him that their sacrifice and the trust it demonstrated would not go unrewarded.

g. Another prediction of his death. 18:31-34.

For the third time in this Gospel, Luke tells how Jesus foretold his death and resurrection to incredulous disciples. This third episode was the most pointed and succinct yet. Taking the Twelve aside privately, he informed them that Scripture was about to be fulfilled at Jerusalem as he would shortly be "handed over to the Gentiles." He would die at their hands but would not be defeated by death. "They will mock [the Son of Man], insult him, spit on him, flog him, and kill him. On the third day he will rise again," said Jesus.

Luke adds that the apostles "did not understand any of this." At this point, the "meaning was hidden from them, and they did not know what he was talking about." In retrospect, we tend to be amazed at their dullness. But would we have been any different? The power of their eventual witness to Christ's resurrection is, if anything, made stronger by the fact that they clearly were not expecting him to be alive on the third day.

**Day 5
Slowness to
Understand**

Read Acts 1:1-11 to see how slow the apostles were to comprehend Jesus' mission.

1. Are you shocked by the disciples' slowness? Explain.
2. Can you point to some issue where your understanding of God's will has come very slowly?
3. How does one prepare his or her heart to hear God?
4. What is a primary obstacle to spiritual insight in your own experience?
5. Pray for God to give you a teachable spirit.

Week Twenty-Six

Luke 18:35–19:28 (IV D 3 h in Outline)

Day 1
Blindness

Read Matthew 15:1-20 and watch for Jesus' comments about blindness.

1. If you knew you had to forfeit one of your five senses, which would it be? Why?
2. Have you ever known someone who was blind? How did he or she cope with the situation?
3. Which would be worse: *physical* or *spiritual* blindness? Why?
4. What causes spiritual blindness? How is it recognized? How cured?
5. Choose a Bible character you would describe as "spiritually blind." Explain your choice.

Day 2
Determination

Read Psalm 116 about crying out to the Lord.

1. How did the blind man show his determination?
2. Why do you think he was so tenacious and persistent?

h. Events at Jericho. 18:35–19:28.

The final episodes in Luke's account of Jesus' journey toward Jerusalem and his appointment there with the cross (cf. 9:51) all occur in the town of Jericho. It is approximately seventeen miles from his destination. In the time of Jesus, there were actually two Jerichos. The old city known to us from the Old Testament was just outside a new Jericho established by Herod the Great. Because Luke places the miracle of healing a blind man on the *approach* to Jericho (18:35) and both Matthew and Mark have Jesus *leaving* it in their parallel accounts of the same event (cf. Matt.20:29; Mark 10:46), it appears likely that the healing took place as Jesus was leaving one site and entering the other.

"A blind man was sitting by the roadside begging" as Jesus passed along. Although neither Matthew nor Luke identifies him, Mark informs us that his name was Bartimaeus. Because of the noise being made by the great multitude accompanying the Lord, the beggar asked aloud for someone to tell him what was happening. The answer came back: "Jesus of Nazareth is passing by."

Bartimaeus obviously had heard of Jesus and knew something about his ministry over the past three years. He immediately and persistently began calling for Jesus. He addressed him as the "Son of David" and effectively confessed his faith that Jesus was the long-awaited Messiah. "Son of David, have mercy on me!" was his cry. Perhaps he knew the prophecy of Isaiah 35:5 that the Messiah would heal the blind. In spite of the fact that the people toward the front of Jesus' entourage "rebuked him and told him to be quiet," Bartimaeus would not let his faith be silenced. Confronted with people telling him to be still, "he shouted all the more."

His unshaken faith was rewarded when Jesus "stopped and ordered the man to be brought to him." Asked what he wanted, the blind man said, "Lord, I want to see." In response, Jesus healed him immediately, and Bartimaeus "followed Jesus, praising God" — as did many others who had witnessed the miracle.

Without turning a miracle story into a parable, it is worth pointing out that this event reminds us how Jesus opens the eyes of all who turn to him in tenacious faith. "How many likewise have found Christ able and willing to give them spiritual vision! Their eyes have been opened to behold things unseen and eternal, and they have been enabled to follow the Master with joyful footsteps as they journey toward the celestial city where they will see the King in his beauty and will be like him when they 'see him even as he is.'" [Erdman, *Luke*, p. 191.]

A second encounter at Jericho was with a man named Zacchaeus. His story is the counterpoint to Jesus' encounter with the rich young ruler. Although Zacchaeus was a man of considerable wealth himself, he saw in Jesus something worth more than his worldly treasures. He had made his money as a "chief tax collector." Since this title occurs nowhere else in the New Testament, we cannot be sure of its precise meaning. It probably means that he either supervised or employed men to work under him to collect taxes. It would have been his duty to raise an amount specified by the Romans for a given district.

Although tax collectors were generally dishonest and had a bad reputation everywhere, one is forced to wonder if Zacchaeus was an exception to the rule — an exception who nevertheless had to bear public

3. Describe the most determined person you ever knew.
4. What has been the greatest obstacle to your spiritual life? How have you exhibited determined faith in coping with it?
5. Why are Bible study and prayer called "disciplines"? How tenacious are you in observing them?

Day 3
The Rejected Rich

Read James 2:1-13 about the duty of impartiality in dealing with people.

1. What is "reverse snobbery"? How might Zacchaeus have been its victim?
2. What unique spiritual challenges do gifted, beautiful, or wealthy persons face? Can such a life situation become a curse?
3. How sympathetic are people likely to be with someone like Zacchaeus? Why?

4. How may a church show acceptance toward all people?
5. Are you impartial in dealing with others? Explain.

scorn. He would eventually offer to "pay back four times the amount" that anyone had been cheated by him, and that was in addition to a pledge to "give half of my possessions to the poor." Someone who had systematically cheated others over the years would know that he could not make good on such promises. Furthermore, would Jesus not have rebuked such an impossible offer as *hypocritical*? Since an important trade route passed by Jericho and the city was famous for its balsam groves, it is not inconceivable that Zacchaeus had become wealthy by honest work as a tax official.

Word may well have reached Zacchaeus that Jesus welcomed people who had been systematically excluded by the Pharisees (cf. 15:1). Hearing that the rabbi was passing through Jericho, he "wanted to see who Jesus was." The presenting problem was that he was a "short man" who could not see over the crowd. The fact that he was a tax collector likely also meant that he could not count on a considerate path being made for him among the thronging citizens. So he ran ahead on the route Jesus was taking and "climbed a sycamore-fig tree to see him."

When Jesus came to the place where the man with a bad reputation was ensconced in a tree, he said, "Zacchaeus, come down immediately. I must stay at your house today." The "I must" of this statement is emphatic and sets the stage for what will come at v. 10. More than simply being open to them, Jesus was on a divine mission to *seek* and *save* people who had been shoved aside by the religious establishment.

In response to Jesus' boldness in inviting himself to his house, Zacchaeus got out of the tree "at once" and welcomed him "gladly." Although the crowd disapproved of his being the guest of a "sinner," Jesus went home with Zacchaeus. What would the short and unpopular man of Jericho say to his gracious act? As grace tends to do when it encounters a tender heart, it moved Zacchaeus to repentance. "Look, Lord! Here and now I give half of my possessions to the poor, and if I have cheated anybody out of anything, I will pay back four times the amount." This was far more than the original amount plus one-fifth required under the Law of Moses for making restitution (Lev. 6:5). It was the sort of unmistakable "fruit in keeping with repentance" that John the Baptist had called for in his preaching (3:8). Such genuine repentance showed that Zacchaeus was a genuine "son of Abraham" — not merely by birth but also by faith (cf. Rom. 4:12). "Today salvation has come to this house," declared Jesus.

We cannot be sure whether the words that close this story come from Jesus' mouth or Luke's pen: "For the Son of Man came to seek and to save what was lost." It is really of no great consequence who made the comment. It is a succinct summary of one salvation story wherein a most unlikely candidate for salvation (i.e., a rich and unpopular man who had a bad reputation) was brought back into the fold; it is also a challenge for the church to understand its mission in service to Jesus more clearly.

The final event recorded at Jericho may have also taken place at Zacchaeus' house. "Because he was near Jerusalem and the people thought that the kingdom of God was going to appear at once," Jesus gave a parable designed to counter their mistaken idea. Like a nobleman going to a "distant country to have himself appointed king and then to return," so would Jesus soon leave his disciples to be glorified at the right hand of the Father (cf. Dan. 7:13-14). It would be the duty of those disciples to use what he entrusted to them during his absence to his glory. Between his ascension and second coming, Christians have something important to do.

Day 4
Your Gift from God

Read Romans 12:1-8 about God's equipping of his church for ministry.

1. "Every Christian has a spiritual gift from God." Do you agree? Explain.
2. What is your special gift for God's glory? How did you identify it?
3. How are you using your gift at this point in your spiritual life?

4. What *encouragement* does the parable of the minas give you?
5. What *warning* do you find in this parable?

The parable actually envisions three types of persons who will give account of themselves at the appearing and kingdom of our Lord. There are faithful servants, unfaithful servants, and nonservants for him to evaluate.

The story has the nobleman entrusting ten of his servants with a "mina" each while he is away. A *mina* was a Greek coin worth about one hundred times a single day's wage or, as a footnote to the NIV says, "about three months' wages." Unlike the parable of the talents (Matt. 25:14-30) which represents the servants of God as having differing abilities, the thrust of this story is different. It simply points out that every believer has *some* responsibility to honor the Lord, has *some* gift entrusted him or her by Christ. Upon the nobleman's return, he called for an accounting. While the behavior of only three of the ten is related, that is sufficient to make the necessary point.

One servant had used his master's mina wisely and "earned ten more," a 1,000 percent return. A second servant had "earned five more," a 500 percent return. Both were praised and given authority over ten and five cities respectively. But the third servant said, "Sir, here is your mina; I have kept it laid away in a piece of cloth." The reason he gave for his failure was fear (i.e., "you are a hard man"), but the nobleman called him a "wicked servant" and took away what he had entrusted to him. His master told him that he could have done something with his gift, even if nothing more than collecting interest on it as an investment. "The smallest gift must be put to good use. In the Christian life we do not stand still. We use our gifts and make progress or we lose what we have." [Morris, *Luke*, p. 276.]

Day 5
Judgment

Read 1 Corinthians 3:1-15 about the judgment of human labors done for God.

With his servants judged as either faithful or unfaithful, the nobleman turned finally to those who had never enlisted as his servants. He called them "enemies" because they "did not want me to be king over them." There is no neutrality in the matter of faith and unbelief, truth and error, life and death. One must either decide for Jesus or, by default, remain under the sovereignty of his enemy (i.e., Satan) and share his horrible fate. The nobleman ordered that those who had rejected him be brought before him and killed. "The parable follows the reality of ancient politics. Refusing the rule of the one in power often meant paying with one's life. Here is the judgment of God. For the leadership in the short term, this would mean Jerusalem's destruction in A.D. 70. But in the long term there was a more permanent rejection to face. It is a terrifying thing to fall into the hands of a judging and rejected God." [Bock, *Luke*, p. 311.]

Luke's Gospel invites people who learn the story of Christ to fall in love with him, acknowledge his sovereignty, and serve him faithfully. But this invitation is not a tepid sentimentality. It is everyone's best and final hope for salvation. To reject Christ is to come under condemnation.

1. What is the central message of the parable of the minas?
2. How does Matthew 25:14-30 supplement the teaching of this parable?
3. What does 1 Corinthians 3:1-15 add to your understanding of how God will judge Christian deeds of service?
4. In this parable, who do the people called "enemies" represent?
5. Are you ready for the Lord's return? What would be his judgment of your life today?

Week Twenty-Seven

Luke 19:29–20:40 (V A to V C in Outline)

Day 1
Fickleness

Read Philippians 3:12–4:1 about the importance of carrying through.

1. Jesus received an emotional welcome as he neared Jerusalem. Why did the crowds turn against him so quickly?
2. Relate Luke 8:13 to this event.
3. What is the value of high emotional expression to faith? What is its liability?
4. How good are you at carrying through on commitments in religion? With your family? At work?
5. Take time to reflect on Numbers 30:2 and Ecclesiastes 5:4-5.

V. A Final Ministry in Jerusalem. 19:29–21:38

A. His Triumphal Entry. 19:29-44.

At this point in the Gospel of Luke, Jesus' announced purpose of going to Jerusalem, presenting himself to the nation of Israel and its leaders, and facing the event for which he had come into the world begins to move swiftly to its climax. In what has come to be called his "triumphal entry" into the holy city, he offers himself as king one final time. It is one of the most emotional scenes in all of Holy Scripture. It was clearly staged by Jesus for maximal emotional impact and produced a great outpouring of celebration. At the same time, however, the scene vividly displays the contrast between mere sentiment and true faith. Many of those who celebrated his entry into Jerusalem on Sunday would be screaming for his death by the following Friday.

The geographical references at 19:29 put Jesus about two miles east of Jerusalem. From there, he sent two disciples to a nearby village to "find a colt tied there, which no one has ever ridden." A reference earlier to his arrival as a "staged" event is based in part on the fact that Jesus seems to have prearranged the use of the donkey. "The Lord needs it" were the code words his disciples were to use if its owners questioned them about taking it.

The colt was one "which no one has ever ridden." From the Old Testament, we know that only such things as were previously unused were suitable for sacred purposes (cf. 1 Sam. 6:7). By means of this lowly animal, Israel's king would enter the city not as a warrior but as a man of peace. This would both fulfill a biblical prediction about the Messiah (Zech. 9:9) and challenge the popular expectation of his role as a nationalistic deliverer.

As Jesus neared the city, masses of people "spread their cloaks on the road" before him (cf. 2 Kgs. 9:13) and cheered his arrival. It is interesting, though, that they did not hail him as Son of God or even as the Messiah — although we may be supposed to see the latter implied in the title "king" (v. 38). They praised him "for all the miracles they had seen" from him and granted that he had come "in the name of the Lord." One of the apostles would later acknowledge that "his disciples did not understand all this" until "after Jesus was glorified" (John 12:16). Only Jesus really understood what was happening in this emotional scene.

The great throng that shouted his praises likely did so out of their misguided desire rather than from spiritual insight. To whatever degree they saw (or *hoped for*) Jesus' kingship over Israel, they almost surely hoped to prod him to a warrior-deliverer role as opposed to a reign as Prince of Peace.

The Pharisees in the crowd who objected to all the excitement and counseled Jesus to "rebuke" his disciples may have come closer than anyone else that day to catching the significance of what he was doing. They certainly were not willing to see Jesus proclaimed as the Messiah. Neither were they willing to provoke Roman intervention. His response to their demand was to say the multitude's excitement was appropriate and that the "stones [along his route] will cry out" if the people with him were to keep silence.

In a lament that Luke alone relates, Jesus "wept" (lit., sobbed out loud) over Jerusalem as the city finally came into view. He prophesied the terrible

**Day 2
When Opportunity
Knocks**

Read 2 Corinthians 5:11–6:2 about responding to God's favor.

1. What was the source of Jesus' sorrow in vv. 41-44? What was "the time of God's coming" for Jerusalem?
2. Comment on the old saying "Opportunity knocks but once, then is gone forever." Is it true?
3. Did you ever let a moment of exceptional opportunity pass by? If so, why?
4. Are you aware of any unique spiritual opportunity before you today? How can one recognize such opportunities?
5. Pray for God to make you sensitive to the opportunities he sets before you.

Day 3
The Authority
Question

Read 1 John 2:28–3:10 about life as God's child.

1. What events lay behind the question of 20:2?
2. Do you believe the question was sincere? Explain.
3. Comment on this statement: "People seldom need more proof of Jesus' credentials so much as a heart that is passionate for God."
4. Why did Jesus answer their question with a question? How did it expose the questioners' hypocrisy?

fate that would come to the city when Rome eventually besieged, encircled, and ravaged it in A.D. 70. All this would occur "because you did not recognize the time of God's coming to you." Leon Morris writes: "There is an ignorance that is innocent, but there is also an ignorance that is culpable. These men had the revelation God had made known in the Scriptures of the Old Testament. They had the continuing evidence that God was active in the life and ministry of Jesus. They could see in Him that God had not forgotten His people. There was every reason for them to have welcomed Jesus as His disciples did. But they refused to accept all this evidence. They rejected God's Messiah. They would now have to live with the consequences of their rejection. It is this that brought forth Jesus' tears." [*Luke*, p. 281.]

B. Cleansing the Temple. 19:45-46.

On Monday following the triumphal entry (cf. Mark 11:11-17), Jesus entered the temple compound and "began driving out those who were selling." What God had meant to be a holy center for worship had been degraded into a noisy bazaar (i.e., "you have made it 'a den of robbers'"). This was apparently the second time in his public ministry that Jesus had done such a drastic thing, for John reports a temple cleansing at the start of the public ministry (John 2:14ff), whereas Luke and the other Synoptic writers tell of this one in connection with the events leading immediately to his death.

C. Questions and Challenges *from* His Opponents. 19:47–20:40.

1. The setting for the events. 19:47-48.

The public enthusiasm for Jesus coupled with his cleansing of the temple for a second time let the "chief priests, the teachers of the law and the leaders among the people" know that he could no longer be tolerated. Because he was a threat to their hold on the people, they were now determined to "kill him." Yet, Luke points out, Jesus still had the respect of the common people. It was his popularity with the masses that briefly restrained the nation's leaders in their purpose to kill him. Therefore it would be necessary for them either to expose and discredit him before the crowds or else to bring some formal charge against Jesus that could result in a death penalty for him.

Thus begins a series of challenges to Jesus from his opponents. Tuesday (cf. Mark 11:27) of his final week was spent in the exchanges contained in chapters 20 and 21.

2. A question about his authority. 20:1-19.

The first question put to Jesus was about the "authority" by which he entered the city to such clamor and — more particularly still — created such a commotion at the temple. "Who gave you this authority?" they demanded. His astute response was to put his critics on the horns of a dilemma with a question of his own: "John's baptism — was it from heaven, or from men?"

No sooner had he posed his counter-question than his enemies realized their hopeless position in trying to answer it. If they conceded that John had the authority of heaven for his ministry and teaching, they would have to explain their rejection of his call to repentance and baptism; if they said John's ministry was "from men" (i.e., presumptuous rather than truly prophetic), they feared the crowd would stone them for attacking someone they believed to be a prophet. After huddling about their options, they returned with this answer: "We don't know where it was from." Having exposed them for their dishonesty in raising the whole authority question, Jesus said, "Neither will I tell you by what authority I am doing these things." As

5. At a practical level, how do we acknowledge the authority of Jesus over our lives?

a matter of fact, of course, this *was* an answer to their question. Jesus both believed and implied in his question that John's authority (as well as his own!) was "from heaven"; anyone unwilling to acknowledge John certainly would not acknowledge Jesus either.

With his enemies reeling from having their devious question turned back on them, Jesus followed with a parable that further exposed — and infuriated — them. In his Parable of the Tenants, the vineyard is Israel (cf. Isa. 5) and its owner is Yahweh; the tenants are Israel's leaders; the owner's servants were the Old Testament prophets and John the Baptist; and the owner's son is Jesus. Although God had sent many prophets to call the nation and its leaders to repentance, the Israelites had refused to acknowledge them as having been sent "from heaven" and had killed many of them. Now Yahweh had sent his own son to them, and they would murder him as well. The owner of the vineyard would therefore punish its original tenants and give it over to others (i.e., Gentiles).

His opponents knew immediately that Jesus "had spoken this parable against them" and grasped its meaning. Although they wanted to "arrest him immediately," his popularity with the masses again forced them to bide their time.

Day 4
Life in Two Worlds

Read 1 Peter 2:13-25 about submission to human authorities.

1. Explain the trap laid for Jesus in the question about paying taxes to Caesar.
2. What was the essence of Jesus' response?
3. Is there any limit to the

3. A question about tribute money. 20:20-26.

Humiliated but undaunted, Jesus' enemies regrouped and decided to send "spies" (i.e., people who would not be known to be opponents) with another question. It focused on the extremely touchy issue of the Roman occupation and Jewish obligation to their hated overlords: "Is it right for us to pay taxes to Caesar or not?" The plan here was to create another dilemma for Jesus. If he said paying taxes to Caesar was right, he would presumably offend many and cease to be a popular teacher with them; if he said paying taxes was not obligatory, he could be reported to the government and charged with sedition.

Jesus "saw through their duplicity" and answered the spies by calling for a denarius. When someone produced the silver coin with the outline of Emperor Tiberius on it, Jesus asked, "Whose portrait and inscription are on it?" When they answered, "Caesar's," Jesus gave this response: "Then give to Caesar what is Caesar's, and to God what is God's." Believers live in two domains simultaneously (i.e., Caesar's and God's, earth and heaven) and are obligated to fulfill their responsibilities in both — until such time as earth's demands contravene God's (cf. Acts 4:19). Earth's civil governments are entitled to our respect and support by taxation, and meeting these duties of citizenship is a vital element of Christian responsibility (Rom. 13:1ff).

Again, Jesus' response silenced his critics. They immediately realized that his perceptive reply made it impossible for them to "trap him" on this point. But the questioning and challenge did not stop with this exchange.

4. A question about the resurrection. 20:27-40.

Since the Pharisees had been unable to catch Jesus with their hard questions, some Sadducees stepped forward to try their hand at it. One of the distinctions between these two groups was their respective positions on the issue of resurrection and afterlife. "The Sadducees say that there is no resurrection, and that there are neither angels nor spirits, but the Pharisees acknowledge them all" (Acts 23:8). Thus the question raised by the Sadducees was designed not only to embarrass Jesus with what they deemed an unanswerable question but to remind the Pharisees of their inability to deal with it — for this was undoubtedly their "stumper" in debates on this topic.

submission a citizen owes his or her government? If so, specify that limit.

4. What duties does a government have to its citizens?

5. Should the Christian religion seek special privileges from the state? Explain your answer.

Day 5
Life after Death

Read Paul's affirmation of life after death in 1 Corinthians 15:12-28.

1. What was the point of the complex question put to Jesus by the Sadducees?

2. How does Yahweh's statement to Moses at the burning bush imply that humans survive death?

3. What did the Sadducees believe about the resurrection? The Pharisees?

4. How does the Christian view of the resurrection of the dead differ from both Jewish views just identified?

5. What insights about the resurrection life do you get from Jesus' statements here? What questions are raised?

Based on the Old Testament provision for levirate marriage (i.e., a provision to keep a man's family name and inheritance intact if he died childless by having his widow marry his brother, Deut. 25:5), they imagined a situation in which seven brothers had been married to the same woman without her bearing a child. One can almost see the smirk on their faces as they ask: "Now then, at the resurrection whose wife will she be, since the seven were married to her?"

Jesus made two points in his reply to their question. First, life following the resurrection will not be a mere resumption of life as we have lived it on earth. The Pharisees' doctrine of the resurrection assumed that the future life would be an indefinite continuation of life as we know it now. Jesus — while not denying that the relationships we have had in this life (i.e., parent-child, brother-sister, husband-wife, etc.) are valid in the world to come — insisted that postresurrection life will be qualitatively different from what we know here. Marriage for the sake of reproduction is necessary in a world where people die, for example, but such an arrangement will not be necessary in a world where life is everlasting. Second, he produced an argument from Hebrew Scripture to prove that human beings survive death. When Yahweh met with Moses at the burning bush (Exod. 3:1-6), he identified himself as "the God of Abraham, and the God of Isaac, and the God of Jacob." This implied, argued Jesus, that the three patriarchs who had died centuries before Moses' time were still alive. "He is not the God of the dead, but of the living," said Jesus, "for to him all are alive." There *is* an afterlife, and the materialist assumptions of both ancients and moderns are wrong.

Even though they had already been bested by Jesus in earlier exchanges, some of the Pharisees still present congratulated Jesus (i.e., "Well said, teacher!") for putting the Sadducees to silence. Both politics and religious dispute can create strange bedfellows! This ending to the questions and challenges *from* his opponents had exposed both the Pharisees and Sadducees as insincere quibblers looking to play the game of one-upmanship not only with each other but with Jesus.

Week Twenty-Eight

Luke 20:41–21:38 (V D to V F in Outline)

Day 1
Incarnation

Read Hebrews 2:5-18 for a unique perspective on the incarnation.

1. Define *incarnation*. What is the significance of the term to the question Jesus asked his opponents?
2. Why did his critics refuse to answer him?
3. Why does Jesus deserve the titles "Son of God" and "Son of Man"? What is the significance of each?
4. Comment on 1 John 4:2-3. Why is the confession that Jesus came "in the flesh" so critical to Christian faith?
5. What is the meaning of Hebrews 2:14?

D. Questions and Challenges *for* His Opponents. 20:41–21:4.

Having put both Pharisee and Sadducee opponents to silence with the answers he gave to their questions, now it was Jesus' turn to pose a question. The one he posed turns out to be the crucial background to the climax of his ministry. It is a question whose answer implies a claim to deity for him. It is this claim that will eventually be used as the basis for a charge of blasphemy against him before the Jewish High Priest and Sanhedrin.

1. His question about the Messiah's sonship. 20:41-44.

The Jews have always understood that the Christ (i.e., Messiah) was to appear in the lineage of David. Yet in Psalm 110:1, David spoke of the Messiah and his enthronement at the right hand of God. In that psalm, the following language is used: "The LORD (i.e., Yahweh) says to my Lord (i.e., Messiah-master) . . ." Thus a difficulty of interpretation emerges. If the Messiah is *David's son*, by what method of reasoning could he also be *David's Lord*?

The implications of this psalm are central to the Christian faith and were brought to the fore by Jesus himself. The only way one of King David's descendants could also be his superior would be for the Messiah to be divine as well as human. Indeed, the Christian doctrine of *incarnation* affirms that Jesus of Nazareth is not only the Son of David but also the Son of God, not only human but also divine.

Because of the implications of the interpretation of Psalm 110 for Jesus' claims, his opponents would not touch his question. They refused to say what was obvious to Jesus and the bystanders listening to the exchange. Their refusal demonstrated again their insincerity and hypocrisy — which Jesus proceeded to expose publicly.

2. His warning about the hypocrisy of the scribes. 20:45-47.

With the "teachers of the law" refusing to reply to the question he had put to them, Jesus turned to his own disciples and warned them against either following them or behaving as they did. Summarizing the extended denunciation of these pious frauds given in Matthew 23, Luke offers "only a few short sentences which sketch three principal features in the character of these unworthy leaders of religious thought. The first is their vanity, their ambition for display and for high position, and their love of flattery. The second is their cruel avarice, expressed by our Lord in the suggestive clause, 'who devour widows' houses.' The third was their shameful hypocrisy; they are described as men who 'for a pretence make long prayers.' It has always been remarked that the most bitter denunciations of Jesus were addressed to the men whose outward lives were most respectable and whose religious professions were most loud." [Erdman, *Luke*, p. 213.]

3. His admiration of a widow's giving. 21:1-4.

Just after his scathing rebuke of hypocrisy among the religious leaders, Jesus witnessed and praised the example of a poor widow whose spiritual life was notable for its contrasting genuineness. In the temple area known as the Court of the Women, thirteen trumpet-shaped collection receptacles were placed. Each was labeled as to what its contents would be used to do. Worshipers could select one or more of these containers in which to place their gifts. It takes very little imagination to figure out

Day 2
False Teachers

Read Romans 16:17-19 for Paul's comments about the motives of false teachers.

1. Why were the "teachers of the law" so opposed to Jesus?
2. Where does the issue of *power* fit into the motives of these teachers?
3. Erdman listed three principal traits of the false teachers Jesus opposed. Do you agree with his summary? Comment on each.
4. How do these three traits fit some of the teachers you have seen exposed in your lifetime?
5. How does one decide which teachers to trust?

Day 3
Deeds and Motives

Read 1 Corinthians 13 for what it teaches about pure motivation.

1. Why did Jesus call attention to the gift of a poor widow?
2. Do gifts or deeds need to be small in order to be pure? Explain.
3. Have you ever called your own motives into

question? Why?

4. What helps you keep your motives pure in living out the requirements of your faith?

5. Evaluate this statement: "We can best measure our offerings not by what we give but by how much we keep."

how this procedure could be exploited for show by a self-seeking person. He could make the rounds, tossing noisy handsful of coins into each of the thirteen treasury receptacles and calling attention to himself as a wealthy, pious, and generous man.

As various people were tossing in their gifts "out of their wealth," Jesus "saw a poor widow put in two very small copper coins." Her gift, worth less than one cent, was offered "out of her poverty." Indeed, in giving those two coins, she had "put in all she had to live on." Jesus praised her deed with these words: "I tell you the truth, this poor widow has put in more than all the others." In our giving, praying, and other acts of religious devotion, God evaluates these actions by the motives prompting them.

Day 4
The Fall of Jerusalem

Read a lament over the destruction of Jerusalem by Babylon at Psalm 137.

1. How was the fall of Jerusalem related to Jesus Christ?

2. How did this event drive a deep wedge between Jews and Christians?

3. What became of the temple when the Romans conquered Jerusalem?

4. In what way might we regard the fall of Jerusalem as a foreshadowing of the end of the world?

5. What lessons should we learn today from Jerusalem's overthrow?

E. Revelations to His Disciples about the Future. 21:5-36.

Matthew, Mark, and Luke all have versions of this discourse about the sacking of Jerusalem and the end of the world. The primary difficulty in interpreting this material is in distinguishing references to an event to take place in A.D. 70 from one that will take place at Jesus' second coming. In the Gospel of Luke, the focus seems to be principally on the former event — with an awareness that it serves as something of a foreshadowing of the latter.

1. The destruction of the Jewish temple. 21:5-7.

The setting for the discourse is a question posed by the disciples. As they were walking about the temple grounds, they not only saw wealthy men and poor widows going about their business but also could not help "remarking about how the temple was adorned with beautiful stones and with gifts dedicated to God." As if to say again that he did not want his disciples caught up in the externals of religion, Jesus startled them with his comment that a time would come when "not one stone will be left on another" in the temple complex they were admiring.

The disciples' shock and dismay over the prospect of the temple's destruction come through in the question they posed: "Teacher, when will these things happen?" More specifically still, they asked about the possibility of a "sign" that would signal the event. In response, Jesus predicted the fall of Jerusalem and the desecration of the Holy City under the Roman General Titus that would not come about for another forty years.

2. The fall of Jerusalem. 21:8-28.

As Jesus sketched an overview of the time between A.D. 30 and A.D. 70, he first warned against interpreting any and every unusual event as a "sign of the end." In a word, he said that wars, earthquakes, outbreaks of disease, and the like are to be expected across human history. The same thing should be kept in mind by those of us who live in the post-A.D. 70 period. California earthquakes, AIDS, and shocking events in the Middle East are *not* signs of the second coming (cf. Matt. 24:36-39) but the "normal" (?) pattern of events to be expected in a fallen world that exists under the curse of sin.

Jesus also told his disciples to expect persecution. "They will deliver you to synagogues and prisons, and you will be brought before kings and governors, and all on account of my name," he predicted. Yet he said they were "not to worry" about such treatment, for God would deliver them. In some cases, deliverance would come in the form of words provided them to say in their defense (v. 15); in others, it would come in the form of eternal life following their martyrdom (v. 16). The promise that "not a hair of your head will perish" is clearly not a prediction of Christian exemption from all *physical* harm (e.g., martyrdom has just been predicted at v. 16) but the Lord's version of Socrates' ancient dictum that a good man cannot be hurt by a bad man. Yes, the bad man can imprison, deprive, or even murder the good one, but he cannot touch his inner person to destroy his faith or to deprive him of his reward (cf. Matt. 10:28).

The clear and distinct sign of the fall of Jerusalem and the destruction of the temple would be this: "When you see Jerusalem being surrounded by armies, you will know that its desolation is near" (v. 20; cf. 19:41-44). The Jewish revolt that began against Rome in A.D. 64 came to its horrendous climax when Jerusalem was besieged, conquered, and humiliated six years later. The Roman armies showed no mercy as they pillaged, raped, and slaughtered the city's residents. It is estimated that they killed fully a million Jews and enslaved countless thousands.

Extrabiblical history about the fall of Jerusalem lets us know that Jesus' warning that his disciples in Judea should "flee to the mountains," those in Jerusalem should "get out," and "those in the country not enter the city" spared them from the worst of Rome's savagery. As the armies of Rome began to encircle Jerusalem, Christians obeyed the Lord and fled — many to a mountain region around Petra. This not only saved the lives of unnumbered thousands of Christians but drove a permanent wedge between them and the Jewish survivors of the war of extermination waged against them. After A.D. 70, ethnic Jews who had embraced the Christian faith were neither welcomed nor tolerated in synagogues.

Although the final paragraph of this discourse is taken by most scholars to refer to the second coming rather than the destruction of the temple, it seems more likely that it rounds out and summarizes what has been said about the Roman conquest of Jerusalem. Even the reference to the "Son of Man coming in a cloud with power and great glory" —

though it certainly sounds like and *may* refer to Christ's personal return at the end of time (cf. 2 Thess. 1:7-9) — need not move us away from the events of A.D. 70. The imagery of God coming on a cloud sometimes simply means that he is bringing judgment on a people, as was predicted against Egypt in Isaiah 19:1. Although the Roman armies would come against Israel in divine judgment for its rejection of the prophets and the Messiah (cf. 20:9-19), those who had accepted Jesus and who would act on his warning to flee to the mountains would experience "redemption" (i.e., deliverance) from that devastation.

3. An appeal for vigilance. 21:29-36.

In the Parable of the Fig Tree, Jesus told his disciples to see the fulfillment of his prediction about Jerusalem's fate as a sure sign of his sovereign purpose to bring all of history to his desired end. As surely as a tree's leaves are precursor signs to its fruit, so should the fate of Jerusalem be seen as an assurance that heaven's purpose of kingly domain would be realized. And the fall of Jerusalem would happen within the lifetime of the Lord's contemporaries. "I tell you the truth, this generation will certainly not pass away until all these things have happened."

What, then, should be the spirit of believers? Constant vigilance and prayer will spare us from being so caught up in this world that we miss the kingdom of God. "Be always on the watch, and pray that you may be able to escape all that is about to happen, and that you may be able to stand before the Son of Man."

F. Summary Statement about His Work in Jerusalem. 21:37-38.

Luke completes his summary of Jesus' final ministry in Jerusalem and prepares us for the climactic

Day 5
Watchfulness

Read 2 Peter 3 and its call to watchfulness before the Day of the Lord.

1. What is the message of the Parable of the Fig Tree?
2. What sorts of things did Jesus warn against that might distract some from readiness for his coming?
3. What sorts of things hold the possibility of distracting you from being ready for the Lord's return?
4. How do you keep your attention focused on his coming?
5. Does the thought of his return bring feelings of *fear* or *hope* to you? Why?

195

events of his passion by telling his readers how the final week of his earthly life was spent. He informs us that Jesus spent the daylight hours teaching large crowds in the temple area and spent the night "on the hill called the Mount of Olives" — perhaps sleeping under the open sky.

With events moving swiftly to their grand crescendo, Jesus continued to teach about the kingdom. While his enemies stayed awake nights to scheme and plot his death, he slept peacefully within the secure knowledge that he was doing the Father's bidding and securing our salvation.

Week Twenty-Nine

Luke 22:1-38 (VI A and VI B in Outline)

VI. The Death and Resurrection of the Son of Man. 22:1–24:53.

A. The Conspiracy against Jesus. 22:1-6.

The recent actions of Jesus had forced the hands of his enemies. They could wait no longer to do something about him, for they justifiably saw him as a threat to their position and power. Yet they faced a problem in that "they were afraid of the people." Since this was a festival time in Jerusalem, it seemed certain that their plan to kill Jesus would have to wait until Passover had passed and the great crowds had left for home. Their dilemma was solved from a most unexpected-to-them source. One of Jesus' own disciples came to them with an offer to give him up.

Judas Iscariot went to the Jewish officials and "discussed with them how he might betray Jesus." Both Luke and John explain his action by saying that "Satan entered Judas" to prompt his evil deed (cf. John 13:27). This explanation should not be taken to mean that he became a demoniac or was caused to do something against his will. Any human being who lies, betrays a trust, or rejects Jesus does so because of the power of Satan to enter our hearts and influence us to do wrong. Perhaps Judas gave in to Satan because of his disappointment over the nature of Christ's kingdom, or perhaps it is to be traced directly to his love of money (cf. John 12:4-6).

The rulers were "delighted" with Judas's offer and "agreed to give him money." With the deal struck between these unlikely partners, Judas began

Day 1
Judas

Read John 12:1-11 for an insight into Judas' character.

1. What do you think lay behind Judas's decision to betray Jesus?
2. How did Judas react to Jesus' eventual death sentence? Why?
3. Was Judas's betrayal fundamentally worse than Peter's denials? Explain.
4. What do you think kept Peter from resorting to suicide?
5. Imagine that you meet Judas on his way to hang himself. What might you say? What would you say to someone threatening suicide today?

watching for a circumstance under which he could "hand Jesus over to them when no crowd was present."

B. The Last Supper. 22:7-38.

Day 2
The Lord's Supper

Read Paul's account of the initiation of this meal in 1 Corinthians 11:17-34.

1. How did the Passover meal provide an appropriate setting for this event?
2. What is meant by these words: "This is my body given for you"?
3. What is meant by these words: "This cup is the new covenant in my blood, which is poured out for you"?
4. Explain Paul's insights at 1 Corinthians 11:27-29.
5. What does the Lord's Supper mean to you? How do you avoid letting it become a mere ritual practice?

In the context of his final meal with the Twelve, Jesus gave them instructions concerning a perpetual rite to be celebrated by his church across the centuries until his return. Against the backdrop of Passover's acknowledgment of a great deliverance by God's power, he set in place a memorial to the far greater deliverance that his death would provide.

1. Preparing for the event. 22:7-13.

Because he knew of Judas' plot to deliver him to his enemies, Jesus had made secret arrangements for a place he could use to eat his final Passover with the apostles. He sent Peter and John ahead of the group to look for "a man carrying a jar of water." Since that was a task for women in that culture, they would be able to spot him in the crush of people. Seeing him, the two disciples followed him, spoke the formula-words agreed upon between Jesus and the man (cf. 19:28-34), and were shown to a "large upper room, all furnished."

Having found everything "just as Jesus had told them," Peter and John made final preparations for the meal to be eaten. Since Judas would know of this place only when he arrived later with the larger group, he could not tip off the Jewish officials to Jesus' whereabouts. Thus Jesus protected himself against losing this important time with the Twelve.

2. Instructions about a kingdom meal. 22:14-20.

In the course of eating the Passover meal with his disciples, Jesus pointed forward again to the "fulfillment" of all things that would come with the fullness of the kingdom of God. With the first of two cups mentioned in Luke's account, he anticipated his passion and departure from their midst by saying that he would not physically and personally drink with them again "until the kingdom of God comes."

Taking bread from the table, Jesus distributed it among them with these words: "This is my body given for you; do this in remembrance of me." Although these words have been the basis of controversy across the centuries, they are no more obtuse than Jesus' claim "I am the door" or "I am the water of life." The bread eaten that night clearly was not the literal flesh of Jesus, for he was physically present with the disciples. His words mean that the bread *signifies* or *represents* his body.

The interpretation that sees the bread as a memorial to Jesus' body rather than its actual presence should not be taken as some sort of weakening of his meaning. The key expressions, after all, are "given for you" and "in remembrance of me." Believers eat the bread in the Lord's Supper as a reminder of his self-sacrifice at Calvary. It testifies to his vicarious suffering and death in our place.

Jesus gave the cup to his disciples with these words: "This cup is the new covenant in my blood, which is poured out for you." The prophets had anticipated the establishment of a new covenant (Jer. 31:31-34), and a covenant is always inaugurated by the shedding of blood. A detailed and insightful development of this new covenant theme is found at Hebrews 8–10.

3. Interactions with his disciples. 22:21-38.

In the context of such a dramatic setting and against the new teaching Jesus had just given, the group was shocked back to reality by a bombshell announcement, but they quickly adopted their customary insensitivity. Unthinkable as it may seem to us in retrospect, we should perhaps reflect on our own spiritual dullness at the most inappropriate of times.

Day 3
Satan's Power

Read Job 1:1-22 and pay attention to Satan's challenge to one man's faith in God.

1. What does it mean to say God is "sovereign over Satan's powers to attack the human race"?
2. Explain the meaning of 1 Corinthians 10:13.
3. In what way did Satan "enter" Judas?
4. Did Judas know what he was doing? Did God hold him responsible for his actions? Explain your answers.
5. What relationship does Satan have to the temptations that come to you? How could he "enter" you?

Day 4
Spiritual Greatness

Read Philippians 2:1-11 for an account of Jesus' exaltation via humble service.

1. What situation produced Jesus' discussion of "greatness"? What do you think the apostles had in mind?
2. Describe the contrast Jesus drew between worldly models of greatness and a kingdom model.

a. The announcement of impending betrayal. 22:21-23.

The "bombshell announcement" following the covenant meal that night was that "the hand of him who is going to betray me is with mine on this table." The significance of this statement relates to several things. "Jesus reveals that his death is no surprise. His passing away is not a sign of a plan disappointed or of salvation gone awry. Still, the betrayer is responsible to God for his betrayal. Judas may have met the leadership in private, but God was not fooled. As with all secretly plotted sin, God was there. . . . As Jesus dies to secure forgiveness for others, he himself meets with betrayal. Even one of his own betrays him (Ps. 41:9). Woe will befall Jesus' rejecter. It is a fearful thing to reject the One who gives his life to secure our forgiveness." [Bock, *Luke*, p. 351.]

The Twelve took his statement seriously and began discussing "which of them it might be who would do this." It is interesting to note that all heads did not turn immediately to Judas. Neither did he say or do anything that gave himself away within the little group. At this pre-Pentecost point, he does not stand out as a villain among the disciples. In fact, the next episode might well have turned the finger of suspicion more toward Peter than anyone else in the room.

b. A dispute over kingdom importance. 22:24-30.

Perhaps it was the discussion among themselves about a betrayer that resulted in a "dispute" that centered on "which of them was considered to be greatest." With their Lord so near his ultimate act of humility, the spirit driving his closest associates was incredibly far removed from his. Luke alone among the Gospel writers tells of this quarrel about greatness. John's contribution on this point is to tell of the action of Jesus in washing the feet of his followers (John 13:1ff).

Concerned as they were about rank and authority in the kingdom of heaven, Jesus warned them against interpreting the things of God against the models they knew best. While he acknowledged the authoritarian posture of Gentile kings (i.e., rulers who "lord it over them") and their desire for titles showing their superiority (i.e., "Benefactor"), he emphatically said it was not to be so among his followers.

What, then, is *greatness* in the eyes of God? "Indeed, the greatest among you should be like the youngest, and the one who rules like the one who serves." The only greatness open to the followers of Jesus Christ is in servanthood with neither expectation nor demand of recognition.

As proof of his thesis, Jesus not only washed their feet that night but reminded them of the pattern of his ministry from the start. "I am among you as one who serves," he told them. Since his disciples wished to honor him as Lord, there should have been no hesitation or embarrassment among them about filling the same role that Jesus accepted for himself. The eventual entry into royal status they were concerned about would not happen in this world but at the great messianic feast that follows the end of the earth experience. Just as Jesus' glorification came at the conclusion of his servanthood and death, so would the exaltation of his followers come following theirs.

c. Peter's denials foretold. 22:31-34.

Having just reminded the apostles of their experiences in standing by him in his trials to date (v. 28), Jesus considered it mandatory to warn them of testings yet to come — Peter in particular. In the most serious of tones, he said, "Simon, Simon, Satan has asked to sift you all as wheat. But I have prayed for you, Simon, that your faith may not fail. And when you have turned back, strengthen your brothers." God is sovereign over Satan's powers of attack against the human race. Although the Almighty will not exempt any of his creatures from temptation — for

3. How did Jesus model greatness in the upper room?
4. Give your personal definition of Christian *greatness*.
5. Using your definition, describe someone you consider an example of Christian greatness.

he will accept only that love and loyalty which are given freely — he will not permit any human to be tested beyond his or her ability to withstand (1 Cor. 10:13; cf. Job 1). Knowing in advance that Peter as well as Judas would fail in the events of the next several hours, Jesus nevertheless prayed not only that the apostle's "faith may not fail" but that he might be able to strengthen his brothers "when you have turned back."

Peter may have been offended by the suggestion that he was susceptible to disloyalty. He protested that his loyalty was without limit, that he would endure not only prison but death for the Lord. Jesus must have looked directly at him with a combination of sternness and compassion when he said, "I tell you, Peter, before the rooster crows today, you will deny three times that you know me."

Day 5
Persecution

Read about persecution suffered by Peter and others in Acts 5:27-42.

1. How had the disciples been received in their previous preaching tour? Why?
2. What would change all this?
3. Comment on Jesus' statement in Matthew 5:10-12.
4. What form does persecution take in your life?
5. What value has come to you through persecution?

d. Announcing a change in their circumstances. 22:35-38.

With Peter silent now, Jesus turned to warn the rest of the group that the situation was about to change for them all. The very atmosphere for their ministry would be vastly different from before.

With very limited resources, the disciples had been sent out earlier to announce the nearness of the kingdom of God (cf. 9:23; 10:4). Due to the hospitality of people among whom they had preached, their needs had been supplied. In the near future, however, that hospitality would become open hostility. They would soon need to provide their own funds, shelter, and protection. After Jesus had fulfilled the messianic prophecy about being "numbered with the transgressors" in his death, the friendly greeting his disciples had received in many quarters for his sake would become persecution because of his name.

Whether purchased by them because of tensions they were already sensing or discovered in the borrowed room they were using, the Twelve told Jesus they had "two swords" at hand. "That is enough," said Jesus — meaning not that two weapons would be sufficient to protect them but that there had been enough conversation for the time. He was speaking of things they could not comprehend, so it was time to cut off the discussion. Things lay ahead for him that night that could wait no longer.

Week Thirty

Luke 22:39-62 (VI C to VI D in Outline)

Day 1
Agony in Prayer

Read Romans 8:18-27 for Paul's description of the struggle believers face.

1. What sense of *struggle* do you experience in your Christian walk?
2. Is there a particular issue or temptation that causes you difficulty?
3. How does prayer contribute to resolving your spiritual struggles?
4. Have you ever experienced a crisis in prayer similar to Christ's in the garden? If so, explain.
5. What is the most agonizing time in prayer you can remember?

C. The Mount of Olives. 22:39-53.

With the comparatively tranquil events of the meal behind him, Jesus went to the Garden of Gethsemane. Luke tells of the intense testing of Jesus that took place there. The inclinations and desires of *flesh* (i.e., all that might oppose God's will) were clearly set over against the *Spirit* (i.e., heaven's holy leading), to use a Pauline figure. We are not to see this event so much as human heroism on Jesus' part as humble submission. "Godet sees this incident as very important, for it differentiates the sacrifice of the freely consenting Jesus from those of animals with no say in the matter. 'At Gethsemane Jesus did not drink the cup; He consented to drink it.' The real battle was fought here." [Morris, *Luke*, p. 311.]

Luke's account of this event is rather brief. It is only from Matthew and Mark, for example, that we learn that the specific site of his prayerful struggle on the Mount of Olives was Gethsemane. Also, Luke records the content of Jesus' thrice-repeated prayer only once. At the same time, however, it should be noted that he alone gives details of the sweat like drops of blood and of an angel's appearance to minister strength to the Savior.

1. His agony in Gethsemane. 22:39-46.

The comment that Jesus went to the Mount of Olives "as usual" likely means that he had spent the night on the sides of that hill on other visits to Jerusalem. This would explain how Judas knew where to find him when he came later with soldiers.

With the disciples in his wake, Jesus declared his

need for a private time in prayer by leaving them at a certain spot and telling them, "Pray that you will not fall into temptation." This is a constant petition that he taught his followers to pray (cf. Luke 11:4b). In the present circumstance, however, he surely had in mind the temptation that would come soon in the face of his own betrayal, trials, and death.

Jesus left his disciples to their own prayers and withdrew to offer his own. Assuming a posture of urgent petition, he "knelt down" and began to plead with his Heavenly Father. He prayed: "Father, if you are willing, take this cup from me." The biblical use of the figure of drinking a cup to signify experiencing wrath is well-documented (Psa. 75:7-8; Isa. 51:17,19, 22; Jer. 25:15-16; Ezek. 23:31-34; Rev. 14:10; 18:6-7). This helps us understand the special intensity of Jesus' agony in this garden prayer. He is not dreading the lash, nails, and physical torment so much as the "cup" (i.e., wrath) which the Father had prepared as the just punishment for sin. Jesus knew that for him to accept the cross was to accept being forsaken by the Father.

In order for Jesus to be our sin-bearer, physical death would not be enough. If physical death is the penalty for sin, each of us can pay his or her own debt. But it is spiritual death (i.e., separation from God, cf. Rev. 20:14) that is required as the just penalty for sin. For Jesus to pay our debt and to experience the wrath due for our sins, he would have to experience not merely the former but the latter as well. And it was this prospect that was so terrifying to him.

His prayers to be spared such a fate became so earnest and anguished that "his sweat was like drops of blood falling to the ground." Attempts have been made by laymen and physicians to explain how someone can "sweat blood" from his pores. Such explanatory contortions are unnecessary, however,

Day 2
Jesus' Agony in Gethsemane

Read Matthew 26:36-46 for a fuller account of what happened in Gethsemane.

1. What was the source of Jesus' agony in Gethsemane?
2. How would you distinguish his agony from cowardice?
3. Was this event a *temptation* to Jesus? Explain.
4. Since Jesus was God in the flesh, why did he need to pray?
5. What place for prayer do you see in the overall experience of Jesus?

for the text does not say that blood came from his body. It simply tells us he sweated so profusely that his perspiration fell off his body as if he were bleeding. The actual shedding of blood did not happen in Gethsemane, but awaited Golgotha.

Despite his anguished and earnest prayers to be spared the fate of being separated from the Father, he qualified his request with these words: "Yet not my will, but yours be done." His Father's will in this matter was not that Jesus endure such terrible and undeserved wrath; his will was that lost humans be given the opportunity to experience repentance and remission of sins (2 Pet. 3:9b). It was simply that the goal of providing salvation could not be attained apart from the offering of an unblemished sacrifice (cf. Heb. 10:4-10). God never wills unjustified suffering to one of his creatures, and suffering occurs in this universe only for the sake of the larger good that is possible by having the natural and spiritual worlds operate by their present methods.

How intense was Jesus' struggle here? It was great enough that he needed the ministry of an angel to "strengthen" him. God never leaves his children without the resources they will need to face pain, opposition, or temptation. By whatever means necessary, he ministers strength to them that will enable them to stand up under their ordeals. What he did here for his beloved Son, Jesus, he continues to do for his sons and daughters struggling in this world.

With his dramatic prayers ended and with his resolve to face the cross settled, he returned to the disciples. He found them "asleep, exhausted from sorrow." They had been so worn down by the series of events that night that they were physically unable to take more. So they slept. When he awakened them, he repeated his earlier instruction to "pray so that you will not fall into temptation." As trying as the night had been for all of them to this point,

Jesus knew that things would quickly escalate and get still worse.

2. His betrayal and arrest. 22:47-53.

As Jesus was "still speaking" his words of admonition to the disciples, Judas appeared with a "crowd" of people. The people the betrayer had with him likely included soldiers from both the temple police and the Roman contingent keeping the peace in Jerusalem during Passover. Leading them to Jesus, Judas approached him to single him out for the soldiers by kissing him. Although such a kiss as a proper form of greeting was proper to its time and place, this one was evil. A sign of goodwill and respect was reduced to an act of betrayal. Thus Jesus asked, "Judas, are you betraying the Son of Man with a kiss?"

Some of the disciples offered to defend Jesus with the swords they had (v. 38). Such methods would not only have been futile against the crowd with Judas, they would also have been inappropriate to the events unfolding. But before Jesus could speak to forbid fighting, one of the disciples swung a wild blow with his sword and "struck the servant of the high priest, cutting off his right ear." Unnamed by Luke, John 18:10 informs us that it was Peter who struck the blow. Jesus immediately spoke to the situation by word and deed. By word, he told his followers, "No more of this!" and put an end to the swordplay. By deed, he reached out to the high priest's wounded servant and "touched the man's ear and healed him."

One wonders how many of the people in Judas's mob saw the quick scuffle and Jesus' resolution of it. Assuming that only Jesus and the man healed knew exactly what had happened, one then wonders how much heart the servant of the high priest had for the rest of the night's developments.

Turning to address the mob — and, in particular,

Day 3
Betrayal

Read Psalm 59 about opposition by traitors.

1. Why did Judas turn against Jesus?
2. Have you ever known someone who turned against Christ? If so, did you know why it happened?
3. Is it possible for a child of God to fall and be lost? Explain your answer.
4. If you were ever to betray Christ, what would be the source of your temptation?
5. Was Judas's situation hopeless after his act of betrayal? Explain.

Day 4
Submitting to Evil

Read Psalm 26 for another man's account of having to confront evildoers.

1. Could Jesus have rescued himself from Judas's act of betrayal? Explain.
2. If he could have escaped, why did Jesus submit to evil here?
3. Why did Paul refuse to submit to evil in Acts 22:23ff?
4. What guidelines help a Christian decide between *accepting* and *resisting* evil at the hands of another?

the "chief priests, the officers of the temple guard, and the elders" leading it — Jesus registered his contempt for their method as well as their intent. "Am I leading a rebellion, that you have come with swords and clubs? Every day I was with you in the temple courts, and you did not lay a hand on me. But this is your hour — when darkness reigns." Their cowardice about arresting him has already been explained by Luke. They were afraid of the masses who regarded Jesus as a genuine prophet. Yet there they were, acting under the cover of darkness to arrest Jesus. Indeed, "darkness reigns" was Jesus' comment not about the night but the spirits of his enemies.

D. Peter's Three Denials. 22:54-62.

With Jesus in the hands of his opponents, his disciples must have been frightened by the awareness that they could easily share in his fate. Thus they scattered, with some of them hanging around the edge of the unfolding events of the night to see what would happen to their leader.

A rapid series of hearings — not all of them official and perhaps some of them even illegal — takes place. First, Jesus goes before the former high priest, Annas, for an unofficial hearing (cf. John 18:12-14). This may have been nothing more than a courtesy to the old man by his successor and son-in-law, Caiaphas [Kī´-ə-fəs], as the latter set things in motion to assemble members of the Sanhedrin. Second, a night hearing takes place before Caiaphas and some members of the Sanhedrin. This is the first trial in Luke's series, for he makes no reference to the hearing before Annas. Third, a second hearing before the Sanhedrin takes place after daybreak. This appears to have been a fuller convening of the great court than in the night — perhaps a quorum to rubber stamp what Caiaphas and his hand-picked cronies had done under cover of darkness. Fourth, Jesus is delivered

Day 5
Denial

Read another account of Peter's denial at Mark 14:66-72.

1. Why did Peter deny being Jesus' disciple?
2. Have you ever known someone who acted similarly?
3. Did Peter do something less serious than Judas? Explain.
4. Why did Peter and Judas come to such different ends?
5. What significance do you attach to Jesus' post-resurrection experience with Peter as recorded at John 21:15ff?

to Pilate by the Jewish leaders. Fifth, Pilate sends Jesus to Herod. And, sixth, the final trial before Pilate brings about a death sentence for the Son of Man.

When Jesus was taken to the house of Caiaphas, Peter was following "at a distance" and sought out a fire in the courtyard as the night became cold. There a servant girl recognized him and said, "This man was with him." A short time later, someone else noticed and confronted him by saying, "You also are one of them." Then, about an hour later, still a third person said, "Certainly this fellow was with him, for he is a Galilean." All three times, Peter denied knowing Christ — becoming more vehement each time.

As Peter was making his third denial, two things happened: a rooster crowed and Jesus caught his eye. Peter not only remembered the prediction Jesus had made about his denials (22:34) but surely also sensed the eyes of Jesus peering into his very soul. Shaken by his deeds, Peter "went outside and wept bitterly." His tears of regret helped pave the way to his postresurrection meeting with Jesus, his reception of Jesus' gracious forgiveness, and his recommissioning to the work of an apostle.

Week Thirty-One

Luke 22:63–23:25 (VI E in Outline)

Day 1
Injustice

Read Amos 5:7-17 to find Yahweh's attitude toward social and civil injustice.

1. How was Jesus treated by his soldier-guards?
2. What feelings are stirred within you by this report of their treatment of the Son of God?
3. Where do you see injustice in the world of your time and place?
4. What feelings do you have about injustice in your own time? Is there anything you can do to address the problem?
5. Why does any culture tolerate injustices such as racism, corrupt officials, and the like?

E. The "Trials" of Jesus. 22:63–23:25.

Prisoners are sometimes abused and mistreated. This likely happened much more often in ancient cultures than in modern ones. The treatment Jesus received at the hands of the soldiers put in charge of him is something of a case study in how such abuse happens. But their approach to the Son of God was little different from that of the officials — both Jewish and Roman — who put him through a series of trials riddled with injustice.

Caiaphas, for example, had earlier joined in a conspiracy to see Jesus dead (John 11:49-53). Ironically, he had justified the plot to kill Jesus by arguing that the Nazarene preacher could bring down the wrath of Rome on Jewish rule of their homeland. He said, "You do not realize that it is better for you that one man die for the people than that the whole nation perish." He was prophetic without realizing it in this statement, and John points out as much in his account of what the high priest said.

Things got no better when Jesus was removed from the Great Sanhedrin to the hands of Pilate, Rome's procurator for Judea. Pilate was concerned only with his own position and career. He caved in quickly to the mob's demand for blood by giving Jesus over to an execution squad.

1. Before the Jewish rulers. 22:63-71.

The soldiers who were in charge of Jesus "began mocking and beating him." Bored by all that was happening and aware that Jesus was regarded as a prophet by many, they decided to have fun at his expense. Thus they put a blindfold over his eyes, took turns hitting him, and demanded, "Prophesy! Who hit you?" This must have gone on for a considerable time, for Luke says the soldiers "said many other insulting things to him."

Sometime during the night, Caiaphas had presided over a preliminary hearing whose concern was anything but the truth. He was merely trying to get a precise charge against Jesus that would hold before the full Jewish court. It was during this hearing that Peter was spotted in the courtyard and denied Jesus three times. The charge that had come out of that hearing was blasphemy. When witnesses could not give consistent testimony, Caiaphas had taken matters in hand personally and asked Jesus, "Are you the Christ, the Son of the Blessed One?" Jesus replied by saying, "I am." It was at this point that he tore his clothes (i.e., a ritual sign of disgust) and told his peers, "Why do we need any more witnesses? You have heard him speak blasphemy. What do you think?" (Mark 14:53-65).

The Great Sanhedrin was the highest Jewish tribunal. It was the court of final appeal for settling all matters related to the Law of Moses and the traditions of the elders. With seventy members, it was presided over by the high priest whenever it was in session. It had wide-ranging powers under Roman authority, and only capital cases required ratification of its sentences imposed on offenders. Caiaphas, high priest during the years A.D. 18-36 not only presided over the trial of Jesus but also was in power during the early persecutions of Christians recorded in the early chapters of Acts.

The Mishnah is a collection of Jewish laws transmitted orally until sometime in the second Christian century. One of its tractates, Sanhedrin, deals with the rules and procedures for the great court. If these

Day 2
Caiaphas

Read Hosea 4:1-9 for a prophet's view of corrupt priests in Israel.

1. What do you know of the history and character of Caiaphas?

2. Was Caiaphas's treatment of Jesus consistent with his general character? Or did he act "out of character" in this setting?

3. What unwitting prophecy did Caiaphas make about Jesus?

4. What admission did he get from Jesus before the Jewish court?

5. Under what charge did the Sanhedrin condemn Jesus to death? Explain.

rules were in effect in Jesus' time, for example, his trial was a miscarriage of Jewish justice in a variety of ways. Trials could not be held at night, verdicts could not be rendered on the same day as the trial, and sentences could not be imposed on the same day they were given. Perhaps the first of these points is at issue in that the court assembled "at daybreak" to ratify what had happened in the nighttime hearing.

When Jesus was brought before the court, he was presented with this ultimatum: "If you are the Christ, tell us." They must have regarded his answer as enigmatic, if not unresponsive. He said they would not believe his answer, but he added that the "Son of Man" would henceforth be seated "at the right hand of the mighty God." Without seeking clarification of his meaning, the court pressed still harder and asked, "Are you then the Son of God?" The affirmative answer Jesus gave this question sealed his fate with the Sanhedrin: "You are right in saying I am."

Before the Jewish court, Jesus was guilty of blasphemy and deserved to die. But a death sentence had to be ratified by the Romans, and the Sanhedrin proceedings had to give way to Pilate's authority.

Day 3
Pontius Pilate

Read more details of Pilate's handling of Jesus from John 19:1-16.

1. Why was it necessary for the Sanhedrin to submit Jesus' case to Pilate?
2. What correct insights did Pilate have into this case?
3. Pilate knew Jesus was innocent of any offense justifying the death penalty. Why did he

2. Before the civil rulers. 23:1-25.

Still early on Friday morning, Jesus was moved to Pilate's court. Modern excavations at the Castle of Antonia beside the Jerusalem temple appear to have identified the place where this trial would have taken place — only a few minutes from the site of his hearing before Caiaphas.

When the religious leaders turned Jesus over to the civil authorities, they made three charges against him: subverting the nation, opposing the payment of taxes to Caesar, and claiming to be "Christ, a king." The first charge was vague at best, the second was flatly false (cf. Luke 20:20-26), and the third was ambiguous. It turned out that the third charge —

involving the claim to kingship — would become the basis of a civil charge against Jesus. It would be made to sound like Jesus was leading a band of revolutionaries wanting to free the Jews from Roman political dominance.

Even so, Pilate was not inclined to take the matter seriously. In Luke's abbreviated account of his conversation with Jesus on this point, Pilate asked, "Are you the king of the Jews?" Jesus responded affirmatively. In John's more extensive report of this exchange, it is clear that Jesus told Pilate that his "kingship" was no threat to Caesar. "My kingdom is not of this world," said Jesus. "If it were, my servants would fight to prevent my arrest by the Jews. But now my kingdom is from another place" (John 18:36). This statement almost invites Pilate to check with his soldiers who were there at his arrest in Gethsemane about his refusal to summon his disciples to fight. Indeed, Pilate may have already checked the soldiers' reports to find out what had happened.

At any rate, Pilate was unconcerned enough about any potential threat from Jesus that he said, "I find no basis for a charge against this man." Enraged Jewish officials protested and said that the Galilean's teachings had stirred up trouble throughout the Jewish homeland. At the mention of Galilee as the point of origin for Jesus' work, Pilate seized on what he apparently hoped would be an out for himself. Since Galilee was under the jurisdiction of Herod Antipas who was then in Jerusalem for the feast, Pilate decided to shuffle Jesus over to him. If Antipas disposed of the case, the procurator could be done with the matter.

Herod Antipas was the Herod who had beheaded John the Baptist. One writer describes him as a "playboy prince" who would have had little concern to dispense justice in any setting; he was more inter-

sentence him to death?

4. How did Pilate display his general antisemitism in handling Jesus' death? Cf. John 19:19-22.

5. What do you discern about the character of this man from his handling of this situation?

Day 4
Herod Antipas

Read Mark 6:14-28 for an earlier episode from the life of Antipas.

1. Why did Pilate send Jesus to Herod Antipas?
2. What interest did Antipas have in Jesus? What did he hope to see?
3. What action did he and his court take toward Jesus?
4. Jesus once called Antipas "that fox" (Luke 13:32). In light of this episode, why do you think he chose that description?
5. How was Jesus' response to Herod different from that he gave Caiaphas and Pilate? How do you explain the difference?

ested in amusement and indulgence. It was this spirit that he exhibited in dealing with Jesus. Though he had never seen Jesus before, he had "heard about him" and was hoping "to see him perform some miracle." It was just possible that Jesus could have saved his life by performing what Herod would have considered an amusing trick. The Son of Man had no interest in jumping through hoops for Herod and his court. The only thing he gave the Galilean ruler was dignified silence.

Unable to get Jesus to amuse him and his friends, Herod provided his own entertainment. "Then Herod and his soldiers ridiculed and mocked him. Dressing him in an elegant robe, they sent him back to Pilate." The humiliation that had started at the hands of the temple soldiers (22:63-64) was escalated. With neither the interest nor competence to deal with Jesus, Antipas sent him back to Pilate. The final jab at his prisoner was to dress him in an "elegant robe" — probably a discarded royal garment that mocked the notion of Jesus as a king.

In closing his brief account of the hearing before Herod Antipas, Luke tells his readers that Pilate's action in sending Jesus to Herod somehow healed an old quarrel between the two men. Unless Luke 13:1 provides a clue to the tension between them, we have no idea what it was. Apparently Pilate's "respect" for Herod in offering him jurisdiction over this case cemented their friendship. The early Christians held both rulers responsible for the murder of their leader. "Indeed Herod and Pontius Pilate met together with the Gentiles and the people of Israel in this city to conspire against your holy servant Jesus, whom you anointed" (Acts 4:27).

With the case now back in his lap for a final disposition, Pilate reminded the mob that his earlier inquiry "found no basis for your charges against him." He added that Herod likewise had found no basis for a capital charge against Jesus. Trying to find a way out of his dilemma, he proposed punishing Jesus as a warning against causing any more trouble among his own people. His proposal only made the now-bloodthirsty mob more agitated.

His next thought was to grant his annual Passover favor of releasing a prisoner, so he gave the crowd a choice between Jesus and Barabbas. On the assumption that Pilate really was trying to find a way to release Jesus, he could not have offered a more impossible choice to the mob. Barabbas was a hero to the Jews because he had participated in an "insurrection" against the Romans. For all we know, the person he had killed could have been a Roman soldier. Although such a character might have been despicable to Pilate, he would have been admired by the Jews of Jerusalem. So the cries went up for the release of Barabbas.

Saying once again that he found "no grounds for the death penalty" in Jesus' case, Pilate repeated his earlier idea of beating and releasing Jesus. But the people would have nothing of it and "demanded that he be crucified, and their shouts prevailed." One weak Roman official against a howling mob was no contest. Although he had no obligation to grant their request to crucify Jesus, he caved in to the pressure of the situation and "surrendered Jesus to their will."

A modern Christian reader should not miss the ironic ending of this pathetic trial before Pilate. It hints of the larger significance of Jesus' substitutionary atonement in that a man guilty of murder and who deserved the death penalty under law was released and the innocent man bore the penalty he deserved. As we are reminded that he died in our place, we fall in love with Jesus again.

Day 5
Death for Another

Read Mark 15:1-15 for a second account of the release of Barabbas.

1. How did Barabbas enter the series of events surrounding the death of Jesus?
2. Why was Barabbas in prison? What sentence did his crimes carry?
3. If Pilate was making a halfhearted attempt to set Jesus free, why was his offer of Barabbas a strategic mistake?
4. How does this episode exemplify the nature of a substitutionary atonement?
5. How do you see the death of Jesus in relation to your own situation? Explain.

Week Thirty-Two

Luke 23:26-56 (VI F and VI G in Outline)

Day 1
Crucifixion

Read John 19:16-27 for another account of the crucifixion of Jesus.

1. What do you know about the details of crucifixion as a form of execution?
2. Why do the Gospel writers not dwell on the physical details of the event? What was their focus?
3. Why did Jesus refuse the analgesic offered him?
4. What sort of mockery was associated with Jesus' crucifixion?
5. What effect does this scene have on you?

F. The crucifixion. 23:26-49.

The Romans did not invent crucifixion as a form of capital punishment. We know it from at least the time of the Persians. Rome did, however, bring this cruel form of execution to its ultimate form. It brought about a slow death, with a maximum of suffering. Crucifixion also humiliated those subjected to its physical torment by stripping victims naked and exposing their death contortions to public view. Although some think the Romans would have allowed Jewish victims a loincloth as a concession to their feelings about nudity, there is no certainty of this. They not only punished criminals by this death form but warned onlookers of the risk they embraced in breaking its laws. Because it was such a horrible form of death, Roman citizens were exempt from it except under the most unusual of circumstances (e.g., treason, desertion by soldiers, etc.).

With an unjust sentence of death having been handed down by Pilate, there were no options left for Jesus. Unlike Paul, a Roman citizen who could appeal his sentence to Caesar (Acts 25:12), he would die. Beyond these purely legal factors, it was for this hour that Jesus had come into the world from the beginning.

1. Events on the way to Golgotha. 23:26-32.

It was customary for one about to be crucified to carry his cross from the scourging post to his crucifixion site. Because the gross weight of the total cross probably exceeded 300 pounds, it was only the crossbar — weighing probably around 100 pounds —

that the victim had to carry or drag. Placed across the nape of a man's neck and tied to his outstretched arms by ropes, it was his duty to follow a lead soldier who carried a sign bearing the condemned man's name and crime.

Although Jesus left Pilate's presence carrying his cross in the customary fashion (John 19:17), he was unable to bear it all the way to his execution site. Exhausted from the events of a sleepless night and weakened by the beating given him by the Roman soldiers, he fell under its weight. Consistent with their rights in an occupied land (cf. Matt. 5:41), the soldiers in charge of Jesus randomly chose an innocent passerby to pick up and carry the crossbeam. The man chosen was "Simon from Cyrene." Because another Gospel refers to his family (Mark 15:21; cf. Rom. 16:13), some speculate that Simon became a disciple as a result of his encounter on this critical day.

Although his own disciples were now scattered and a mob of his opponents had bullied Pilate into condemning him to death, Jesus was not without friends in Jerusalem. Along the route he was forced to take, there were many citizens of the city who lamented the fate of this pious and loving man. Consistent with one of the unique features of this Gospel, Luke singled out some "women who mourned and wailed for him" as Jesus moved toward his execution. "Our Lord turned to these women with a message of sympathy and told them that they were not to weep for him but for themselves and their children. He was not rebuking them for their compassion; he rather meant to indicate that while his sufferings were pitiful, their own were more worthy of tears, for they were to be even more intense. He had in mind the destruction of the city due to its impenitence and made certain by its rejection of the Redeemer. Jesus declared that the days would come when childlessness would be a ground

Day 2
The Fate of Jerusalem
Read Matthew 24:15-35 for a prediction of Jerusalem's fate.

1. What circumstance called forth Jesus' comments about the future of Jerusalem?
2. What do you understand his statement about the "green" and "dry" trees to mean?
3. Why was Jerusalem to experience such a terrible fate?
4. What other cities in the Bible were punished because of their rebellion against God's holy purposes?
5. What does this episode tell you about God's sovereignty in human affairs?

217

for congratulation because of the universal distress. He predicted that the horror would be so great that men would call upon the mountains to fall on them and the hills to cover them, preferring such forms of death to the torments which threatened from the armies of Rome." [Erdman, *Luke*, p. 242.]

The final thing Jesus said to the women is in the form of a parable or enigmatic saying: "For if men do these things when the tree is green, what will happen when it is dry?" His meaning was probably something akin to the following: If the Romans do something this horrible to someone they admit is innocent (i.e., Jesus, the "green tree" who is filled with the life of God), you should certainly fear what they will do to people who are guilty (i.e., Israel, the "dry tree" that has no good fruit).

In addition to Jesus that day, "two other men, both criminals, were also led out with him to be executed." From Matthew 27:38, we learn that their specific offense had been theft.

Day 3
"Father, Forgive Them"

Read Acts 7:39-60 to find a disciple who appears to have been deeply moved by this prayer.

1. What does Jesus' prayer for his tormentors say about his state of mind during the crucifixion?
2. What had Jesus taught about loving one's enemies? How does this exemplify his teaching?
3. What did the people's *ignorance* have to do with the possibility of their forgiveness?
4. Is there such a thing as

2. Events at Golgotha. 23:33-49.

a. Crucifixion and mockery. 23:33-38.

Jesus was crucified at 9 a.m. (cf. Mark 15:25) between the two thieves at a site known as "The Skull." The Greek word is *kranion*, and this term becomes in Latin *calvaria*; it is from the latter that the King James renders "Calvary" at this verse. Its Aramaic name from Jesus' time was Golgotha (Mark 15:22). It is commonly held that the place was called The Skull because of the skull-like shape of the hill. Used for crucifixions, the resemblance would have needed to be only slight to bring about such a name.

It was customary to give someone about to be crucified a bitter potion of wine mixed with myrrh (or "gall") which would serve as a mild analgesic. When offered it, Jesus refused (Matt. 27:34). He would experience the cross to the fullest and be in possession of his senses for the seven statements he made from it — three of which are cited by Luke. Crucifixion proper would have proceeded with the victim's arms being nailed to the crossbar at his wrists. He would have then been lifted onto the upright pole already in place. A sharp protrusion that looked much like a rhinoceros horn would have been between his legs. With his legs flexed upwards slightly, his feet would have been nailed to the upright post. The only movement a crucified man could make to relieve the pressure on either his wrists or genitals would be to lift the full weight of his body by pressing up against the nails in his feet.

"Father, forgive them, for they do not know what they are doing," said Jesus. This statement is unique to Luke and reveals that Jesus was compassionate toward sinners to the end. The ignorance Jesus pleaded for his tormentors meant neither that they had not committed a sin nor that they would not be held accountable for what they were doing. It meant that their offense was pardonable, if they chose later to seek forgiveness (cf. 1 Tim. 1:13). Pentecost and the subsequent preaching of the gospel of repentance and remission of sins in Acts constitute the answer to this prayer.

Roman execution squads were given whatever clothing or other belongings the condemned persons brought to their last moments. As was likely their custom, the men in charge of Jesus' crucifixion "divided up his clothes by casting lots."

Meanwhile a cruel mockery was going on near Jesus. The Jewish rulers "sneered" at him and taunted him by saying, "He saved others; let him save himself if he is the Christ of God, the Chosen One." They neither knew nor cared that such a demonstration of his power — which was well within the limits of possibility for him — would have defeated his purpose in coming into the world. He would not accept

an "unpardonable sin"? If so, what is it?

5. Under what circumstances did these people receive forgiveness? Explain.

Day 4
Two Robbers

Read Matthew 27:32-44 and notice what is said about the two criminals.

1. Both robbers initially mocked Jesus. Why? Why did one stop?

219

2. What did the penitent thief ask of Jesus? What was his meaning?
3. How did Jesus respond? What does this tell you about salvation?
4. What is "paradise"? What becomes of people between death and resurrection?
5. How do the two thieves symbolize all humanity?

their challenge, but it would be for different reasons than they would have supposed. With the taunting already under way, the soldiers joined in and mocked his claim to be "King of the Jews," a title Pilate had included in the statement written above Jesus' head that gave the reason for his execution.

b. The penitent thief. 23:39-43.

The two criminals crucified with Jesus wound up demonstrating the two possible positions that all others take toward him. Although both were guilty and under sentence of death, only one expressed repentance and faith in Jesus. Although both initially chided Jesus over his fate (Matt. 27:44), one eventually rebuked the other and said, "Don't you fear God? . . . We are punished justly, for we are getting what our deeds deserve. But this man has done nothing wrong." Perhaps it was Jesus' reaction to what was happening to him that touched the criminal's heart. Jesus had prayed for his murderers to be forgiven. He had not cursed his tormentors. Surely this man was who he claimed to be! Finally, then, the robber turned to the man on the center cross and said, "Jesus, remember me when you come into your kingdom." The response he received was an assurance of salvation: "I tell you the truth, today you will be with me in paradise." The other brigand apparently died impenitent and unbelieving.

c. The death scene. 23:44-49.

Day 5
Forsaken by God

Read 2 Corinthians 5:11-21 for Paul's teaching about reconciliation.

1. Was Jesus really "forsaken" by God while on the cross? Explain.
2. What was required to pay humanity's sin debt: *physical* or *spiritual* death?

The death scene of the Son of God was made all the more dramatic by a great "darkness" that began at noon and continued until 3 p.m. Furthermore, "the curtain of the temple was torn in two" — symbolizing the opening of access to God's favor that was being created by his death (Heb. 9:3,8; 10:19-20). Then, approximately six hours after being nailed to his cross, Jesus cried, "Father, into your hands I commit my spirit." With those words, his physical life ended.

The more important truth of the cross event is that there Jesus experienced his fullest identification with humanity as our sin-bearer and was made sin for us (2 Cor. 5:21). This explains his cry, "My God, my God, why have you forsaken me?" (Matt. 27:46). In his holiness, God cannot have fellowship with sin. He must withdraw and detach from it. Thus the Father and Holy Spirit were required by their very holiness to withdraw from the perfect and beloved Son of God that day. Now we know what Jesus was dreading in his Gethsemane struggles. He did indeed drink the undiluted cup of divine wrath for our sakes in his death on Golgotha.

His ordeal over, the centurion in charge of the proceedings "praised God" by acknowledging that he had seen a righteous man suffer that day. Many others who had come out to see what was happening were also touched by what they saw. They returned home in heaviness (i.e., "they beat their breasts") to ponder the meaning of what they had witnessed.

G. The Burial. 23:50-56.

With Jesus' death verified by the execution squad (John 19:34), "Joseph, a member of the [Sanhedrin] Council, a good and upright man, who had not consented to their decision and action" stepped forward and requested permission from Pilate to bury the corpse. This believer who had kept his views about the Messiah to himself (cf. John 12:42) had been emboldened by what had happened. He dared to go public, with whatever risks that might have for his future rule as a leader of Israel. Joined by his friend Nicodemus (John 19:39; cf. 3:1ff), he removed the body from the cross, wrapped it in a linen cloth, and placed it in his own new rock-hewn tomb. Since Jesus had died around 3 p.m. and since the sabbath would begin at sundown, there was no time to be leisurely about the burial.

What is the significance of your answer?
3. Is it correct to say that Jesus "tasted hell for us" on the cross? Explain.
4. Relate this moment to Jesus' agony in Gethsemane. What did he dread most about his death?
5. Explain 2 Corinthians 5:21 in light of what happened on the cross.

"The women who had come with Jesus from Galilee" watched Joseph and Nicodemus closely. They carefully marked the tomb's location in their minds and made plans to return after the sabbath to add their own "spices and perfumes" to the burial provisions the two men had made. What a surprise lay ahead for them on Sunday morning!

Week Thirty-Three

Luke 24:1-12 (VI H 1 in Outline)

H. The Resurrection and Appearances. 24:1-49.

The bodily resurrection of Jesus of Nazareth from the dead is the capstone doctrine of the Christian faith. Everything else stands or falls with this. Paul put it this way in his correspondence with the church at Corinth: "If Christ has not been raised, our preaching is useless and so is your faith. More than that, we are then found to be false witnesses about God, for we have testified about God that he raised Christ from the dead. And if Christ has not been raised, your faith is futile; you are still in your sins. Then those also who have fallen asleep in Christ are lost. If only for this life we have hope in Christ, we are to be pitied more than all men" (1 Cor. 15:14-15a,17-19).

When Jesus was pronounced dead Friday afternoon, his body had been put in a nearby tomb that belonged to Joseph of Arimathea. Joseph and Nicodemus had quickly washed the corpse, patted it down with some of the 75 pounds of spices Nicodemus had brought, and wrapped it mummy-style in linen strips with more of the spices sprinkled throughout the wrappings. Custom would have called for the head to be wrapped separately, with the initial strips of linen being carried around the chin to hold the deceased's mouth closed (cf. John 11:44).

Shortly after the burial was complete, some of the Sanhedrin went to Pilate and requested that a guard be placed at the tomb. They had recalled a report that Jesus had predicted that he would rise from the dead after three days. Pilate granted their request

Day 1
The Critical Doctrine

Read 1 Corinthians 15:12-28 to see why the resurrection of Christ is such a critical doctrine.

1. Why is Jesus' resurrection so critical? Why was his crucifixion not enough by itself?
2. Do you think Christianity would have "gotten off the ground" without the doctrine of Christ's resurrection? Explain.
3. What things did Paul say depended on the truthfulness of this doctrine?
4. If you could not believe in Jesus' bodily resurrection, what would that do to your ability to embrace the demands of Christian discipleship?
5. What do you believe about the resurrection of your own body?

and posted soldiers at the scene. "So they went and made the tomb secure by putting a seal on the stone and posting the guard" (Matt. 27:62-66).

The godly women who had stayed close to Jesus through the ordeal of his crucifixion and who followed to see where he had been interred had made plans from late Friday afternoon, through the sabbath, and into Sunday morning to add their own loving touches to their Master's corpse. Luke eventually identifies these women as Mary Magdalene, Joanna, Mary the mother of James, and certain "other women" (v. 10; note: the only additional person we can identify with certainty is Salome, cf. Mark 16:1). They prepared spices and perfumes of their own. Since the sabbath had not ended until sundown Saturday, they had been forced to delay until sunrise Sunday morning to make their way to the tomb.

Day 2
Sunday Morning

Read Mark 16:1-14 for another account of Easter Sunday.

1. Who took care of Jesus' corpse Friday afternoon? What sort of burial had he received?

2. What plans had been made by a group of Jesus' female disciples? What did they find at the tomb Sunday morning?

3. Did the women go to the tomb expecting to find it empty? Explain how this strengthens their testimony.

4. What reaction did the women get when they reported an empty tomb?

1. The empty tomb. 24:1-12.

As the women walked toward the tomb "very early in the morning" on that Sunday, a variety of concerns must have gone through their minds. If they knew of the guard, would the soldiers permit their intended deed? Could they move the heavy stone at the mouth of the tomb? What would happen to them if they were found tampering with the burial site? This much is certain: they did not go to the tomb expecting to find it empty!

Arriving at the site, the women were shocked that they "found the stone rolled away from the tomb." Summoning the courage to investigate, they actually "entered" the burial chamber but "did not find the body of the Lord Jesus." What they saw left them "wondering about this" and trying to figure out what had happened. "The following point cannot be stressed too strongly: these women did not go believing in resurrection. They did not go to check and see if the tomb was empty. The fact that they took spices along to anoint the decaying body shows what they expected to find, and this despite six predictions in Luke. So the first people who had to be convinced of the resurrection were the disciples themselves. They may have belonged to the era of the ancients, but they did not think as a matter of course that resurrection would occur. In a real sense they were the first skeptics to become convinced that Jesus was raised!" [Bock, *Luke*, p. 380.]

While they were sorting out their thoughts, "suddenly two men in clothes that gleamed like lightning stood beside them." Although Luke does not call these two men angels, there can be no doubt that his description identifies them as such. The women were naturally frightened and "bowed down with their faces to the ground." The message from the angels was in the form of a gentle rebuke: "Why do you look for the living among the dead? He is not here; he has risen!"

They reminded the women that Jesus had spoken of his betrayal, death, and resurrection during his Galilean ministry (cf. 9:22; 18:32-33). If modern readers tend to be shocked that the women appear not to have understood this prediction, we should remind ourselves that all the disciples were equally unwilling to hear him talk about his death. In Matthew's parallel account of the Luke 9:22 prediction, for example, Peter responds with particular vehemence to the idea of his Lord's death. "Perish the thought, Lord! This shall never happen to you!" he said. As with so many after-the-fact understandings that come to human beings, it was only after the angels had reminded them of Jesus' predictions that the women "remembered his words."

The women then did a natural and appropriate thing. They sought out the eleven remaining men who had been chosen to be Christ's apostles and reported what they had experienced. Further proof

Day 3
Women and Angels

Read more about the angels and women from Matthew 28:1-7.

1. When did the women see the angels? What was their reaction?
2. What message did the angels give them?
3. From Hebrews 1:14, what is the primary role of angels? How were they filling that role here?
4. Why did the angels leave the message to the women? Why did they not appear to the apostles?
5. What do angels do today on behalf of God's people? How does their work relate to human responsibility?

Day 4
A Predicted Event

Read Luke 9:18-27 for a prediction by Jesus of his death and resurrection.

1. Jesus spoke of his death and resurrection several times in advance. Why were his disciples caught off guard?
2. Knowing they were not hearing and understanding him, why did Jesus continue to speak of these events in advance?
3. Of what value were his predictions after the fact? Explain Luke 24:8.
4. Have you ever realized later that you had been told something that you had refused to hear? Seen a biblical truth that you had refused earlier?
5. What can we do to guard ourselves against prejudiced readings of Scripture?

that the earliest disciples were not credulously eager to foist off a claim of resurrection is evident in their response to the report. "But they did not believe the women, because their words seemed to them like nonsense." The word translated "nonsense" (Gk, *leros*) is found in nonbiblical texts and points to the sort of babbling that people sometimes do when they are in intense pain or emotional distress.

To his credit, Peter "got up and ran to the tomb" — along with John (cf. John 20:3ff) — to investigate for himself. He crouched down and looked into the tomb. Apparently the angels who had spoken to the women earlier were no longer present. He did see "the strips of linen lying by themselves"; that is, he saw the empty grave clothes in which Jesus had been buried. My curious mind cannot resist wishing that he had had a camera with him! What I would give to see the sight of those empty burial wrappings!

The fourth Gospel gives this more detailed description of the sight from the second eyewitness who was present then: "He saw the strips of linen lying there, as well as the burial cloth that had been around Jesus' head. The cloth was folded up by itself, separate from the linen" (John 20:6b-7). Scholars continue to debate the sight described with these words. Did the two men look in and see what we would describe as a body cast, with linen, water, and spices having combined to create a rigid shell for the body that had miraculously passed through both it and the rock walls of his borrowed tomb? Did they see carefully removed linen strips which had been neatly folded before the risen Christ departed his temporary tomb? No definite answer can be given to our questions.

What is certain from the description of the tomb contents is that it is not the scene of a plundered and desecrated burial site. There is no trace of someone having broken in and stolen away the body. The condition of the grave clothes alone — whether as a turtle's empty shell or a housekeeper's neatly folded laundry — speaks of a deliberate and unhurried departure. Believers across the centuries have proclaimed what the reluctant earliest disciples gradually came to believe: *God raised up Jesus Christ from the dead, and he is alive forever!*

What other explanation fits the facts? Some unbelievers dismiss the New Testament accounts by saying that the confused women simply went to the wrong tomb on Sunday morning and mistakenly spread the word of an empty tomb. With all that followed on such a claim, it would have been easy enough for the Jewish or Roman officials to quiet it. They would have needed only to take people to the sealed tomb that the soldiers had guarded and whose location was different from the one the distraught women had mistakenly identified as having held the body of Jesus.

Another attempt at setting aside the resurrection claim is the so-called "swoon theory." It holds that Jesus only became comatose on the cross, was buried quickly in a cool tomb, and revived. A recent variant of this is Schonfield's theory of a "Passover plot" in which Jesus receives a soporific drug while on the cross that put him in a deathlike trance; Joseph and others in on the scheme hurriedly removed him from the cross and resuscitated him. Can anyone be so gullible as to think that a squad of professional executioners could not ascertain the certain death of Jesus before releasing his body? Was the upward thrust of a Roman javelin into his side insufficient to prompt a pain response that would show some flicker of life still remaining in his body? Would a "sudden flow of blood and water" (John 19:34) — blood cells already separating out from its plasma — that resulted from the spear blow come from the body of someone still alive?

Day 5
Other Explanations of the Resurrection

Read the soldiers' account of the empty tomb at Matthew 28:11-15.

1. What do you make of the soldiers' explanation for the empty tomb?
2. What is the so-called "swoon theory"? Evaluate it.
3. What unbelieving accounts have you heard to account for the claim of Jesus' bodily resurrection? How do you respond?
4. How did Peter argue the case for Jesus' resurrection on Pentecost Day of Acts 2?
5. How would you make a case for the resurrection as historical fact? If one believes this, how should she live?

Perhaps the most absurd explanation of all is the one offered by the Roman and Jewish hierarchy in Jerusalem when the first reports of the empty tomb began to circulate. They bribed the soldiers who had been posted to guard the tomb to say that Jesus' disciples came and stole the body while they were asleep (Matt. 28:12-14). Men who admit to being asleep cannot give credible testimony in anyone's court as to what happened during their sleep! Furthermore, if they had allowed the body to be stolen from them — whether awake or asleep — they would have been deserving of death for their dereliction of duty. After all, does anyone really believe that a group of disspirited men who did not even understand — much less believe — the prediction Jesus had made about his resurrection overpowered a group of Roman soldiers?

But maybe the Romans and/or Jews moved the body to another location to protect it from the disciples' attempts to retrieve it. Then all they would have had to do to stop nascent Christianity dead in its tracks was to produce the corpse of Jesus they were keeping in protective custody. Their failure to do so proves that this was not the fate of the body.

The empty tomb on Sunday morning was neither a cool couch, frantic emergency room, nor plundered grave site. It was an elegant and powerful evidence of the truth that would be proclaimed henceforth to all the world: "God raised him from the dead, freeing him from the agony of death, because it was impossible for death to keep its hold on him" (Acts 2:24).

Week Thirty-Four

Luke 24:13-35 (VI H 2 in Outline)

2. The walk to Emmaus. 24:13-35.

The empty tomb would not be evidence in itself of the resurrection of Jesus from the dead and would need to be supported by a variety of bodily appearances of the once-dead-but-alive-again Son of God. These appearances would need to be numerous enough and experienced under a wide enough variety of circumstances to eliminate the possibility of mere dream, wishful thinking, or hallucination. Since no one witnessed the resurrection itself, it would take a series of strong proofs of a raised Jesus of Nazareth to establish a resurrection claim.

Against the strongest possible demands for authentication, the resurrection of the Son of God may be accepted as factual. Paul's summary of post-resurrection experiences of Christ includes appearances "to Peter, and then to the Twelve. After that, he appeared to more than five hundred of the brothers at the same time, most of whom are still living, though some have fallen asleep. Then he appeared to James, then to all the apostles, and last of all he appeared to me also, as to one abnormally born" (1 Cor. 15:5b-8). When a total list of post-resurrection appearances is compiled from Paul's list and all of the Gospels, we can account for at least eleven such episodes.

Of the eleven times Jesus showed himself alive, fully five were on the Sunday of the resurrection. One of the most interesting and intimate of these five is Luke's moving account of an appearance to two men who were walking toward Emmaus [E-mā´-əs].

Emmaus is identified in the Lucan text as a village "about seven miles from Jerusalem." Two disciples

Day 1
"Many Convincing Proofs"

Read Luke's second account of the post-resurrection period at Acts 1:1-11.

1. Why is an empty tomb not proof in itself of Christ's resurrection?
2. How many post-resurrection appearances do we know about? Can you list them?
3. What do you find particularly interesting about the Emmaus Road episode?
4. Why was it important for Jesus to appear to many people under a variety of conditions?
5. Do you agree with Luke's claim at Acts 1:3 about the "many convincing proofs"? Explain.

were walking away from Jerusalem toward the village on "that same day" as the resurrection, visits to the empty tomb, and the women's report of a sighting of angels at the tomb. It appears that they were leaving Jerusalem disappointed and without expectation of seeing the risen Christ. They had heard reports from the women about the claim that he had risen, but they had hoped for more. So, on the Sunday afternoon of the resurrection, they started for Emmaus and "talked and discussed these things with each other."

These men were leaving Jerusalem in unbelief. They had apparently discounted the women's report in much the same way the apostles had; it seemed nothing more than the "nonsense" of their grief-stricken yearnings. So, as in the cases of the women and Peter, we must see these as people who were anything but inclined to posit that Jesus had been raised from the dead. As they walked and talked, "Jesus himself came up and walked along with them; but they were kept from recognizing him." The implication seems to be that some action on Jesus' part prevented the two men from identifying him. Perhaps this is Mark's meaning in his brief report of this same episode: "Afterward Jesus appeared in a different form to two of them while they were walking in the country" (Mark 16:12). The point of his disguise or clouding of their senses must have been to give himself the opportunity to walk these two men through the systematic presentation of himself and his mission found in the Old Testament. They needed not only an experiential confirmation of the resurrection but a solid scriptural background for its significance.

Jesus began the conversation by asking, "What are you discussing together as you walk along?" The slant taken above on their attitude toward the possibility of Jesus' being alive from the dead is con-

Day 2
Dashed Hopes

Read Psalm 42 for a biblical statement of discouragement by a believer.

1. What was the state of mind for Cleopas and his friend as they traveled toward Emmaus?
2. What information did they have about the resurrection as they left Jerusalem?
3. Do you fault the men for not waiting longer at Jerusalem? Explain.
4. Recall a time when you suffered a major disappointment or loss of hope. How did you deal with it?
5. What are some modern life situations where we encounter people with dashed hopes? How can we best minister to them?

firmed by their response. There was no animated excitement or eagerness to share the good news of hope. Instead there was a "downcast" look of sadness, disappointment, and failed hopes on their faces. One of the men even voiced something of a bemused rebuke to their new travel partner. Cleopas [Klē´-ŏ-pəs] — the only one of these two disciples ever named, unknown to us except from this story — asked, "Are you only a visitor to Jerusalem and do not know the things that have happened there in these days?"

In order to take the conversation in the direction he wanted, Jesus did not answer Cleopas directly. Without disclaiming knowledge of what had happened during the weekend just past and without jumping ahead of the issues he and his friend were discussing, he simply replied, "What things?"

If the two men had been morose and despondent before, they seem to have become animated in answering Jesus. One wonders if there was a tone of frustration in their voices as they told this presumed stranger of hopes that had been raised for them only to be dashed. So they began telling the third party whose identity they do not know about "Jesus of Nazareth." As we read these lines today, we feel somewhat like insiders with Jesus to a joke being played on them. We hear two people who obviously don't understand either the man or his mission trying to describe Jesus and his ministry to the man himself!

The minimum they were willing to assert about Jesus was this: "He was a prophet, powerful in word and deed before God and all the people." While it is no small compliment to be considered a "prophet" (i.e., one who speaks for God), that would be a low estimate of Jesus in light of his true identity. Yet it would appear that they once believed far more about him. "We had hoped that he was the one who was going to redeem Israel," they said. It is hard to know whether the emphasis here is on the word "hoped" or "had"; the former could imply that they still entertained the belief that Jesus was the Messiah, whereas the latter would make us think that they had abandoned any such notion they might have held earlier.

And what had caused them either to doubt or to abandon faith in Jesus? "The chief priests and our rulers handed him over to be sentenced to death, and they crucified him. . . . And what is more, it is the third day since all this took place." Jesus had been put to death. Insofar as they knew, he was still dead. So everything was over for them! They were on their way out of Jerusalem — leaving behind them whatever level of commitment they once had to Jesus.

What of the reports about events earlier that day? They had been "amazed" by the report of some women about an empty tomb and their alleged "vision of angels, who said he was alive." They also knew that Peter and John, identified by them as "some of our companions," had subsequently gone to the tomb and "found it just as the women had said." So why were they leaving Jerusalem with downcast faces rather than rejoicing that Jesus was alive from the dead? "But [Jesus] they did not see." They were abandoning hope because the living body had not been discovered by Peter and John. "This empirical note seems to be the key for the two, since it seems they are not yet convinced that Jesus has been raised from the dead. Thomas gets all the contemporary press as a doubter of the resurrection, but Luke 24 makes it clear that he was merely one of a crowd, including these two followers. Like modern people in their skepticism, they will be persuaded only if they actually see Jesus. As readers we almost want to yell at the two, 'Take a close look!' " [Bock, *Luke*, p. 384.]

Day 3
Seeing the Obvious

Read John 9:13-41 about spiritual blindness.

1. These two disciples on the Emmaus Road did not recognize Jesus. What did Jesus do to keep them from recognizing him?
2. Do you think the state of mind for these two men contributed to their inability to recognize Jesus? Explain.
3. What kept the people in John 9 from recognizing Jesus as their Messiah?
4. Have you ever known anyone who could not "see the obvious" about himself or herself? About Jesus?
5. How may we keep our hearts open to the truth God wants us to see?

Cleopas and his friend were not only downcast by unbelief but were also in the process of cutting themselves off from the place and circumstances that could most likely address their issues. They apparently did not go to the tomb themselves. They did not even wait through the duration of the third day to see if Jesus would reveal himself alive to his apostles. They were going home and giving up.

So we should not be shocked that Jesus rebuked them by saying, "How foolish you are, and how slow of heart to believe all that the prophets have spoken!" Please notice that he did not rebuke them for questioning the reliability of the women or making too little of what Peter and John had reported. He rebuked them for failing to believe Scripture. "They had accepted it in part; as men often accept just so much as suits their prejudices and tastes and notions; but they failed to believe in all that the prophets had spoken, and particularly the predictions of Jesus' atoning death, and of his return to the glory which he would share when he ascended." [Erdman, *Luke*, p. 253.]

Like so many of their contemporaries, these two men apparently knew the Old Testament predictions about the Messiah's glory, power, and triumph. But they knew nothing of (or chose to disregard!) the equally emphatic texts about his role as a suffering and rejected servant of God (cf. Isa. 53). So Jesus began with Moses and worked through the Prophets in order to explain to these dispirited disciples "what was said in all the Scriptures concerning himself." What a Bible School lesson that must have been! Scripture was systematically interpreted by the Son of God for two discouraged souls!

As the threesome came near the village to which Cleopas and his friend were going, presumably Emmaus, "Jesus acted as if he were going farther." Perhaps the ruse was to test their hearts. Were they

Day 4
Knowing the
Scriptures

Read Psalm 119:57-72 about the value of knowing and heeding the Word of God.

1. Jesus explained what the Old Testament said about him to these two men. What are some of the texts you think he cited?

2. Why did Jesus ground his teaching of these two men in Scripture rather than in their direct personal experience of him that day?

3. What values are there in serious Bible study for Christians today?

4. Does Scripture-based faith deny the daily experience of God in a Christian's life? How do the two relate to each other?

5. How has the "Falling in Love with Jesus" series contributed to your knowledge of Scripture? Would you recommend it to others?

Day 5
The Resurrection Body

Read Paul's discussion of the resurrection body at 1 Corinthians 15:35-58.

1. The same physical body buried in Joseph's tomb was raised on Sunday morning. How can we be sure?
2. Do you realize that your *physical* body will be raised? What issues does that raise for you?
3. In what ways was Jesus' body different after the resurrection? The same?
4. What of those who will still be living when Jesus returns? What will happen to their bodies?
5. In what ways do you expect to be the same after your own resurrection? In what ways different?

hearing the Word of God? Did they want to know the fulfillment of these things? Or were they so committed to their misunderstandings that they had no interest in what he was saying? They "urged him strongly" to stay with them in view of the fact that it was getting late and the road could soon become not only cold but unsafe for travelers. Jesus agreed to their urging and sat down to eat with them. Taking the role of table host to himself, Jesus "took bread, gave thanks, broke it and began to give it to them." It was only at this late point in the day and conversation that the two men were allowed to recognize Jesus.

Perhaps he exposed his nail-pierced hands to them as he broke the bread. Maybe there was something in his prayer that reminded them of others they had heard him pray before. Or perhaps it was simply time for the Lord to remove whatever obstacle to recognition he had erected. Luke says: "Then their eyes were opened and they recognized him." Consistent with other postresurrection accounts of things Jesus could do in a resurrected body that we have no record of his having done previously, he then "disappeared from their sight" (cf. John 20:19,26).

At that point, the two men appear to have chided themselves for not recognizing the Lord earlier. "Were not our hearts burning within us while he talked with us on the road and opened the Scriptures to us?" they asked. Then, even though it was late and the roads were less than fully safe, they "returned at once" to Jerusalem, found the apostles, and heard them relating an appearance of the risen Lord to Simon. "It is true!" the apostles were reporting, "The Lord has risen and has appeared to Simon." To this fresh report of an appearance to Peter (cf. 1 Cor. 15:5), Cleopas and his forever-unnamed friend added their own witness about seeing Jesus alive.

The news was beginning to spread, and the accounts of eyewitnesses were beginning to multiply. The Son of God was alive and turning skeptics into committed believers.

Week Thirty-Five

Luke 24:36-53 (VI H 2 to VI I in Outline)

Day 1
"Peace Be With You"

*Read another statement
about peace from Jesus at
John 16:17-33.*

1. Why did Jesus begin
   this encounter with an
   affirmation of peace?
2. What does the word
   peace mean in its
   Christian context?
3. Do you have a sense of
   God's peace in your life
   now? Explain.
4. What happens to a life
   without peace?
5. How does one enter
   more deeply into the
   peace of God?

Day 2
A Ghost?

*Read John 20:19-29 for
another episode of proof
about the nature of Jesus'
postresurrection body.*

1. Why was it important
   for Jesus to deal with the
   question of whether his
   disciples were seeing a
   "ghost" or real person?

3. Appearing to the apostles. 24:36-49.

a. Proof of his resurrection. 24:36-43.

Appearing to the apostles. 24:36-49. The impression one gets from reading of the conversation between the apostles and the two men who had just come to them from the Emmaus Road is that it must have been an animatd one. The apostles were telling of their experiences — especially of the personal appearance of the risen Christ to Peter. Then Cleopas and his friend told of their experiences. This would not have been a ho-hum session.

Into this tumult stepped Jesus himself! "While they were still talking about this, Jesus himself stood among them and said to them, 'Peace be with you.'" From the parallel account in the Gospel of John, we learn that the group was in a room "with the doors locked for fear of the Jews" (John 20:19). Their reaction of shock at his presence should therefore not surprise us. At least for those who had seen him already (i.e., Peter, Cleopas, and Cleopas's friend), the shock may have been less that they were seeing Jesus than that he had somehow materialized among them without opening a door.

Luke tells us that the assembled disciples were "startled and frightened, thinking they saw a ghost." After all, there is no evidence that Jesus exhibited such abilities prior to his resurrection. He had an ordinary physical body that moved from one place to another just as ours do. He had used doors for their customary purpose and had never come into a closed room this way. So the startled men began to speculate that what they were seeing was perhaps not Jesus' resurrected physical body but its ghost (i.e., non-material essence). Jesus was very deliberate in his efforts to set them straight on this point. He was not appearing to them as a disembodied spirit but in the same physical body they had always known — although it clearly had new possibilities in its resurrected and transformed state.

Jesus addressed their confusion directly. Were they only dreaming? Were they seeing a ghost? Was this the same man they had known as Jesus of Nazareth? To put all these issues to rest, he offered himself to them and invited empirical testing. "Look at my hands and my feet," he said. "It is I myself! Touch me and see; a ghost does not have flesh and bones, as you see I have." He then proceeded to let them see — and, presumably, touch — the nail wounds in his hands and feet.

It is hard to think that this episode was not in the writer's mind as one of the men present in that room wrote this 60 years later: "That which was from the beginning, which we have *heard*, which we have *seen with our eyes*, which we have *looked at* and *our hands have touched* — this we proclaim concerning the Word of life" (1 John 1:1). As a matter of fact, John was writing that epistle to counter a Gnostic-type account of Jesus that would have denied a literal flesh-and-blood body to the Son of God. "This is no hallucination. The disciples have not fabricated the stories that they heard. Psychosis has not created an account to fill an emotional hole. This is no immaterial Jesus, as the Gnostics later claimed had come, a Jesus who walked but left no footprints. No, this is the crucified Jesus with the marks of nails in his hands to prove he had gone the limit to overcome sin. It is Jesus raised from the dead, pure and simple." [Bock, *Luke*, p. 387.]

When Luke says that the men "still did not believe it because of joy and amazement," we should

2. How did he deal with their misgivings?
3. Why is it important for us to know how Jesus handled this issue?
4. What does 1 John 1:1 tell us about the importance of this issue to the early church?
5. If you could have any question answered about Jesus' post-resurrection body (or your own), what would it be?

Day 3
"Too Good to Be True!"

Read Revelation 22:1-6 about the glory awaiting believers.

1. The disciples could hardly believe their eyes for joy over having Jesus back among them. Can you understand such a reaction?

2. Have you ever seen or heard something so wonderful that you reacted in stunned disbelief? Explain.

3. The gospel is God's "good news" to humankind. Have you ever known people who thought the message was too good to be true?

4. Have you ever had difficulty believing what lies ahead for you in heaven?

not hear him saying that they were obstinate in their unbelief. Instead, we should hear him saying that what they were experiencing was all just too good to be true. Their joy had them pinching themselves to be sure these things were real! As a definitive evidence that it was his physical body that had been raised and presented to them, Jesus asked for something to eat. When they gave him a piece of broiled fish, "he took it and ate it in their presence."

b. The last words to the apostles. 24:44-49.

Although Luke does not make it clear, there is a gap of nearly six weeks between verses 43 and 44. The appearance in a closed room took place on Easter Sunday; the discussion and instruction that parallel the Great Commission in the other Synoptics took place at the end of the 40-day period between his resurrection and ascension.

In his final visit with the apostles, Jesus talked at length about the Old Testament and his mission. The important prediction-fulfillment motif was explained as it relates to the Hebrew Bible and the things he did. The events of his betrayal, death, and resurrection should not have caught his disciples by surprise. They were spoken of "in the Law of Moses, the Prophets and the Psalms." This tripartite way of referring to the Old Testament canon clearly indicates that Jesus saw every major division of the Old Testament being "fulfilled" in his work.

Just as he had done earlier with the two men walking to Emmaus (24:27), "he opened their minds so they could understand the Scriptures." Perhaps reviewing basically the same texts he had with Cleopas and his walking partner — and maybe many others during his 40 days of appearances — Jesus explained how they pointed to his death, burial, and resurrection.

In what we call the Great Commission, Jesus moved beyond Old Testament exposition to specify the mission he had for the apostles after his departure: "repentance and forgiveness of sins will be preached in [Christ's] name to all nations, beginning at Jerusalem." They were not to begin preaching immediately, however, for they were not yet fully equipped for the task. They were told: "Stay in the city (i.e., Jerusalem) until you have been clothed with power from on high." That power would be tied directly to the promise of his Father to send the Holy Spirit to empower them. Only then were they to offer themselves publicly as "witnesses of these things."

The fulfillment of the promise to send the Holy Spirit and the gospel proclamation that followed that dramatic event would become Luke's narrative in Volume Two of his two-volume history of the beginnings of Christianity — *The Book of Acts*. Luke was apparently the only one of the four men chosen to author a Gospel who wrote a sequel to it. His two books contribute more to the total volume of the New Testament than any other writer, including Paul and his thirteen epistles.

I. The Ascension. 24:50-53.

The ascension of the Lord Jesus Christ is the linking event that binds Luke's Gospel to Acts. Closing out the former with a brief account of it, the latter opens with a more detailed version of what happened.

With his personal ministry on Planet Earth complete, Jesus must have been eager to return to the presence of the Father and Holy Spirit, to regain the glory he had known from eternity until the Incarnation (cf. John 17:1-5). He led the apostles "to the vicinity of Bethany," a town on the slopes of the Mount of Olives. There, as he was "blessing" his followers, "he left them and was taken up into heaven." After a time of worship at the site, the men

Day 4
Everyone Needs to Know

Read another account of the Great Commission from Matthew 28:16-20.

1. What message did Jesus entrust to his apostles to share with others?
2. Did his followers begin publishing the message that day? Explain.
3. When did their work begin? With what result?
4. What responsibility do you have to this task?
5. When will Christ's disciples know we have completed our task of making the gospel known to others?

Day 5
Enthronement

Read Daniel 7:15-27 for a predictive view of Jesus' ascension and coronation.

1. Try to imagine any "mixed feelings" Jesus might have had as he prepared to go back to heaven.
2. From the Daniel 7 reading, try to visualize the "homecoming" Jesus experienced in heaven.
3. From John 14, we know the disciples were "troubled" at the thought that Jesus would ever leave them. Why?

4. Luke 24:52 lets us know that the apostles experience great "joy" on the heels of Jesus' departure. Why the change from an earlier attitude?

5. What is Jesus doing in his current heavenly role? How does that affect your life today?

"returned to Jerusalem with great joy. And they stayed continually at the temple, praising God." Most students who write on Luke call attention to the ending of the Gospel at the same geographical center where it had opened. "Luke began and ended his gospel in the Temple, but what a change had taken place. The old covenant had been set aside, and the new covenant with all its hope, power, and reality had been established." [Benware, *Luke*, p. 147.]

Luke has told us the story that had radically changed his own life. He has explained his own love for Jesus and has invited men and women across the centuries to fall in love with him. His carefully researched and Spirit-guided narrative is a strong foundation for faith among those of us who, like Luke himself, believe on a Savior we have never seen with our eyes. Because of Jesus' faithfulness in fulfilling every promise of Scripture, we know that we will see him yet when he returns in his glory.